ALFRED HITCHCOCK

Also by Peter Ackroyd

FICTION

The Great Fire of London
The Last Testament of Oscar Wilde
Hawksmoor
Chatterton
First Light
English Music
The House of Doctor Dee
Dan Leno and the Limehouse Golem
Milton in America
The Plato Papers
The Clerkenwell Tales
The Lambs of London
The Fall of Troy
The Casebook of Victor Frankenstein
Three Brothers

NONFICTION

Dressing Up: Transvestism and Drag: The History of an Obsession
London: The Biography
Albion: The Origins of the English Imagination
Venice: Pure City
London Under

NAN A. TALESE

DOUBLEDAY

New York   London   Toronto   Sydney   Auckland

A·L·F·R·E·D

HITCHCOCK

A Brief Life

Peter Ackroyd

www.nanatalese.com

DOUBLEDAY is a registered trademark of
Penguin Random House LLC. Nan A. Talese and the colophon are
trademarks of Penguin Random House LLC.

Book design by Maria Carella
Jacket design by Michael Windsor
Jacket image: Alfred Hitchcock, 1963. Ullstein Bild/Getty Images

Library of Congress Cataloging-in-Publication Data
Names: Ackroyd, Peter, 1949– author.
Title: Alfred Hitchcock : a brief life / Peter Ackroyd.
Description: First United States edition.
New York : Nan A. Talese Doubleday, 2016.
Identifiers: LCCN 2016021521 (print)—LCCN 2016023999 (ebook)
ISBN 9780385537414 (hardcover)—ISBN 9780385537421 (ebook)
Subjects: LCSH: Hitchcock, Alfred, 1899–1980.
Motion picture producers and directors—Great Britain—Biography.
Motion pictures—Production and direction—Anecdotes.
Classification: LCC PN1998.3.H58 A675 2016 (print)—LCC
PN1998.3.H58 (ebook)—DDC 791.4302/33092 [B]—dc23
LC record available at https://lccn.loc.gov/2016021521

MANUFACTURED IN THE UNITED STATES OF AMERICA

1 3 5 7 9 10 8 6 4 2

First United States Edition

CONTENTS

ALFRED HITCHCOCK

1

THE CHILD WHO NEVER CRIED

Alfred Hitchcock was born on 13 August 1899 on the floor above his father's shop at 517 High Road, Leytonstone; Leytonstone was by the time of his birth a soft forgetful suburb, sweltering in summer and sullen in winter. It was marked by a sense of vacancy, deriving from the time when it was simply a hamlet on the Roman road to London. It was situated five miles to the northeast of the city, and at the time of Hitchcock's birth was still nominally part of Essex, but the vast roar of London was coming ever closer. In 1856 the Great Eastern Railway arrived and Leytonstone soon became a "dormitory town" filled with the modestly affluent who made their way each morning into the City and its environs.

William Hitchcock was a greengrocer, selling everything from cabbages to turnips. It was as busy as any other high road, with horses and carts and carriages passing incessantly; the scent of bananas ripening, and the musty dusty odour of potatoes, were mingled with the keener stench of horse dung. The pervasive smell of manure was in fact only alleviated by the arrival of the electric tram in 1906, an event that Hitchcock vividly remembered. A photograph was taken of him and his father outside the family business on what looks to be the recently established Empire Day; he is astride a horse, no doubt the one that brought the produce from Covent Garden market. William Hitchcock was a successful merchant, whose business soon expanded, and Hitch-cock told one biographer that "I remember my father going to work in a dark suit with a very white starched shirt and a dark tie." In this, at least, the son came to resemble the father. William Hitchcock was also a highly nervous man, who suffered from various neuralgic conditions such as skin lesions.

Emma Hitchcock was by all accounts also smartly dressed, meticu-lous and dignified; like most lower-middle-class housewives, Hitchcock's mother took great delight in cleaning and polishing the appurtenances of the home. She was also adept at preparing family meals, a process she immensely enjoyed.

Hitchcock claimed he was told that, as a baby and small child, he never cried. Yet he also adverted to his terror when, as an infant in the cradle, a female relative put her face too close to his own and uttered baby noises. He also remarked that when a baby is about three months of age, the mother will try and scare it; it is an experience that suppos-edly both of them enjoy. On another occasion he recalled his mother saying "Boo!" at him when he was six months old. Even if he never cried, he was not devoid of fear.

He had an older brother, called William after his father, and an older sister, Ellen, known as "Nellie"; but they seem to have left no lasting impression on his life. The Hitchcocks were a deeply Catholic family, with three of his grandparents Irish Catholics amongst whom religion was instinctive and almost primordial. His father called him "my lamb without a spot," and Hitchcock himself remembered stand-ing at the foot of his mother's bed at the end of the day to recite his adventures or misadventures; it was a form of familial confession.

The family moved down to Limehouse when Hitchcock was six or seven. Limehouse had become an integral aspect of the East End of London by the latter part of the seventeenth century, when it harboured a population of some 7,000 with close connections to the river. These were the men and boys who went down to the sea in ships. In the eigh-teenth and nineteenth centuries it was one of the most important centres for shipbuilding in London. So now the boy can truly be claimed as a Londoner and even, by the common consent of the time, a cockney. A Chinese colony had moved into Limehouse twenty years before his own arrival, and provided another distinctive colour in Hitchcock's boyhood world.

William Hitchcock had expanded his business by purchasing two fishmonger shops in the aptly named Salmon Lane; the family lived above one of them, at number 175. The lane was a few yards north of Limehouse Basin and the Thames, so the penetrating smell of fish was compounded by the more settled odour of the murky river. In 1905, just before the Hitchcock family's arrival in the neighbourhood, Henry James wrote in *English Hours* that by the Thames a "damp-looking dirty blackness is the universal tone. The river is almost black, and is covered with black barges; above the black house-tops, from among the far-stretching docks and basins, rises a dusky wilderness of masts."

Limehouse was a rough and raucous neighbourhood, the very essence of what was known as "the stinking pile" of East London. The river Lea, which runs through it, had for centuries been the site of industries banished to the outskirts of the city, among them dye works and chemical works and glue factories. In an essay that the young Hitchcock devoured, "On Murder Considered as One of the Fine Arts," Thomas De Quincey described the area in 1812 as "a most dangerous quarter," a "perilous region" replete with "manifold ruffianism." It had not changed a great deal by the time of Hitchcock's arrival. It was a neighbourhood of small shops and houses standing a few feet back from the pavement, little plots of impoverished humanity. Most Londoners shunned the area. When Hitchcock was growing up here the public houses were open from early morning to half-past midnight, with a glass of gin or a half-pint of beer for a penny.

Hitchcock rarely alluded to this fusty frantic world in interviews, but it is manifest in his early English films where the street life of London emerges on to the screen with its music halls and its public houses, its picture palaces and its street markets, populated by the animated and quick-witted cockneys whom he knew so well.

As a boy he was called by his parents "Alfie" or "Fred" which, as soon as he reached mature years, he changed to "Hitch." He was always reticent about his childhood, and his family, but he did manage to recall certain episodes. He enjoyed telling of the occasion when, for a minor misdemeanour, his father colluded with a local policeman to have him locked in a police cell for two or three minutes. The boy had returned late after one of his expeditions through London. The event is meant to "explain" his apparent lifelong fear of policemen as well as his obsessive interest in guilt and punishment. It is not at all clear, however, why William Hitchcock would arrange for his "lamb without a spot" to undergo what would be for a small boy a terrifying ordeal. One caveat may be entered. Throughout his films vertical bars, parallel bars, and dark slashes of shadow become a familiar motif.

It is clear enough, however, that fear fell upon him in early life. He may have created the little symbolic drama of the father and the policeman, endlessly repeated to interviewers, as a litany to dispel darkness. Yet something already marked him out as a shuddering, shivering human being, afraid of judgement and punishment. Many interpretations and explanations for this have been adduced, from his relationship with his mother (never mentioned by him) to his Jesuitical education (always introduced by him). The sexual fantasies of his adult life were lavish and peculiar and, from the evidence of his films, he enjoyed devising the rape and murder of women. He said that he always followed the advice of the French playwright Victorien Sardou, to "torture the women!" So it is possible that even as a child he harboured desires and instincts that could not be admitted. Hence the fear of the world that became his familiar characteristic. He was afraid of crossing the floor of the studio canteen in case someone approached him. He fled disorder. He arranged his life as if it were a military campaign, although it is not clear who or what the enemy might be.

He had a horror of life that could only be assuaged by his imagination. And, essentially, he never changed. The fears and obsessions of his childhood remained with him until the end of his life. In certain respects, he was always a child. His absorption in the plots of his films, imagining a sequence of powerful scenes, parallels the fantasies of attack and private calamity on which he obsessively dwelled. That, at least, is part of his story.

. . .

From an early age he seems to have been obsessed with travel and transportation; perhaps in fantasy he wanted, somehow, to get away and to be anywhere other than Limehouse, the East End and the riverine world. He collected maps and timetables, tickets and schedules, and all the other paraphernalia of journeying; he pinned a map on his bedroom wall and with small flags charted the progress of ocean-going vessels according to the latest information he had read in *Lloyd's List*; he memorised the stations along the routes of the Orient Express and the Trans-Siberian Railway with the help of *Cook's Continental Time Tables*. Even by reciting the names of destinations, and contemplating the portions of blue sea upon the map, he was transported in imagination. Yet at the same time he kept a meticulous record of the hours of departure and arrival, so that all his tickets and schedules were arranged in precise fashion. Even as a child he kept tight control over his fantasies. On his office desk, in later life, he kept a European train schedule.

But he was not only an armchair traveller. He said that by the age of eight he had travelled on every route, from beginning to end, of the London General Omnibus Company. Its maps advertised journeys "by motor and horse." He was a passenger on the London Tilbury and Southend Railway that stretched from Fenchurch Street to Shoeburyness. Here lies the origin of that fascination with boats and trains which begins in his early silent films and continues through *Strangers on a Train* and beyond. He kept precise timing on his film sets and, as he said in *The Stage* in 1936, "I have to know where I am going every second of the time." This is the creed of the nervous traveller.

. . .

His early schooling was that of an orthodox Catholic. At a young age Hitchcock was enrolled as an altar boy, and seems to have enjoyed the ritual that accompanied the office. He loved the sweet sense of guilt relieved, of bells and incense announcing a sacred sense of the world. At the age of nine he attended as a boarder the Salesian College in Surrey Lane, Battersea, over the river; it was established by the order of the Salesians of Don Bosco, with a mission to educate "the children of the urban poor" and "aspiring working class." Hitchcock lasted only a week, no doubt horrified by the regime of a boarding school and the enforced absence of his family. He was then enrolled at a local convent school on the East India Dock Road, Howrah House, run by the Sisters of the Faithful Companions of Jesus.

At the age of ten he moved to St. Ignatius College in Stamford Hill, a school run by Jesuits in the strict fashion of that order; the motto of Ignatius himself is popularly supposed to be "Give me the boy and I'll give you the man." Hitchcock's pupil number was 343, and in the register of admissions he is named "Alfred Hitchcock, son of William Hitchcock, Fishmonger."

He told an interviewer that he had learned from the Jesuits the virtues of order, control and precision; the Jesuits were well known for their ability to fabricate arguments on tortuous questions, and for turning equivocation into an art form. This may partly have come from their experience as hunted missionaries in Elizabethan England, when many were tortured in the Salt Tower of the Tower of London before being killed.

Hitchcock absorbed knowledge quickly and expeditiously, so the wide curriculum would not have presented any great difficulty to him. He was obliged to study Latin and mathematics, physics and English; the notable authors, such as Longfellow and Shakespeare, were memorised and recited on special occasions. He never came top of the class, but he usually earned a respectable third or fourth place. He did also gain a distinction in mathematics.

The routine itself was unchanging. The daily Mass was conducted, in Latin, at 8:45, and the boys genuflected to the Blessed Sacrament before making their way to class. Each classroom possessed its own altar dedicated to the Blessed Virgin Mary, in front of whose image were placed flowers and candles. The boys went to confession every Friday where their sins were revealed and absolved. A "retreat" of three days was ordained each year, during which time they meditated on the spiritual exercises of St. Ignatius and contemplated the seven deadly sins and the four last things. In an interview with the school newspaper, many years later, Hitchcock wrote that "a Catholic attitude was indoctrinated into me. After all, I was born a Catholic, I went to a Catholic school and I now have a conscience with lots of trials over belief." What his training most firmly instilled in him, however, was a sacred rather than a secular view of the world where mystery and miracle are as important as logic and reason.

Of Irish Catholic stock he was always something of an "outsider," at least in England. But, more importantly, a Catholic education instilled in him a powerful conscience together with a tremulous sense of guilt. He feared and hated the body. He felt unease with all bodily functions. After he went to the lavatory, he cleaned it so that it seemed as if no one had been there. His was always a life of the mind, isolated and apart.

The priests and brothers of St. Ignatius College also had a predilection for punishment, not unknown in that period in most London schools. It was not quite as hellish as Dotheboys Hall in *Nicholas Nickleby*, perhaps, but it was tough. Discipline was administered with the aid of a hard rubber strap; three strokes would render the hand numb, so a sentence of twelve strokes had to be extended over two days. In a refinement of anxiety the boys themselves could choose the time for the ordeal; most of them of course put it off to the end of the day, so that their anticipation of pain naturally increased. It is not known how often Hitchcock received this penalty, but it is likely to have been rare. He had a preternatural fear of authority of every kind, and the black-robed Jesuit no doubt instilled nervous terror. He explained once that "I was terrified of the police, of the Jesuit fathers, of physical punishment, of a lot of things. This is the root of my work." The remark has a further application. He once said that "I spent three years studying with the Jesuits. They used to terrify me to death, with everything, and now I'm getting my own back by terrifying other people."

His nickname was "Cockie," and he was not widely popular. He portrayed himself as a lonely boy, without playmates. This is easy to believe. He was plump, and shy, and without physical skills of any kind; he may have exhibited that mild effeminacy that was evident in later life. It is also reported that he smelled of fish, from close proximity to his father's fishmongery. This is the sort of detail that boys remark. He was not necessarily bullied, but he was known to be odd.

So he invented games for himself, and played alone. He was also too defensive, and too proud, to encourage intimacy. One journalist, observing him sitting on the set waiting for the crew to prepare, noted that "he is likely to be sitting alone, with the look of a fat boy who has run away from the cruelty of his contemporaries." In later life he seemed to have had a hatred of small boys. He scared the life out of one young actor, or "minor," Bill Mumy, when he bent down and whispered, "If you don't stop moving about, I'm going to get a nail and nail your feet to the mark, and the blood will come pouring out like milk."

And he watched. He watched the others in the class and in the playground. He said the same about his family life. "At family gatherings," he told an interviewer, "I would sit quietly in a corner, saying nothing. I looked and observed a good deal. I've always been that way, and still am." Watching provides a definite form of pleasure. It involves the mastery of the observer, absorbing the details of people and of places, even discerning plots and patterns not seen by the participants. It is the gaze that captures the world. It also furnishes a sense of safety, and even of invulnerability. The observer is removed from any threatening consequences. It may of course also lead to voyeurism, a theme much explored in Hitchcock's films.

Watching was accompanied, or enlarged, by another passion. From an early age he began to visit the picture palaces. He saw his first films at the age of eight or nine. They were short, running for three or four minutes, with titles such as *A Ride on a Runaway Train* or *Hal's Tours and Scenes of the World*. They exploited the realism and immediacy of the new medium. When a train seemed to hurtle towards the screen, some of the audience would scream and duck under their seats. Hitchcock himself recollected how others would wet their seats in excitement or terror. "The stories weren't much, you know," he recalled, "but it was a wonder to watch them."

He came of age with the cinema itself, and in his teenage years he saw the films of D. W. Griffith, of Douglas Fairbanks senior, Harold Lloyd and Mary Pickford. The first Chaplin silent films were released in England when Hitchcock was fourteen. Picture palaces had become as popular in the East End as music halls; in Hitchcock's own neighbourhood stood the Palaceadium on White Horse Road, around the corner from the fish shop in Salmon Lane, the Poplar Hippodrome and the Gaiety Cinema on East India Dock Road, the Ideal Picture Palace on Ming Street and the Premier Electric Theatre on Leytonstone High Road.

By strange coincidence Hitchcock's early North-East London neighbourhood was the first home of the British film industry, with the river Lea and Epping Forest providing a suitable setting for short tales of adventure and intrigue. The first purpose-built studio was constructed at Whipps Cross, while the British and Colonial Kinematographic Company was located on Hoe Street, Walthamstow. Broadwest Films, who made *The Merchant of Venice* in 1916, was based in Wood Street, Walthamstow, while Tiger Films could be found in a nearby tram depot. Walthamstow itself became known as "the English Hollywood," with one fifth of all studio space to be found there. So Hitchcock was in the right environment.

From an early age he was reading the trade papers. From a bookshop off Leicester Square he bought *The Bioscope* as well as the *Kinematograph and Lantern Weekly*. He already evinced what might be called a professional interest. With his parents he also attended the annual circus on Wanstead Flats and visited the Stratford Music Hall with its diet of variety acts, dioramas and Italian operettas.

He had other interests. It was not difficult to take the bus into Fleet Street and alight at the stop just before the Old Bailey. It was an institution he relished. In later life he could recall the exact floor plan of the central criminal court. He was attracted to the trials of murderers and, in particular, murderers of women. He collected a library of criminal cases and of crime fiction, and on at least one occasion visited the Black Museum of Scotland Yard. "I have always," he wrote, "been fascinated by crime. It's a particularly English problem, I think." Even in later life he took particular pleasure in reading the transcripts of sensational cases, such as an episode when the judge started interrogating the notorious serial killer, John Christie, at the trial in 1953. The judge emphasised the following words, with slight emendations.

JUDGE: And you killed her.
CHRISTIE: Yes, Your Honour.
JUDGE: And assaulted her, too?
CHRISTIE: I believe so, Your Honour.
JUDGE: Before, during or after death?
CHRISTIE: During, Your Honour.

This case against the killer, whom Hitchcock called "that adorable Christie," so fixed itself in the imagination of the film-maker that he used the same set of circumstances in *Frenzy* in 1972.

In later life he confessed that he might have enjoyed the role of a prosecuting barrister or a hanging judge. But he never, ever, wished to be a policeman. His interest in crime, therefore, can be seen as part of his passion for theatre. With his parents he visited the West End and saw the latest plays. According to his authorised biographer, John Russell Taylor, he could happily sit for hours discussing the theatrical world of his youth "about which . . . his knowledge was encyclopaedic and his enthusiasm profound." There is much that is intensely and innately theatrical about Hitchcock's work. Several films, such as *Rope* and *Murder!*, were based on stage plays, while the principal scenes from a number of others are set upon a literal stage where the camera simply moves beyond the proscenium arch. The theatre and the cinema are deeply intertwined in Hitchcock's imagination, deriving from those early days when they were closely linked, with films often shown in theatres.

· · ·

He left school at the approved age of thirteen, by which time a child was deemed ready to choose a profession for life. Hitchcock told his parents that he wanted to be an engineer, an eminently safe and suitable career, and so he was enrolled at the London County Council School of Marine Engineering and Navigation on Poplar High Street; he studied mechanics and acoustics, but was also engaged in making working drawings of various machines. This period of training was enough to gain him employment, in November 1914, at W. T. Henley's Telegraph Works Company Limited in Blomfield Street off London Wall in the City. This was the head office of a company that specialised in manufacturing insulated wires and cables with a special interest, during this period, in submarine cables and other forms of bombproof communication.

Hitchcock was a junior technician associated with the sales department. He worked as a "technical estimator" for the size and voltage of electric cables. By his own account he was often idle and allowed the estimates to pile up on his desk until he had no choice but to deal with them; then, again by his own account, he worked at a prodigiously fast rate. His choice of engineering as a steady career must have been confirmed by the death of his father from chronic emphysema in the month after Hitchcock joined Henley's. His older brother took over the fish shops, while Hitchcock and his mother still lived above 175 Salmon Lane from where Hitchcock commuted to his job in the City. There are some reports that mother and son moved back to Leytonstone but this cannot be verified.

Neither Leytonstone nor Limehouse, however, were immune from the steady bombardment of the First World War. For a young man of Hitchcock's nervous condition, the diet of terror from the skies would have been something of a genetic shock; nothing could destabilise the order of the world more savagely. In early 1915 the Zeppelins were seen in the sky above Leytonstone; Limehouse and the area of the river were prime targets for the German bombs; Poplar was hit particularly badly. German submarines were spotted in the Irish Sea, and from everywhere came talk of sabotage and saboteurs. Some of Hitchcock's earlier films reflect that mood of panic and even of hysteria. He never forgot it. He re-created the first Blitz in his direction of *The Birds* when the birds attack the beleaguered Brenner household. "The bombs are falling, and the guns are going like hell all over the place!" he said. "You don't know where to go . . . You're caught! You're trapped!"

Yet in most later interviews Hitchcock tended to suppress the memories of the terror he must have experienced, and chose to concentrate instead on some of the war's tragi-comical moments which he associated with his mother. One evening he returned home to find that artillery fire had exploded near his house. He rushed into his mother's bedroom, to find her trying to put on her clothes while still wearing her nightgown. On another occasion, during an air raid, he remembered "my poor Elsa Maxwell plump little mother, struggling, saying her prayers, while outside the window, shrapnel was bursting around a search-lit Zeppelin." In a third anecdote he was sheltering under a table with his mother while, kneeling, she continually crossed herself.

. . .

At the age of sixteen, Alfred Hitchcock encountered the life and work of Edgar Allan Poe. "I felt an immense pity for him," he noted, "because, in spite of his talent, he had always been unhappy." The childhood of Poe had been one of fear and trembling; he had been sensitive and vulnerable to every slight, and thus had become retiring and unsociable. As an adult he always dressed in black, and adopted an almost ritualistic manner of living in the world; he sought formal restraint to discipline the miseries and longings of his morbid nature. But he had also an abiding need for female sympathy and protection; as a result he idolised certain women with disastrous consequences. Poe's unhappy life made a deep impression upon the young Hitchcock.

He began reading Poe's short stories. The victim in "The Pit and the Pendulum," never named, first sees the white lips of the judges issuing the decree of Fate. He is taken down—down innumerable steps—to a stone dungeon in the centre of which opens a vast pit. It is a world of all-pervasive fear and threat. He has been removed to a claustrophobic arena of horror without knowing the reason. He is not guilty of any offence but he is being punished. He is perhaps aware of being watched by an unseen audience, somewhere in the darkness, which takes a particular interest and even pleasure in his unhappy condition.

Then he glimpses with horror a monstrous scythe descending upon him inch by inch with slow and steady sweep; he could hear its hiss and sense its acrid smell even as it cuts through the outer layer of his garments. It hangs down like a figure of dread. But then the enemies of his accusers suddenly appear, and he is freed. Was it a dream? What is its meaning? Poe carefully calculated and planned his narratives to create a surreal logic of anxiety and dread; they deal in doubles, in self-destruction summoned by "the imp of the perverse," in idealised heroines, and in protagonists who have a horror of the invading eye. This is the world of Poe that Hitchcock pondered. Forty-five years later Hitchcock wrote that "I can't help comparing what I've tried to put in my films with what Edgar Allan Poe put in his novels."

. . .

He enrolled with a cadet regiment of the Royal Engineers at the age of seventeen; he and other young workers at Henley's received evening briefings, with marches and drills at the weekend. It was one of the war's futile gestures, of course, but he could not be accused of lack of patriotism. In 1917, he came of age to be called up for service, but he was excused with a "C3" classification; whether this was due to his size, height, or some unnamed medical problem, he was consigned to a group of men who were "free from organic diseases" and able "to stand service conditions in garrisons at home." He could then have undertaken "sedentary work" as a cook or storeman but, fortunately for him, the war was almost over and his services were not required.

He found sedentary work of a more pleasurable kind, however, when he enrolled for night classes at the Art Department of Goldsmiths College, part of the University of London, where he honed his skills in draughtsmanship and indulged his burgeoning love of art. He was sent out to sketch people and buildings, with particular attention to light and shadow. At a later date he explained to his fellow director François Truffaut that "one of the first things I learned in the School of Art was that there is no such thing as a line; there's only the light and shade." Light and darkness form the figure.

He was also encouraged by his teachers to frequent museums and art galleries in search of inspiring work, and in a period of greater affluence he purchased work by Dufy, Utrillo, Roualt, Sickert and Klee. According to his daughter, Patricia Hitchcock O'Connell, he appreciated non-figurative art as long as it was agreeable to the eye but he had no interest in any symbolic significance or inner meaning.

His presence in the evening classes at Goldsmiths did not go unnoticed by the managers of Henley's and, in 1919, he was moved from sales to advertising. Here he learnt how to design layouts as well as to write the copy that accompanied them; he illustrated brochures, and edited them. Promotion, and publicity, now became his forte. His skill may have lent him confidence because he was no longer the shy and lonely schoolboy. There is a photograph of him on board ship for a company outing down the Thames; he is wearing a straw hat and double-breasted suit, and is smoking a cigarette. He was already well known for his "fooling" and an almost irrepressible stream of wit and humour. He organised the Henley soccer club and took part in billiards. It may have been in this period that he began taking dancing lessons at the Cripplegate Institute in Golden Lane.

In 1919 he founded and edited the *Henley Telegraph*, sold to the staff for threepence. Like most editors of small publications he was obliged to provide some of the copy himself, and in the first issue of

June 1919 a curious short story appeared. "Gas" is a piece of Grand Guignol with an ironic twist, heavily influenced by Poe with a small dash of Saki. He may, perhaps inadvertently, have aspired to the condition of the "fat boy" in *The Pickwick Papers*. "I wants to make your flesh creep." It demonstrates that Hitchcock had a macabre imagination and a sense of humour; six stories followed in other issues of the little magazine, all of them marked by parody, comedy and melodrama. These characteristics would quickly become evident in his first work for the cinema.

At this age, by his own account, he was indeed already fat but also ambitious; he may have been ambitious because he was fat. He was always self-conscious about his weight. He was never entirely committed to Henley's; it seems that he was too light-hearted, and too casual with the necessary reports and records. He did not quite fit in. He had by now lost interest in advertising and was not happy with a salary of fifteen shillings per week.

He had kept a keen eye on the film trade papers, and soon learned that "Famous Players-Lasky" had decided to set up a studio in Poole Street, Islington, in North London. This was the company that provided the films for Paramount Pictures. On its arrival in London, Famous Players-Lasky British Producers Limited, as it was called for the occasion, inserted advertisements for various employees—among them "captioneers" who wrote and illustrated the captions that directed the narrative of the silent films. After two years of illustrating and writing advertisements for Henley's, this was Hitchcock's opportunity.

He discovered that Famous Players-Lasky had chosen, for its first film, *The Sorrows of Satan* by Marie Corelli. He read the novel and, with some help from his colleagues in the advertisement department, he created a series of designs and captions for the proposed film. He also compiled a portfolio of his recent work for the department. He took these to the new studio in Poole Street, where he received an unpleasant surprise. *The Sorrows of Satan* had been discarded, and instead Famous Players-Lasky had decided to concentrate upon two other films, *The Great Day* and *The Call of Youth*.

It was at this point that his perseverance and energy won through.

Immediately he began work on the newly chosen films and, within a day or two, arrived at Poole Street with the appropriate material. His speed and evident talent impressed the managers of the company, and he was employed on a part-time basis to provide the designs and graphics. He was in effect moonlighting, working for the film company while at the same time being employed by Henley's, but it appears that he paid a portion of his supplementary income to his immediate superior who allowed him the time and space to create a world of film.

His persistence was successful and, at the end of April 1921, Hitchcock became a full-time employee of Famous Players-Lasky. The *Henley Telegraph* announced his departure: "He has gone into the film business, not as a film actor, as you might easily suppose, but to take charge of the Art Title Department of one of the biggest Anglo-American Producing Companies. We shall miss him in many ways, but we wish him all success." That success would be greater than anyone at the time could possibly have imagined.

2

I'LL DO IT

Thomas Burke, a novelist and essayist, was invited to visit the recently established studio in Islington. He remarked, in a piece entitled "In the Streets of Film Land," that it was "a dismantled power station—a tremendous barn of a place which, despite the warm day, struck coldly." It was "lofty and full of echoes, and its floor was littered with thick lines of lighting cables." Little islands of fabricated sets were placed along the sides, and next to some of them costumed actors waited for their cues. Since the films did not require their own sound to be recorded, more than one film could be made at the same time.

The camera and the cameraman were placed in front of the set in use, close to a more bulky stills camera. The continuity girl sat nearby, making notes. Burke had expected tumult and shouting but "the only persistent noise was the hiss of the arc-lamps." Then he heard the voice of the director or producer. "We'll just have that over again, Miss Gwyn. Like this, you see." Strange phrases were uttered. "Cross it." "Kill it." "Iris." And then came the call "Light 'em up!" The director took up his megaphone and without any excitement or urgency issued his directions: "Camera. Come on, butler. Come on, detective. Come on, lady's maid . . . Now for his right arm . . . Knee in his back . . . Down him . . . Struggle . . . Fix him. Fine!" Then the call came of "Lights out!" The action was over.

The producer called together his team and conferred while still photographs were taken of the most dramatic moments. Burke noted that there were "No Smoking" signs everywhere but that everybody smoked. When the cast and crew went upstairs to the canteen for lunch, he also observed that a great equality prevailed—the junior electrician sat next to the star, and the commissionaire sat beside the producer. He felt that all were "intensely interested" in the novel process of making a film.

This was the beginning of the world in which Alfred Hitchcock would remain for the rest of his life.

.   .   .

Famous Players-Lasky was in essence an American studio with a largely American staff; there were in fact two large studios, one on the ground floor and one on the first floor, filled with what *The Times* called "the most up-to-date devices from the United States." The London fog, always a threat, was expelled through the roof. Alfred Hitchcock was first employed to design the title cards for the films then in production. His was a practical discipline with the purpose of signalling the action and characters for the audience. From the beginning he learned how to cooperate with the studio's scenarists, essentially scriptwriters, who were usually American women; he once said he was steeped in the cinematic learning of "the middle-aged American women" who worked in Poole Street. It was under their guidance that he also learned to write scripts. He learned also that it was possible to change the tone or meaning of a film by inserting very different title cards from the ones intended; in this manner, a poor film might be saved. He composed titles for such films as *The Mystery Road*, a romantic adventure, and *Dangerous Lies*, now lost to the world.

In this setting he also met the woman with whom he would share all the stages of his life and career. Alma Reville, born just the day after him in the same year, was already a professional of film production. At the age of sixteen she joined the cutting department of the London

Film Company at Twickenham Studios; her parental home was just a short distance away. She became the girl on the cutting-room floor, quick and skilful. In an article written in early 1923 for the *Motion Picture News* she remarked that "the art of cutting is Art indeed, with a capital 'A,'" and she emphasised the importance of smooth continuity and the subtle use of close-up. Her expertise was such that one of the directors at Twickenham Studios promoted her to be studio floor director and then second assistant director. It was a young profession. If she had been a man, she might have moved ahead of Hitchcock very rapidly. In the same year as Hitchcock, 1921, she joined Famous Players-Lasky in Islington where she continued her roles as doyenne of the cutting room and second assistant director.

For the first two years he barely seemed to recognise her; already ambitious and determined, he had little or no interest in the opposite sex. She herself recalled a plump young man, swathed in a large overcoat, who walked unhurried across the studio floor with title cards under his arm. If he had looked properly he would have seen a short girl, four feet and eleven inches in height; she was a redhead, pretty, quick and efficient with a total dedication to the exciting industry of film-making.

Famous Players-Lasky did not last long at Islington. Anglo-American cooperation was not working. Films like *Three Live Ghosts* and *Love's Boomerang* were not popular with English audiences, especially in contrast with the genuine American product coming from studios such as Goldwyn Pictures and Universal Pictures in Hollywood. Alma was obliged to leave Islington, and a paragraph in the *Motion Picture News* announced that "Alma Reville, the continuity writer, late of Famous Lasky . . . is now at liberty to accept engagements." Islington Studios continued life as a rental studio and Hitchcock remained there as general factotum, but aspiring to greater things.

Eventually, in 1923, she received a telephone call. "Is that Miss Reville? This is Alfred Hitchcock. I have been appointed assistant director for a new film. I wonder if you would accept a position as a cutter on the picture?"

He later confessed to her that he was very shy with women, but there had been a further cause for his reticence. Alma said that "since it is unthinkable for a British male to admit that a woman has a job more important than his, Hitch had waited to speak to me until he had a higher position."

He had not been idle at Islington. He wrote the treatment of a film comedy, *Good Night Nurse!*, which was never filmed; all that survive are eight pages of perfectly handwritten notes. In late 1922 he also seems to have borrowed some money from his uncle, Joseph, to finance an independent film of his own entitled *Mrs. Peabody* or *Number Thirteen*; it was to be a drama set in lower-middle-class London, which Hitch-cock knew well, concerned with one of the low-income housing estates known collectively as Peabody Buildings. Production closed down after a couple of reels had been completed, for lack of further finance. This first failure must have seemed at the time to be catastrophic, but he said only that it had been a "somewhat chastening experience" which taught him always to watch the money trail of any production.

At the beginning of 1923 a famous actor-manager, Seymour Hicks, joined forces with an independent director to remake an old film comedy, *Always Tell Your Wife*. When the director fell ill Hicks looked around for someone in the studio to complete the work; his gaze fell upon the portly young employee who was, according to Hicks, "tremendously enthusiastic and anxious to try his hand at producing." One reel survives, of no great quality. Yet in the summer Hitchcock began work on a film that was received with much greater enthusiasm.

A group of independent film-makers descended upon Islington Studios as their ideal space. Michael Balcon was an aspiring producer; Graham Cutts had already directed three films and in those early days of the cinema could be described as experienced; Victor Saville came in as co-producer with Michael Balcon. Balcon was by far the most influential of the three, becoming in time the head of Ealing Studios and the *éminence grise* of the British film industry. In later days Hitch-cock explained to an interviewer, "I have been allowed to experiment.

This I owe to one man, Michael Balcon . . . It is he who has allowed me to follow my celluloid whims."

Their association began with *Woman to Woman*. Hitchcock was as enthusiastic and anxious as ever. It soon became clear that the three men needed a scriptwriter; Hitchcock volunteered and showed them examples of a script he had already finished. They needed an art director. Yes, this was also something Hitchcock could do. Even as he was writing the script and designing the title cards, he was also creating the sets and supervising the costumes. His phrase was "I'll do it." It was this energy and adaptability that Balcon, ever the professional, admired. But Hitchcock could be dogmatic; he would build a set and then call out to the director "Here's where it's shot from." He also knew an expert cutter. This was the occasion for the unexpected telephone call to Alma Reville.

Woman to Woman, directed by Graham Cutts, concerns a dancer with the Moulin Rouge who has an affair with an English soldier; the baby is born, the soldier suffers amnesia and marries again. All the complications that ensue leave plenty of room for sensation and melodrama. When the film was released in the spring of 1923 it was a great success with audiences in Germany, England and the United States. The *Daily Express* remarked that it was "the best American picture made in England" which, at the time, must have seemed to be a compliment. Alfred Hitchcock, although uncredited as assistant director, had proved his worth. In that year the *Motion Picture News* printed a caricature of him, now known as A. J. Hitchcock.

In the following year Balcon and his associates took the further step of purchasing the Islington Studios from Paramount, the managers of which seemed only too eager to rid themselves of what had been for them a failed enterprise. With Hitchcock still as an assistant director they completed two films within three months. *The White Shadow* and *The Passionate Adventure* are now forgotten but they were all part of Hitchcock's cinematic education. In *The Passionate Adventure*, for example, he had to construct a stretch of derelict canal with the houses beside it. Later in his career, he always preferred to work on a set, rather than on location.

The film-makers had now taken the title of Gainsborough Pictures, and were eager to acquire more capital. Germany was at that time one of the great centres of European cinema, and it was natural for Balcon to arrange a co-production agreement with one of its more significant companies. In the early autumn of 1924 Hitchcock was sent, with Alma and Graham Cutts, to the new glass studios of Universum Film-Aktiengesellschaft (UFA) at Neubabelsberg, near Berlin, where they would eventually complete work on two Anglo-German productions. *The Prude's Fall* and *The Blackguard* both starred the expensive American actress Jane Novak, in a number of exotic European locations.

Neither Hitchcock nor Alma could speak a word of German and were at first reduced to sign language and a sort of technical patois, but they persevered. They learned more than a language. They learned an art form. On an adjoining set the German director F. W. Murnau was working on *The Last Laugh*, a silent film with no subtitles and only one title card at the end. It was a triumph of expressive film-making. Murnau took the young Englishman into his confidence and, as Hitchcock said later, "from Murnau I learned how to tell a story without words." From Murnau he also learned the technique of the fluid camera which can rove like any character. He learned another device. If you need to show a mansion or a cathedral you do not need to create a version of the mansion or cathedral. You need only show a marble pillar, or a great wooden door, or just part of a door. The imagination of the audience will do the rest. "What you see on the set does not matter," Murnau told him. "All that matters is what you see on the screen."

Murnau created the chiaroscuro of dark puddles shimmering with opalescent light, of the sad mistiness of street lamps in the rain, of the sheen of wet pavements in the glare of shop windows. There was no light without darkness, and no substance without shadow. And then might come the close-up of a face, bewildered or fearful. The unchained melody of the "mobile" camera could follow a figure wandering, or stumbling, through an indifferent or hostile setting. This was a place of endless corridors, perilous staircases and wild fairgrounds.

In that sense the German cinema unlocked the door of Hitchcock's imagination. This world is hazardous and uncertain; it is tremulous and frightening; it is deadly and unpredictable. It elicits anxiety and disorientation. It is always precarious. Hitchcock may have learned the techniques of German expressionism as a filmic exercise, but it is more likely that the works of Murnau and others touched something that lay deep within his personality.

It also became clear to him that in the German system of film-making the director was always the most important element—not the actor, not the scriptwriter, not the cameraman, but the man sitting or standing beside the camera who gave the orders. Murnau treated his actors as puppets who had only to obey his instructions. It was Murnau who was responsible for the budget and, more importantly, for the editing. Hitchcock took these lessons to heart. When asked whom he considered to be his true mentors, Hitchcock replied, "The Germans! The Germans!"

Other German episodes were less agreeable. He and Cutts were taken by the managers of the studio to a nightclub in Berlin where men danced with men, and women with women. This was not a situation with which Hitchcock, at least, was familiar. The two Englishmen were later propositioned by German prostitutes as Hitchcock quietly reiterated, "*Nein, nein.*" In sexual matters he seems not only to have been naïve but also unknowing. Even though he was patiently and quietly courting Alma, their relationship was almost entirely professional. They talked about films, and of course analysed the ones they were then making. In some respects Alma still had a better technical sense than Hitchcock himself, and throughout his life he would defer to her judgement. If she thought that something was not effective, he lost interest in it. As for sex, that was not nearly so important. Companionship and shared enthusiasm were the reasons for their long association.

Their working relationship also involved protecting Graham Cutts, a married man who was pursuing an affair with his difficult Estonian mistress; Hitchcock and Alma were forced to find alibis, to cover his movements and generally to waste valuable time on the director's unpredictable behaviour. Their mood was not helped by their joint realisation that Cutts was not even a very good director. Hitchcock tried to be as discreet as he could about the matter, but would sometimes whisper advice on the set. Eventually Cutts left the studio with his lover and did not return, leaving the last remaining scenes of *The Blackguard* to be directed by Hitchcock himself. Alma once admitted that Cutts "wasn't really a pleasant man; he knew very little, so we literally carried him." Cutts himself was jealous of Hitchcock's talent and expertise; he no doubt sensed a rival in the making, and wasted no time in trying to belittle him. Hitchcock, a man normally consumed with anxiety, seems to have remained unperturbed.

Neither *The Blackguard* nor *The Prude's Fall* was a success. In New York the latter was jeered by the audience, and *Variety* described it as "film junk." Cutts tended to blame everyone except himself, and now stated that he could no longer work with that "know-it-all son of a bitch." Balcon duly noted his opinion, and then asked Hitchcock if he might consider directing on his own account. Hitchcock, obviously surprised by the offer, cheerfully accepted it. "All right," he is supposed to have said, "when do we start?" They started in Munich. He and Alma, now his indispensable assistant, were sent back to Germany for another co-production.

. . .

He did not learn the lessons of German cinema simply in the film studios. On their return to England he and Alma became involved with the newly established London Film Society that was dedicated to the showing of foreign films that would otherwise have gone largely unnoticed. The society had been set up under the aegis of Ivor Montagu, a supporter of Soviet Russia whose enthusiasm encompassed the works of Eisenstein and Pudovkin. From watching films such as Eisenstein's *Battleship Potemkin*, and Pudovkin's *Mother*, Hitchcock was formally introduced to the art of montage which became a key element in his cinematic technique. "Pure cinema," as he put it, amounted to "complementary pieces of film put together, like notes of music make a melody." The director in the editing room could establish patterns of tone and of movement, of mood and of imagery, that could dominate the experience of the film. The actor was no longer the principal agent of meaning; his feelings, his expressions, his thoughts, could now be manipulated by cutting and splicing. The actor smiles; there is a baby; he is a nice man. The actor smiles; there is a nude woman; he is a lecher. These early lessons were invaluable to Hitchcock's art.

Among those who came to the earliest viewings of the London Film Society, held at the New Gallery in Regent Street on Sunday afternoons, were Augustus John, Roger Fry, John Maynard Keynes and the American graphic artist E. McKnight Kauffer; a more technical participant was Sidney Bernstein, who would later collaborate with Hitchcock on projects such as *Rope* and *Under Capricorn*. Montagu said in an interview that "we thought there are such a lot of films that we are interested in that are being made abroad that we would like to fertilise British film ideas by seeing some of them . . . In this way we could draw into film artists, sculptors, writers who up to then disdained films."

Russian and German films at the time excelled their English counterparts, much to the chagrin of Hitchcock and his associates. Who would not prefer *The Cabinet of Dr. Caligari* and *Destiny* to *Flames of Passion* and *Too Many Crooks*? It could plainly be seen that the English cinema was in a dreadful state, dwarfed by that of America and Europe, and considered so rudimentary that actors and writers were inclined to shun it as a low populist sideshow. In turn the established film industry tended to despise the efforts of the London Film Society to expand critical awareness.

So Hitchcock and others were moved to set up the smaller Hate Club, which organised Hate Parties in which the latest English releases were analysed and as often as not condemned. Ivor Montagu recalled that, at one of the meetings of this club, Hitchcock made a general statement of intent. Hitchcock told them that a film was not made for the public "because by the time the public sees it, it doesn't really matter what happens to it." The director was making the film for the press and for the critics, because only through them would his name become known. Publicity was the key. Once he was known and recognised, he was more free to do what he wished. Montagu added that Hitchcock said this in his usual manner, "drily, sarcastically, cynically, teasingly," so that no one could take offence. Hitchcock was not proclaiming a divide between film as art and film as commerce, although most of his colleagues in the London Film Society would prefer the former course, but suggesting as a practical man that art and commerce were not necessarily to be distinguished. He followed this creed for the rest of his career.

He was keenly aware of all the cinematic developments that were taking place around him, from the spectacle of Cecil B. DeMille to the melodrama of D. W. Griffith. In true English fashion he absorbed everything and changed it in translation. His career as one of the most distinguished directors in the world was just beginning.

3

SOUND, PLEASE

In the spring of 1925 Hitchcock and Alma set out for Munich to embark on their new German co-production arranged by Michael Balcon. *The Pleasure Garden* marked Hitchcock's debut as a director. It was financed by Emelka, the studios of which were close to the city; this was a more frankly commercial establishment than Hitchcock's previous employer, UFA, but there is no reason to believe that he balked at the association. This was his chance.

The enterprise was beset by problems from the beginning, largely as a result of inadequate finance. The two female stars from Hollywood, Virginia Valli and Carmelita Geraghty, were not exactly thrifty in their arrangements; misunderstandings with Customs were compounded by problems with bulky luggage, all of which exacerbated Hitchcock's bouts of anxious fear. He was also nervous with the direction of his leading lady, Valli ("I was terrified of giving her instructions," he confessed), and made sure that Alma was always by his side. "Was that all right?" he asked Alma after every take. He and Valli must have struck up some kind of rapport, however, because there were times when he was obliged to borrow money from her. He was often down to his last pfennig.

The film was completed by the end of August. It bears the marks of Hitchcock's characteristic style. In the opening shots a line of chorus girls spin down a spiral staircase and then display themselves on stage to the admiring and lascivious gaze of elderly males in the front row. The rest of the narrative, concerning the conflicting fates of two chorus girls, is played out with what would become Hitchcock's signature amalgam of comedy and suspense.

Another aspect of Hitchcock's films also makes its first appearance here, as male indifference and brutality towards women are exemplified by betrayal and attempted murder. Voyeurism and violence towards women were to become Hitchcock's twin motifs. But comedy was to keep on breaking through. In *The Pleasure Garden*, a cockney couple bring with them the cockney drollery which he knew very well. Comic allusions to homosexuality, male and female, can be found in an extravagantly effeminate costume designer and a female secretary (complete with the Hitchcock device of spectacles) who ogles the chorus girls.

It was, for the time, clever and inventive, with camera angles and techniques of cutting that were still considered by some in England to be too experimental or innovative. Balcon flew over to Germany to see the finished film, and loved it. He said that it had an "American look," by which he meant that it was more sophisticated and more fast-paced than its English counterparts. The press reaction, on its eventual release, was equally satisfying with Hitchcock himself described as "the young man with the master mind." He had proved himself, on his first film, to be an expert director.

But he could not have done it on his own. Alma was of course always there, ready to lend support and give advice. She was his second pair of eyes. He had also gained the inestimable help of a seasoned scriptwriter, Eliot Stannard, to whom Alma had introduced him. Stannard was well known and well respected in the trade, and had already written essays on the formal art of film-making; this would have been enough to endear him to Hitchcock. Stannard in fact went on to write, or adapt, the scripts for eight of the nine films that Hitchcock completed between 1925 and 1929; he already had a firm grasp on the techniques of montage, and on the creation of suspense, so that he could be said to provide the scaffold on which Hitchcock built. In any case the director wished to create a familiar "team" with which he could work. The cameraman on *The Pleasure Garden*, Gaetano di Ventimiglia, worked on the next two films. Throughout his career Hitchcock preferred to surround himself with recognisable faces. This may have been an aspect of his general nervousness.

With *The Pleasure Garden* a public success, the "team" returned in November 1925 to the studios of Emelka to make *The Mountain Eagle*. All that remains of this venture are a few stills of a melodramatic kind and some striking photographs of Hitchcock and Alma making the best of their situation in the thick snow of the Ôtztal Alps which they had chosen for their location filming. While there, Hitchcock was attacked by a violent fit of nausea which was later diagnosed as a form of "mountain madness"; he had been afflicted by a sudden and uncontrollable desire to shout out to the mountains "Let me speak English to someone!" That at least is the story. The film itself was not considered to be a success, and the *Kinematograph and Lantern Weekly* noted that it was "rather wandering and not too convincing." It was wandering so much that it was quickly lost, with no surviving copy to confirm the impression of the stills that Hitchcock was continuing to experiment with German filmic techniques.

The journey had one successful outcome, however. On their way back to England by ship, on Christmas Eve, during a violent storm, Hitchcock proposed to Alma. She was in her cabin, prone with seasickness, when he knocked on the door and asked her simply if she would marry him. Their daughter, who no doubt heard the story first-hand, wrote that "Alma was too sick to lift her head from the pillow. She groaned, nodded her head, and burped." And that was that. The burp said it all. He would later state that "I married her because she asked me to," but that was just another way of sloughing off any hint of sexual desire on his part.

While Hitchcock was in Germany a new film under his direction had been announced. It was to be entitled *The Lodger: A Story of the London Fog*, and was directly influenced by the criminal career of Jack the Ripper in the streets of Whitechapel some thirty-seven years before.

It was based on a novel by Marie Belloc Lowndes and in fact Hitchcock, at the age of sixteen, had seen it played in a London theatre. He was naturally drawn to such material, with murder in the dark streets of the East End as irresistible to him as the image of the stranger with the scarf over his mouth, stalking vulnerable females with a little black bag in his hand.

Eliot Stannard had already started work on the script in the early months of 1926, and Hitchcock began to break down the narrative into hundreds of small drawings which were designed to specify, in his words, "the exact grouping and action of the characters and the placing of the camera." This was the technique, known familiarly as "storyboarding," that he used intermittently for the rest of his life; he conceived his films in purely visual terms. He told aspiring cameramen that they should go to art galleries to learn the effects of the great masters; they should study Rembrandt or Vermeer in order to learn the use of shadow and reflection. In his visual meditation upon characters and objects he became the camera, or an extension of the camera: the camera was for him the pivot of any film. This was not filmed theatre, or a filmed story; it was simply film. The use of light was its music, rising in intensity from piano to forte, and in the process creating a unique rhythm of meaning.

. . .

In February 1926 Gainsborough Pictures announced that the star of *The Lodger* was to be Ivor Novello, a matinee idol whose previous career both as a composer of musical comedies and romantic lead of silent films did not necessarily prepare him for the role of a suspected killer of women. By the end of the story, of course, he would have to be vindicated, but Hitchcock was good at compromise.

In March he began what he called variously "the first real Hitchcock film" or "my first picture," with its combination of Victorian melodrama and expressionistic techniques. He and his cameraman were at one in preferring shafts of light and intense shadows, sudden close-ups and vertiginous staircases. The story was a simple one: at the time of a series of killings, a mysterious stranger arrives at the Bunting household in search of lodgings. The camera roams through the Bunting house as if it were intent upon laying a ghost, but the atmosphere of suspense and suspicion has already been very carefully established. The film opens with the face of a screaming woman, a device Hitchcock would use again as an emblem of female hysteria and sexuality, and then the night sky of London is punctured by a neon sign announcing "To-Night Golden Curls."

Enter Novello from the London fog like a wraith; the gas lamps of the house flicker and dim as he crosses the threshold into the Bunting world of cosy domesticity. The lower part of his face is covered. The eyes do all the work. To today's audiences it might look like overacting, but at the time it was simply intensity. He is led up to his rooms on the second floor, and at once the staircase becomes one of the themes of *The Lodger*; it might be seen as an image of spiritual mystery, mounting ever higher, but it also prompts the fear of falling. In one of the most technically expert scenes, lasting no more than ten seconds, Hitchcock turns a ceiling into glass so that the Buntings can actually see the pacing footsteps of their lodger; this effect would have come as a shock to contemporary audiences. At the end of the film the lodger, known as "The Avenger," is pursued by a ferocious London mob and is suspended by handcuffs from a set of railings. Hitchcock always liked handcuffs.

The filming took six weeks, but Hitchcock sensed trouble even before the first screening. There were still whispers of resentment against him at Gainsborough Pictures, orchestrated in part by Graham Cutts who could not forgive his erstwhile assistant's rise in the company. Cutts had as an ally the chairman of the distribution company attached to Gainsborough, C. M. Woolf. Both men believed that Hitchcock's experimental techniques would alienate an English audience. "I don't know what he's shooting," Cutts told someone at the studio. "I can't make head or tail of it." He prophesied disaster.

Neither Hitchcock nor Alma attended the formal screening in front of Woolf and others. Instead they trudged the stones of London together

Hitchcock in 1926, the year before *The Lodger* came out.

© *National Portrait Gallery, London*

for an hour and a half. Both of them were praying, since Alma had just been on a Catholic induction course in preparation for her marriage. They were eventually greeted, on their return, to devastating news. *The Lodger* was declared to be a fiasco, too "arty" and too "highbrow." It would have to be shelved. Hitchcock's career looked as if it might be over just after it had begun.

Michael Balcon, desperate to see a return on his investment in Novello, came to Hitchcock's rescue. He called in Ivor Montagu, who earned a precarious living by re-editing foreign films and translating foreign titles. It was Montagu's task to rework the film into a more acceptable form. He was actually delighted by the quality of *The Lodger*; he wished only to shorten some scenes and to reduce the number of title cards so that the narrative flowed more naturally. Hitchcock was, as always, highly practical. The title cards were cut from 300 to eighty, but it was still the original film in all of its important elements, and Hitchcock's vision was sustained.

The repairs were completed by July and the press and trade screening took place in the middle of September, when it became clear that Hitchcock's original confidence in *The Lodger* had been well placed. The critic of the *Daily Mail* called it "brilliant" and *The Bioscope* believed it to be "the finest British production ever made." Cutts and Woolf were confounded, Balcon vindicated, and Hitchcock celebrated as the radiant boy. *Picturegoer* had already called him "Alfred the Great."

On its release at the beginning of 1927, *The Lodger* proved to be a popular success; the scenes of the city in shadow, the doubt and suspense hovering over the suspected killer, the lighter touches of London domesticity, would all become Hitchcock's hallmarks; but here for the first time they were conveyed to an English audience without the black mark of being a "foreign" film. The sexual suggestiveness, already one of the weapons in Hitchcock's arsenal of cinematic themes, was also appreciated.

· · ·

Hitchcock, however, did not immediately follow a predictable path. He decided that he wished to create films associated with current events. This was the period when Robert Flaherty and John Grierson were beginning to experiment with projects, in Grierson's phrase, "of documentary value." Hitchcock was alert to any development in the new art of film, and began to consider the possibility of making a film about the General Strike of the previous year; he was not concerned with a simple news story but wanted, as he explained later, to create a "magnificently dynamic motion picture" with "fistfights between strikers and undergraduates, pickets and all the authentic drama of the situation." The proposal was immediately turned down by the British Board of Film Censors who disliked any reminder of a recent social crisis.

Throughout his career he aspired to a different form of cinema— a picture about sabotage in a dockyard, about a pit disaster, about a City scandal, featuring the lives of real people. But this was not a direction which the studios or censors wished to follow. In these early years, however, he never ceased to think about his art. In an open letter to the *Evening News* in November 1927, he made it clear that "when moving pictures are really artistic they will be created entirely by one man," just as a symphony is conceived by one composer. His ambitions were growing with every success.

It is of some relevance, then, that in *The Lodger* he made his first appearance in a "cameo" role; he played the part of a news editor, with his back turned to the camera, in a sequence that lasts two or three seconds. He said at the time that he was obliged to do so because of the shortage of actors, but his subsequent delight in such walk-on performances suggests otherwise. He was making his presence known and, subliminally, alerting the audience to the fact that he was in charge of what they saw. They could not have known who he was in *The Lodger*, of course. It was still a private pleasure.

He and Alma married on 2 December 1926, in a formal Roman Catholic ceremony at the Brompton Oratory in South Kensington. For their honeymoon they travelled to the Palace Hotel in St. Moritz, to

Hitchcock and Alma on their wedding day, 1926.

Courtesy of Evening Standard/Stringer

which resort they returned on their wedding anniversary as often as they could. The marriage endured until his death, with Alma following him into the dark two years later. He once said of her in a magazine article that "she has a consistency of presence, a lively personality, a never-clouded expression and she keeps her mouth shut except in magnanimously helpful ways." Her liveliness did much to dispel his nervous fear, of which she was well aware, and it is doubtful whether he would have been able to make his way in the world without her support. She had what she called "peppery" opinions about films, filming and of course film people, but they were for his ears only. She could spot charlatans and amateurs from a great distance, and he immediately bowed to her opinions. She was in the sound suites, the editing rooms and on the studio floors; she was the first one to see the finished picture, and the last one to deliver her opinions. She was in truth, according to contemporaries, a little "bossy"; but, as she said, she was never terribly ambitious and channelled all her hopes and aspirations into the work of her husband. They were like working partners rather than husband and wife; and that is how both of them wished it to be.

They were in some respects an odd couple. Alma was an almost boyish figure, and tended to wear "pant-suits" in a period they were not considered to be entirely proper. Their daughter, Patricia, recalled that her father arranged to have his wife's trouser suits tailored by Austin Reed, the gentlemen's outfitters, in London. Hitchcock called her "Madame," and on occasions "the Duchess," which is a cockney endearment for wife or mother. With the one exception of the conception of Patricia, he always claimed that theirs was a sexless marriage, and there is no reason to doubt him. He told Truffaut that he was celibate, and "that's why they call me the celibated director."

One intimate family friend, Dorothy Wegman, came to admire what she called "this odd, weird, little faggish man and this sweet little boyish woman." "Faggish" suggests an inclination towards camp or effeminacy. He was graceful to the point of gentility in his gestures and attitudes; he was nimble and dainty on his feet, not at all like the ponderous and serene figure of his public appearances. One of his colleagues and close collaborators, the American producer David O. Selznick, told his wife that "he's not a bad guy, shorn of affectations, although not exactly a man to go camping with."

Hitchcock once said that if he had not met Alma, he might have become a "poof." We may take his word for this, amplified once in a letter to Joan Crawford where he remarked that "in my very rare homosexual moments" he began to leaf through *Vogue*. He said that an actor had to possess a masculine and feminine side to enter the life of any character; the same undoubtedly would apply to an artist such as Hitchcock. He worked easily and naturally with homosexual actors (Ivor Novello was one such). And of course he showed a keen interest in homosexuality in most of his films; it is almost a leitmotif, and it would be an interesting parlour game to name any of his principal characters who were not intimated to be bisexual.

Before he married, he had still been living with his widowed mother in East London while Alma had been with her parents at Twickenham; but now they made a decisive change by setting up home together at 153 Cromwell Road, one of those great anonymous avenues of West London. They lived on the two top storeys of an early Victorian house, unfussy and unremarkable; they climbed ninety-six steps to their door, which may have helped Hitchcock's general fitness. The flat was furnished in contemporary commercial style by Liberty's of Regent Street. It was comfortable, and even cosy. At the back, down below, lay the tracks of the Underground coming up for air from the bowels of South Kensington so that, according to the film director Michael Powell, "the thunder of the passing trains was distant like the waves on the pebbles of Sandgate beach." They ate, and worked, on the dining-room table.

It was here they planned the last stages of *Downhill*, the film that directly followed *The Lodger* and was designed to reap the rewards of the previous film's popularity. Once more it starred Ivor Novello, as fresh and youthful as ever. It is a highly melodramatic narrative of a public schoolboy wrongly accused of seducing a female employee.

Novello was of course the lead. The transition from suspected serial killer to wronged public schoolboy may seem a large one, but for an audience in love with its matinee idol it was not a leap too far.

Yet *Downhill* has its moments. Theatrical as it may have been in execution, it is a successful study in deceit, cruelty and perversion. The interiors are like prison scenes illuminated by shafts of sunlight and, as Novello begins his ineluctable journey downwards, Hitchcock conveys his characteristic sense of the world as perilous and unstable. The protagonist is once more "the wrong man," as he had been in *The Lodger*, and some of his travels take him through scenes of London at night wonderfully striated by neon lighting. It becomes a Hitchcock landscape. The images of the young man's fevered delirium are startlingly clear since, as Hitchcock said, "I tried to embody the dream in the reality, in solid unblurred images" at a time when dreams were generally presented as dissolves. It was an aspect of his instinctive cinematic intelligence.

When it came to be known that Hitchcock would be directing Novello at Maida Vale Underground station, after midnight on a Saturday, a large crowd clustered at the entrance. Novello was to be filmed descending an escalator, an effect never before attempted, with the obvious intent of suggesting the downward movement of his life together with vertigo and general instability. It took five takes in almost four hours as the actor, caked in greasepaint, made the journey down the wooden escalator. Hitchcock held the camera still for twenty-three seconds in each take, where other directors might have allowed five or six seconds. He himself was dressed in white tie and tails, having previously attended the theatre.

There was another instance of what might be called the heroic age of film-making. At one showing of *Downhill* in a London cinema the lights and the screen went up in the middle of the production to reveal Novello himself on the stage, dressed in the part he played, who then proceeded to enact the next ten minutes of the narrative for the benefit of the no doubt surprised audience.

Such was the speed of production, and appetite for new films, that Hitchcock began his next project while still working on *Down-hill*. When the cameraman fell ill on this new production, he readily stepped forward and took up the role. *Easy Virtue* was the account of a woman whose wicked past catches up with her after she marries a suitably rich and respectable young man. It is an old story, but Hitchcock directs it with panache as a study in guilt and voyeurism. The eyes have it, whether they are the eyes of the accusing characters or of the cinema audience. The interiors are full of mirrors and reflections, and the image of the camera becomes central. A newspaper photograph reveals her past. "Shoot," she says to the photographers in the most memorable line in the film, "there is nothing left to kill!"

.   .   .

Easy Virtue was Hitchcock's last film for Gainsborough Pictures. He had been persuaded by John Maxwell to move to the Elstree studios of British International Pictures (BIP) that had recently been founded by Maxwell; he was promised better facilities, better control and, just as important, a better salary. Hitchcock would be paid, at £13,000, an annual salary three times larger than before; by the middle of 1927, he was the highest paid director in England. The terms and conditions must have been acceptable since, in the course of the next five years, he completed ten films with Maxwell as producer. British International Pictures was more commercial, and perhaps more professional, than Gainsborough; John Maxwell himself was a Glaswegian solicitor who knew business better than a businessman. It is a measure of Hitchcock's own professionalism that he was happy to work under such auspices, and indeed take advantage of them.

Much of his work for the next few years consisted of literary or theatrical adaptations that were guaranteed to please an English audience. The first of the Elstree films, however, *The Ring*, seems to have been from a concept of his own devising. For the first time in his career it was announced as "written and directed by Alfred Hitchcock," but it can be assumed that his wife had some part in the composition of the screenplay. He said later that this was the second "real" Hitchcock picture, but he had also taken into his small circle a new cameraman, Jack Cox, who had been working in the film industry since 1913. He would stay with Hitchcock for eleven films, culminating eleven years later in *The Lady Vanishes*, and was partly responsible for the Hitchcock "look," both intimate and impersonal. Cox's assistant recalled how Hitchcock would pull out a sketchbook and draw foreground and perspective for a particular scene, saying "I want you to use a 50 mm lens."

The Ring is a story of two prizefighters challenging one another for the hand of the same woman. There is much play with the notion of the "ring" itself—the boxing ring, the engagement ring, the wedding ring together with the swings and roundabouts of the fairground. Hitchcock liked fairgrounds. The pugilism is itself part of the fun of the fair, with a cast of carnivalesque characters who turn up in later Hitchcock films. Hitchcock had what might be called a cockney vision of the world as part pantomime and part spectacle; he was not interested in the moral complications of characters, only in the scene and the striking image. This was the source of his visual sense. He was not creating a real world, indistinguishable from that outside the cinema, but a carefully crafted artifice. Comedy is in fact the key tone of *The Ring*, together with the suspense of which he had become a master. He had made an art out of the nervous stomach; he pinned the butterflies to the wall.

While directing *The Ring* Hitchcock was everywhere at once. He was not so much interested in the boxing as in what he called "the shop," all the details and business that happen around the fight itself. He experimented with these details; he focused upon them. A fairground was constructed, and a newspaper article confirmed that "the film's director, Mr. Alfred Hitchcock, will be moving among the crowds giving instructions to his cameramen . . . disguised as a showman wearing the traditional frock coat and red silk handkerchief and ebullient silk hat." He was directing the crowds but at the same time he was directing the audience. He knew how to manipulate its attention and moods in the manner of a showground busker. "It is amazing," a journalist wrote, "how he manages to maintain his energy and keenness, considering that since the beginning of the year he has been on the floor, working practically every day." Every new film was now crucial to him, eager as he was to capitalise on his new association with BIP. He had memorised the saying that a director is no better than his last picture.

The premiere of *The Ring* in the autumn of 1927 was a success, with the audience clapping a sequence of montage that Hitchcock had learned from the Russians. "I never heard a montage get a round of applause before," he said, "but this did." The film seemed to come as a revelation and was described in the *Daily Mail* as "the greatest production ever made in this country" and, in the *Daily News*, as "a devastating answer to those who disbelieved in the possibilities of a British film." *The Bioscope* commented that "if future British films only approach *The Ring* in quality, we need have no fears for the ultimate success of the entire producing industry in this country." So Hitchcock, at the age of twenty-eight, was being identified as the saviour of British film. Yet the film was not as successful at the box office, which may have prompted him to meditate further upon the relationship between art and commerce. Was there a point at which both could meet?

He had gone down to Devon by the time *The Ring* was released, ready to start work on *The Farmer's Wife*. This could be described as a pastoral comedy concerning a farmer's desperate attempt to find a bride after the death of his first wife. The brides, each one less attractive than the one before, kept on saying "no"; in that context Hitchcock taps the rich vein of English character acting which he always admired. It was in fact an adaptation of a play but Hitchcock opens it out, as it were, by bringing the camera into the action with fluid and subtle movements.

He said later that "it was a routine job" and merely "a photograph of a stage play with lots of titles instead of dialogue," but he did less than justice to his youthful skills. *The Farmer's Wife* is, in pictorial terms, an impressive and even beautiful piece of work with the landscapes of Devon and of Surrey summoned up as a suitable backdrop for gentle comedy. Nor was it an affair of talking heads, or photographs with titles. A farmhouse was built on the set of Elstree to allow the camera unimpeded access so that it could weave through each room; it was an experiment, following an actress from the sitting room to the kitchen and then upstairs to the bedroom, and he was not sure that it would be successful. But it was. The rhythm of the film was important to him; he said in an interview that "I had to film a little scene in *The Farmer's Wife* six times the other day because the players took it too slowly to fit in with the mood of the picture." The result was impressive, despite Hitchcock's later disclaimer, and a critic remarked that "it has been left to Alfred Hitchcock to put England on the screen."

At a party to celebrate the end of filming Hitchcock invited the members of cast and crew to a West End restaurant; but he had hired the smallest room he could find. The forty guests were crowded into a space designed for twelve, in which rude and clumsy waiters were played by actors. It was one of the practical jokes for which he was well known. On one occasion he arranged a dinner party for the actress Gertrude Lawrence in which every item on the menu was blue. On one opening night Sir Gerald du Maurier found a horse, rather than flowers, in his dressing room courtesy of Alfred Hitchcock. When friends were abroad or away on holiday, he would order the largest and most awkward furniture to fill their rooms. He had a set of whoopee cushions at home, and brought them out for the more grand or formal guests. He painted clown faces on his sleeping daughter.

He often directed his macabre humour at his players. He contrived to get Montgomery Clift hopelessly drunk at the end of filming *I Confess* by plying him with alcohol. Some of his jokes were demeaning to their victims. He made a bet that a property man would not be able to spend the night chained to a camera in a darkened studio; the man accepted the bet, and Hitchcock presented him with a bottle of brandy to beguile the hours away. It was laced with a very strong laxative, with the intended consequences soon apparent. When filming *The Birds* with Tippi Hedren he presented her daughter with a tiny image of Tippi lying in a coffin.

Alma once confessed that "he never stopped playing jokes on people, and now and then I got a little apprehensive." The psychology of the practical joker has been much discussed. It is a form of indirect revenge, and of the need for mastery or control; it also suggests an instinctive scorn for the human race, as exemplified in Edgar Allan Poe's equally celebrated "hoaxes" of an unkind nature. Poe, too, enjoyed gallows humour. It was Hitchcock's speciality, and he eventually made a television series out of it.

For their first wedding anniversary in early December 1927, the Hitchcocks returned to the Palace Hotel at St. Moritz; they preferred familiar places as well as familiar faces. And, at the end of the year, he sent out a caricature of himself in the form of a jigsaw.

.   .   .

In the New Year, Alma made it known that she was pregnant. "I did it with a fountain pen," was his often reported comment.

At approximately the same time his next film was announced with the simple title of *Champagne*. New English films were now considered to be highly desirable, and at the end of 1927 a new Cinematograph Films Act, designed to end the American monopoly of English cinema screens, had stipulated that by 1935 one fifth of all films should be made in England. In fact the quota was reached by 1932. There was even talk of an "English Hollywood."

Champagne was not really the film to lead the charge. It was, as its name suggests, a light and frothy affair; its heroine, Betty Balfour, was as bubbly as can be, but she did not meet with Hitchcock's approval. He described her to a young photographer on the set, Michael Powell, as "a piece of suburban obscenity." He had wanted another, more resourceful, actress for the part of the daughter of a rich man suddenly fallen on hard times. He had also wanted a more serious story of exploitation but, as he said later, "we ended up with a hodge-podge of a story that was written as we went through the film and I thought it was dreadful." Betty Balfour, the ultimate "flapper," frothed and glistened throughout an improbable plot but she was not taken to the public's heart. The film was described as "champagne that had been left in the rain all night." Hitchcock himself was not in the best of tempers during the filming and did all he could, for example, to stop Powell taking stills of Balfour.

Powell himself left a description of the disgruntled director. "He really was the fattest young man I had ever seen. He had a fresh, rosy, complexion, his dark hair was sleeked back, and he was correctly dressed in a suit with a watch-chain across his waistcoat. He wore a soft hat. He observed me out of the corner of his piggy eyes sunk in fat cheeks. There was not much that Hitch missed with those piggy eyes."

Just before the production of *Champagne* was completed, Alma went into labour. It was her husband who panicked. Unable to bear the anxiety he left the flat and went for a long walk through London; he purchased en route a sapphire and gold bracelet in Bond Street, so he might be able to offer her some recompense for his unwarranted absence. Their ensuing conversation seems to have been so much part of familial tradition that it appeared in their daughter's memoir of her mother.

"But you didn't have to go out," Alma told him. "I wasn't really feeling bad at all."

"I know you weren't, dear. But consider my suffering. I nearly died of the suspense."

In his imagination he had taken on the agonies of the woman. Alma said later that "he might as well have changed places with me."

The Hitchcocks had already decided, for the sake of the as yet unborn child and themselves, to purchase a cottage outside London in the neighbourhood of Shamley Green about five miles south of Guildford in Surrey. It is now designated as an area of outstanding natural beauty and in the early part of the twentieth century it was part of still rural England surrounded by farmland and distant hills. They bought a large cottage of Tudor origins, "Winter's Grace," with comfortable if rackety rooms and a large garden; it was renovated in the 1930s, and made more imposing. The new family, in traditional fashion, spent the weekdays in London and their weekends in the country. In Shamley

Green he seemed noticeably to relax. They employed a housekeeper, Mary Condon, who remarked of her employer that "you could not meet a nicer gentleman and a very good Catholic, too." His religious observances might have been part of the duty he felt to his daughter, and to his mother who paid regular visits.

Life in Cromwell Road and in Shamley Green was well ordered and well directed; Alma reported that "our home had to be as orderly and tidy as one of Hitch's film sets." Everything had its place; the taps were shining; the wood well polished, and the meals (generally cooked by Alma) always arrived on time. The lawns and garden beds were tended by employees who were rarely visible. The Hitchcocks worked in both locations, sometimes on the dining table of Cromwell Road and sometimes in the garden of Shamley Green. Hitchcock still had the high spirits of ambition and achievement; as a party trick he would strip to the waist and paint a sailor's face on his belly so that the guests might see the sailor's expressions gyrate. On at least one occasion he dressed up in drag as "Lady Agatha"; a surviving photograph shows a most respectable middle-aged lady.

·   ·   ·

Then he was off again, to the coast of Cornwall, to make *The Manxman*, based on a novel by Hall Caine of a suitably melodramatic nature. The harbour of Polperro posed as the Isle of Man for the setting of a film that rings changes on the triangle of love which Hitchcock had already used in earlier films. It was an altogether more serious production than its predecessor, *Champagne*, with the wild seas and cliffs of Cornwall providing the setting of overwhelming passion, guilt and loss which are for once not dissipated by a happy ending. It is in some respects a simple piece, but one of the highest distinction; the simplicity and directness are compelling and, with the concentration upon facial expressiveness, it draws on the best qualities of the silent cinema. No sound or dialogue could achieve more significant effects. Silent drama can evoke the fears and fantasies of the audience in a unique fashion.

He remarked later that "it was a very banal picture," but he was wrong. *The Manxman* is one of the best of Britain's silent films.

It is also one of the last. Change was in the air. In the autumn of 1927 *The Jazz Singer* had proved the possibilities of synchronised sound, and in the following year *Lights of New York* became the first all-talking picture. Hitchcock was more attuned than most to the development of film and by the close of 1928, after the completion of *The Manxman*, he was ready to take advantage of the new situation. He orchestrated another change; the scriptwriter on his silent films, Eliot Stannard, was no longer considered suitable.

Hitchcock had agreed to direct *Blackmail*, a capable thriller derived from a West End success. The chronology is unclear, but it seems that he had already begun a silent version of the film when it was decided to issue a sound version as well. Hitchcock had in fact anticipated the studio's instructions. An assistant cameraman on *Blackmail*, Ronald Neame, agreed that Hitchcock "loved the idea of sound." Unlike Charles Chaplin, who considered it to be a blow to "pure film," Hitchcock was immediately aware of its possibilities. He planned the sound version even while he was working on the silent alternative; he imagined dialogue even before the first words were spoken. In an article for the *News Chronicle* he revealed that "I did it by shooting a lot of scenes where sound could be tacked on afterwards and making a lot of other scenes, not in the script, with sound. When they were all assembled the whole picture was a talkie." The first reel remains essentially silent but the rest of the film takes advantage of a new range of sound effects. The earliest scenes, showing the arrest of a thief, are played entirely in the old tradition of silent melodrama; after booking their man, the two detectives walk down a corridor in Scotland Yard. Slowly but subtly their voices begin to be heard and the audience is formally introduced to the world of sound. This moment was doubtless both unsettling and exciting.

He had first to test his players. A short piece of unrehearsed film survives of his conversation with his leading lady from Czechoslovakia, Anny Ondra, which gives some clue to his relationships with his actors.

On the set of *Blackmail*, showing primitive audio equipment, 1929.
Hitchcock can be seen in the top right of the photograph.

Courtesy of Imagno

HITCHCOCK: Now, Miss Ondra, we are going to do a sound test. Isn't that what you wanted? Now come right over here.

ONDRA: I don't know what to say. I'm so nervous!

HITCHCOCK: Have you been a good girl?

ONDRA [LAUGHING]: Oh, no!

HITCHCOCK: No? Have you slept with men?

ONDRA: No!

HITCHCOCK: No?

ONDRA: Oh, Hitch, you make me embarrassed! [She giggles.]

HITCHCOCK: Now come right over here, Miss Ondra, and stand still in your place—or it won't come out right, as the girl said to the soldier.

It is perhaps worth adding that Hitchcock would have known exactly when and with whom Anny Ondra was sleeping. He was an indefatigable gossip on sexual matters. He was fascinated by what would be ordinarily concealed and what might be called the hidden life of those he met. One of his screenwriters, Arthur Laurents, remarked that "he thought everyone was doing something physical and nasty behind every closed door—except himself." The fat boy was still watching alone while the others played.

The plot itself is intriguing. A cockney shop-girl stabs to death a man attempting to rape her but her boyfriend, a detective, manages to pin the murder on a petty criminal; the girl is seized with guilt and confusion throughout the action, but on this occasion she is relieved of any consequences when the criminal falls to his death during a pursuit. It leaves her guilt unresolved and cannot be seen as a conventional happy ending.

There were problems with the sound. Anny Ondra, playing the shop assistant, had a strong accent. There was no question of dubbing in those early days, so the leading lady moved her lips to pronounce the words while an English actress spoke them into a microphone. The sound equipment was cumbersome in the extreme, introducing into the film studio an obstacle course of booths and boxes, cables and lamps.

The camera itself had to be placed in a soundproof booth to conceal its cranking noise, while the players had to position themselves immediately below the low-hanging microphones. The new lamps, designed not to hum or splutter, created intense heat. The director, wearing outsize earphones, was close to suffocation in a tiny recording booth.

Yet Hitchcock was already proving himself to be a master of sound. One of the first indications of this emerges in a scene where the heroine, distraught after the stabbing, returns to her family shop. A garrulous neighbour has already heard the news of the horrible murder. "What a terrible way to kill a man. With a *knife*! Now I would have used a brick maybe, but I'd never use a *knife*. A *knife* is a terrible thing. A *knife* is so messy and dreadful." The sound is so modified that the word rings out like a clarion, thus augmenting the heroine's fear.

The final sequence of pursuit is equally significant, but only as a triumph of the soon-to-be-outmoded silent genre. The wrongly suspected murderer escapes from the detectives into the Reading Room of the British Museum, the great dome itself filmed as a work of mystery. In a climactic moment the fleeing man is seen dangling from a thin rope beside the giant visage of Rameses the Great, a monstrous image of imperturbability and indifference before the man's imminent death. Hitchcock used the effect later, with the Statue of Liberty in *Saboteur* and the heads of Mount Rushmore in *North by Northwest*. The image also recalls the sphinx-like demeanour he himself used to affect, concealing his permanent state of anxiety; it might also be considered as a way of representing death.

Blackmail is often considered to be Britain's first "talkie," but that honour must be conferred upon *The Clue of the New Pin*, which cannot now be found in the haystack. The advertising poster for *Blackmail*, however, did not hold back. "The First Full Length All Talkie Film Made In Great Britain . . . See & Hear Our Mother Tongue As It Should Be—Spoken . . . Hold Everything Till You've Heard This One!" The film was, perhaps inevitably, a popular success in Britain. The *Daily Chronicle* celebrated the fact that after the nasal sound of American accents, "the English voices in *Blackmail* . . . are like music."

At the public screening in the Regal cinema in the summer of 1929 the film was, according to *To-day's Cinema*, "punctuated at times with almost continual bursts of applause," one of which lasted for seven minutes. This was a wholly new way of understanding the world, and when it was accompanied by Hitchcock's brilliant renditions of the London ambience—the traffic, the streets, the advertisements, the domestic interiors, the Lyons tea shops, the back alleys—it amounted to a unique vision of the city. In an interview with the *Evening News* at the time of the film's release, Hitchcock remarked that "it has created a demand for realism that is not demanded in the ordinary theatre." He also had a private response. According to their daughter, "my parents were in heaven."

4

I WAS GREY

B*lackmail* had not been a success in foreign markets, and American audiences professed not to understand English accents. So the profits, if any, were very modest. Elstree needed a more solid and durable product. Despite Hitchcock's growing fame he was still a professional working for a company, and he was obliged to turn his hand to whatever the managers considered feasible.

In the summer of 1929 he met Sean O'Casey to discuss an adaptation of the playwright's *Juno and the Paycock*, performed five years before to great acclaim. It would be Hitchcock's first thoroughly conceived and consistent talkie, and it was most certainly filled with talk. *Juno and the Paycock*, as it had been played by the actors of the Abbey Theatre in Dublin, was sustained by O'Casey's particular blend of wild declamation, impassioned prayer and broad Gaelic humour with a music of its own.

The Hitchcocks visited O'Casey at his home in St. John's Wood to discuss this and other future projects. O'Casey recalled that Hitchcock "was a hulk of a man, unwieldy in his gait, seeming as if he had to hoist himself into every movement, like an overblown seal," whereas Alma was "sitting silent but attentive, registering every gesture and every word." He soon realised that it was she who would make the final decisions. Alma was in fact responsible, with her husband, for the script; it does not differ markedly from the theatrical version, except for two or three exterior scenes to lend a degree of verisimilitude.

Sound was always the key question. In one scene a record is being played on a brand-new phonograph but, as family and friends sing along with it, their voices are joined by those of a passing funeral procession which are in turn interrupted by machine-gun fire. Hitchcock had to improvise. A prop man held his nose to create the "tinny" sound of a phonograph while, on camera, the players sang along with him; in another part of the studio a choir began their funeral dirge, while the stagehands beat with canes on pieces of leather to simulate gunfire. Nothing could be pre-recorded. It was as surprising as any performance at an avant-garde concert.

Otherwise Hitchcock remained faithful to the rhetoric and melodrama of the original. Since most of the cast actually came from the Abbey Theatre in the first place, the director let them get on with it. In the process he was plunged into the faith of his childhood. That is why he treats the story with a respect bordering on sentimentality. It would not be wise to be ironic about invocations of the Virgin. It is a lurid narrative of betrayal and vengeance during the Irish Civil War but set in the half-comic and half-pathetic world of the Boyles, a lower-class Dublin family with a drunken father and a perpetually frustrated mother. The studio may have hoped that an American audience would be better able to understand an Irish, rather than an English, accent.

It was a success, largely because of the writing and acting, rather than Hitchcock's own contribution. James Agate in *Tatler* believed that it "appears to me to be very nearly a masterpiece. Bravo, Mr. Hitchcock!," but the director himself confessed that he had been "kind of rather ashamed when it got terrific notices." He did not believe himself responsible for its quality. But he never disavowed it, as he did others of his early films. It evoked the Irishness of his immediate ancestry, and the prevailing note of piety and prayer was deeply congenial to him. He was asked if he had been bored by it. "No," he replied, "because the characters were so interesting."

The success of *Juno and the Paycock* confirmed the nature of Hitchcock's next films. He and Alma would now be the principal screenwriters of four successive pictures, all of which would be based on successful novels or stage plays. They may have been a long way from Hitchcock's concept of "pure cinema" but, as he knew well enough, business was business. He directed, for example, portions of what was essentially a musical variety show called *Elstree Calling*. Hitchcock told one interviewer that it was "of no interest whatsoever"; and so it has proved.

Immediately afterwards he began work on *Murder!* which, as its name suggests, is in part a detective thriller. In later life he disparaged this genre as reliant upon the elements of a puzzle, rather than on genuine suspense or fear, but he brings to the narrative a certain wit and inventiveness. A leading actress has been convicted of murdering a female colleague but one of the jurors, who happens to be a distinguished actor-manager by the name of Sir John Menier, disagrees with the verdict; he must find the real killer.

The crime is essentially set in the theatre, or at least in a theatrical atmosphere, and Hitchcock lights a circle of stage fire to contain his characters. In a world of stage doors and dressing rooms, the proscenium arch is never far away. By the time the murderer turns out to be a transvestite circus acrobat, trying to conceal the fact that he is a "half-caste" (we can justifiably read "homosexual"), the curtain is almost ready to fall. Except that, in the closing scene, it is revealed that the whole story is being played as a drama on the London stage.

What is real and what is unreal? Is performance an intrinsic aspect of the human condition? Is London simply a great stage on which we all are players? Who knows? Who cares? Hitchcock does not. It is on one level simply entertainment, similar to that of the theatre and the circus which provide the settings. There are moments, however, which show the director at his best. In one early scene the amateur detective muses in front of the shaving mirror, thus providing the first example of interior monologue in the British cinema. He is mentally soliloquising to the music of *Tristan and Isolde* issuing from the wireless, but Hitchcock found it necessary to import a thirty-piece orchestra to play the music on the set while the actor's pre-recorded voice is being heard.

It was a very ingenious use of sound, although some at the time considered it to be too highbrow.

In the autumn of 1930, after *Murder!* had been completed, Hitchcock picked up another play ripe for filming. He began negotiations with John Galsworthy whose play *The Skin Game* had been a popular success ten years before. It dramatised a case of class warfare, when a parvenu industrialist wishes to buy up land contiguous to the estate of a member of the classic agricultural order known then as "old money." In advance of filming Hitchcock explained to the players the gestures, words and intonations that he wanted; there was to be none of the improvisation which he had allowed in *Murder!*

The Skin Game is a genuinely arresting and intriguing film, with an auction scene as good as any; the camera weaves and ducks with the characters as they bid for the disputed land, displaying that technical mastery which was Hitchcock's most important asset. The filming was completed in three months and, after its release in January 1931, it proved to be a success with both critics and public. Hitchcock was still the *wunderkind* of British cinema.

.　.　.

After *The Skin Game*, the Hitchcocks embarked upon a cruise. Ever since he had charted the progress of ships across the Atlantic as a schoolboy, he had relished the idea of travel without inconvenient complications—such as disembarking. They sailed down the coast of West Africa before crossing to the West Indies, and returned to England by way of Gambia, but perhaps Hitchcock was too much of a cockney to pay much attention to foreign attractions. He said that the most important lesson was that cruise passengers "get to hate one another after being cooped up for a while on board ship."

Travel may not broaden the mind, but it may stir the imagination. It seems that in the course of their journey Hitchcock conceived an idea for his next film. *Rich and Strange* would consist of the perilous adventures of a middle-class London couple, the Hills, who find out that travel can mean nothing but trouble. It could be viewed as a fantastic reworking of the Hitchcocks' own cruise, but it is performed in a quite different key. The couple, having unexpectedly acquired funds, leave tedious London for the delights of the Orient. They fall out during the course of the voyage and are only reunited by a series of threats and perils that seem to come out of nowhere.

Their funds are depleted; they are obliged to travel on a second-rate liner; the liner sinks; they are picked up by the Chinese crew of a pirates' junk; inadvertently they eat cat in a chop suey before the skin of the cat is shown stretched out to dry. They have entered a fantasy world full of threat, the sum of all their fears. The husband is awkward, bad-tempered and petulant, while the wife has a more amiable or at least less excitable temperament. Allusions to the Hitchcocks themselves are permissible but perhaps not appropriate. The ordeal leaves the Hills none the wiser, however, and when they return to their suburban home they begin once more to bicker in the old fashion. That is, more or less, that.

Much of the film is silent, shot by a second crew in exotic locations where sound equipment would have been too cumbersome. The point of the exercise, if any, is not immediately clear. *Rich and Strange* turned out to be neither. It might be classed a comic melodrama, except that it is not particularly funny. In a cameo at the end, later cut, the two unfortunate travellers talk to Hitchcock himself about their travails. "No," Hitchcock tells them, "I don't think it will make a movie." The sequence may have been discarded for stating the obvious. The veteran film-maker John Grierson wrote that "in trying new material Hitchcock has found himself outside both his experience and imagination . . . his mind does not quite appreciate the wonders of the world he is trying to use." He was in effect accusing Hitchcock of being parochial. The director himself defended the film for having "lots of ideas . . . I liked the picture. It should have been more successful." The English public did not agree. His relations with British International Pictures were in any case becoming strained.

He had taken the precaution of arranging his own publicity. He could not, and did not, rely upon BIP. He formed a small company, Hitchcock Baker Productions Limited, the sole purpose of which was to keep Hitchcock's name and achievements before the public; he had embarked, in other words, upon an endless course of self-advertisement. He had already explained to Ivor Montagu, and others of the Hate Club, the importance of the critics and the press in general in creating a marketable "name." Now he was to achieve it in a thoroughly professional manner. There was self-regard, but not necessarily vanity, in his desire to present himself to the public. He realised, for example, that his weight could be used to advantage in conveying an image of himself and on occasion he granted interviews with journalists while wearing pyjamas and dressing gown to amplify the figure of a fat man. He never ceased using similar techniques throughout his career. He also pondered the financial possibilities of his position, and employed a tax adviser to manage his earnings and his investments.

Even as he was editing *Rich and Strange* he was asked to direct at Elstree Studios what was known in the business as a "quota quickie," a film hastily brought out to complete the number of English productions stipulated by the Films Act of 1927. The picture chosen for him, *Number Seventeen*, was not to his taste. The rambling narrative of jewel thieves, mysterious detectives and hanging bodies borders on the incomprehensible. Hitchcock could not take it seriously, and in fact made sure that no one else took it seriously either. It became a parody of an adventure thriller, played out in what could easily be a haunted mansion. The sinister interiors become the setting for the cheapest thrills, with sudden shadows, locked rooms, disappearing corpses and footsteps without feet. "It's like the pictures, isn't it?" one character suggests. "Too much for my liking," comes the reply.

Hitchcock was essentially playing with his audience and perhaps also with his employers. There are moments in most of his films when the cinematic illusion is displayed, when the audience knows in his words that "it's only a movie." But *Number Seventeen* is based on that premise. The climactic chase scene, for example, is comprised of what are obviously toy models of cars and trains, adding to the atmosphere of farce. He later confessed that the whole enterprise had been a "disaster"; but he had only himself to blame.

There was one last gasp. In the summer of 1932 it was reported in *The Times* that Hitchcock had been "recently appointed by British International Pictures Limited to supervise all their productions at the Elstree Studio." It is not clear of what this "supervision" consisted, except for the fact that he was credited as producer rather than director of another "quota quickie" entitled *Lord Camber's Ladies*. He described it as "a poison thing. I gave it to Benn Levy to direct." It had an illustrious cast, including Gerald du Maurier and Gertrude Lawrence, but it seems notable only for the practical jokes that Hitchcock as producer played on the leading actors. Du Maurier's daughter, Daphne, recalled that "hardly a moment would pass without some fateful telegram arriving, some bogus message being delivered, some supposed telephone bell ringing, until the practical jokers were haggard and worn with their tremendous efforts." This may have been a sign of Hitchcock's contempt for BIP. His contract was terminated shortly afterwards.

He was already dreaming of America. He was beginning to feel that he was in the backwaters of cinematic development. England was too insular. There was no appreciation, except by a few, of Soviet and German cinema. He also believed that American film was technically superior, with its larger resources combined with much greater sense of purpose. He complained in a newspaper article that "one of the chief disadvantages of British film production is the scarcity of people with an instinct for films—who can, in fact, think pictorially." So he set his sights across the Atlantic. He allowed an American agency to suggest his name to various studios, but the time was not appropriate; the Hollywood industry was about to enter a slump. His opportunity would come a little later.

Nevertheless he wanted to begin again under new auspices. He had agreed with an entrepreneur and independent producer, Tom Watson, to direct *Waltzes from Vienna*, a run-of-the-mill musical comedy concerning the professional relationship between Strauss senior and Strauss junior. It is an elaborate setting for the waltz "The Blue Danube." It is not clear why he accepted the assignment. He may have needed the money; he may have wanted to keep busy after his displacement from Elstree. It is not an unsuccessful musical, as musicals go, and Hitchcock made some effort to knit the songs with the narrative in the interests of formal coherence. It is light comedy which manages to be engaging and entertaining.

But he was not happy with the enterprise, and vented some of his frustration on the leading players. Jessie Matthews, the star of the film, complained that "he was then just an imperious young man who knew nothing about musicals. I felt unnerved when he tried to get me to adopt a mincing operetta style. He was out of his depth and showed that he knew it by ordering me around . . . I thought the film was perfectly dreadful." She said also that "he sent me up mercilessly" as "the Quota Queen" and that she "was always anticipating some ghastly practical joke." Hitchcock himself best summed up the experience when he announced on the set that "I hate this sort of stuff. Melodrama is the only thing I can do."

The film was shot at the studios of Gaumont British, at Lime Grove in Shepherd's Bush, of which Michael Balcon was now head of production. Balcon had of course worked with Hitchcock at the Islington Studios, a period which Hitchcock regarded with increasing pleasure. It was Balcon, after all, who had given him his first directorial role. That may have been one of the reasons Hitchcock accepted *Waltzes from Vienna*. Now Balcon was about to rescue his career once more. They had been discussing possible future projects, and Hitchcock mentioned that he had been working from time to time on a script concerning Bulldog Drummond, a gentleman of adventure who might be described as the James Bond of the 1920s and '30s, and Balcon reacted enthusiastically. So a partnership was re-formed that lasted for a further four years.

Another member of this partnership was Charles Bennett. Bennett had originally been a playwright but it was he who had written *Blackmail* and had subsequently written a screenplay entitled *Bulldog Drummond's Baby*; this was the script which Hitchcock mentioned to Balcon. The time was right. Bennett had also left BIP and was looking for a new studio. Hitchcock and Bennett were back in business under the benign management of Balcon.

Bennett recalled that "Hitchcock and I used to go to a local pub— not far from the studio—and we used to spend most of the afternoon just talking. Sometimes we talked very little about the film we were writing." This was Hitchcock's preferred way of working, allowing the scenes and ideas to emerge unprompted rather than in the forcing house of office sessions. Bennett added that "Hitch referred to me as his constructionist and felt I was the best. For dialogue he would bring in someone else—but no one else could build a story like I could." Hitchcock always needed a strong story on which to hang his own ideas. He seems to have worked out individual scenes and images in his head, but had no real idea of how to connect them in a living whole. This was where Bennett was at his best.

Hitchcock had imagined two distinct settings for the new film. One was of Alpine bleakness and the other was of the dark mass of London streets. He was a poet of cinematic imagery. At some point he suggested to his writer that "we just drop the Drummond business"; and out of their new scenario emerged *The Man Who Knew Too Much*. Hitchcock and Bennett would walk the streets or take bus rides in search of possible settings; in particular Hitchcock liked the ambience of the Royal Albert Hall.

Eventually Bennett would work on four of Hitchcock's films, and Balcon would produce them. These were the people substantially responsible for Hitchcock's first great period of English thrillers, and Bennett in particular has never received the credit for his close collaboration with the director. Consistency was further maintained by working again with cinematographer Bernard Knowles, the art directors Otto Wendorff and Albert Juillon, and the editor Charles Frend. All of these now almost forgotten names also contributed in part to the essential spark of the "light thrillers" or "thriller sextet," combining comedy and suspense, which rescued Hitchcock's reputation in the early 1930s.

Charles Bennett and the Hitchcocks started final work on the script in Cromwell Road. What did Hitchcock know about Switzerland, where the film begins? "They have milk chocolate," he said, "they have the Alps, they have village dances, and they have lakes. All of these national ingredients were woven into the picture." He had scenes in mind even before he could assimilate them. But darker elements were also at work. Ordinary people, living in a familiar setting, are suddenly plunged into a "chaos world" where no one is safe. That is where all the suspense and terror start. On the first day of shooting, 29 May 1934, Hitchcock walked on to the set and put the finished script on a table, announcing "Another picture in the bag!"

Peter Lorre, fresh from his success as a child murderer in Fritz Lang's M, had already arrived in London to play one of the central roles. Hitchcock liked Lorre's combination of menace, sarcasm and decorum. Lorre recalled that "all I knew in English was yes and no, and I couldn't say no because I would have had to explain it. Sidney [Bernstein] put me wise to the fact that Hitchy liked to tell stories; so I used to watch him like a hawk and whenever I thought the end of a story was coming and that was the point, I used to roar with laughter and somehow he got the impression that I spoke English and I got the part."

Hitchcock's judgement was correct and Lorre's fascinating manner, like that of a snake hypnotising a victim, came to dominate The Man Who Knew Too Much. It was his visage that was most prominent on the film posters. He plays the leader of a group of assassins who intend to murder a foreign leader but, alas, their secret is revealed to an ordinary English couple on an Alpine holiday, whereupon their daughter is kidnapped by Lorre and his associates; his previous role as child murderer no doubt added a frisson to the adventure. The chase is now on for the daughter, and it takes various turns through a temple of sun-worshippers, a dentist's surgery in the East End and the Royal Albert Hall, before culminating in a siege within the dark streets of Wapping.

Hitchcock made another version of the same film twenty-two years later, with Doris Day and James Stewart, but the differences are far more interesting than the similarities. The American product is more technically assured and more carefully executed, while the English version is funnier, faster and lighter.

He had crafted a thriller of his own devising that would profoundly affect the nature of his later films. The idea that civilisation is as thin as ice, beneath which lie depths and darknesses, is one that stayed with him. The idea that the course of ordinary life is unexpected and full of threat is another of his constant themes. So also is his association of terror with comedy, of threat with pantomime, of the most subdued realism with the most contrived theatricality. It is a cockney vision, adumbrated by Dickens and Chaplin. He had first explored it in such films as *Downhill* and *Rich and Strange*, but now it came fully to fruition. Yet it can also be construed as a Catholic vision which is designed to have power that is emotional and unconscious, rather than rational and intellectual. Hitchcock did not want his audiences to think. He would rather titillate them, bludgeon them, or excite them with unbearable suspense. Hidden laws govern the universe. Individuals are at the mercy of impersonal forces. That is all you know or need to know.

Another device, unveiled in *The Man Who Knew Too Much*, came to be known as the "MacGuffin"; it might be described as the nonsense clause in his films which ties together the improbabilities and implausibilities. It is, to use a more familiar phrase, the red herring, the device that sends the plot and the characters on their way—such as the attempt to assassinate a foreign leader in this film—but remains of little or no interest to the audience; it is simply an excuse for all the activity on the screen.

With Balcon temporarily away in the United States, the managers of Gaumont British, as well as the cinema bookers, were cautious, not to say cool, about the new film. They had seen nothing quite like it before, and their collective suspicions seemed about to consign it to the shelf; but Balcon returned to the studio, not a moment too soon, and persuaded the doubters with a financial agreement in their interest. When it was released in December 1934 it was, much to everyone's surprise (except perhaps the director's), a great success. The reviewer of the *Daily Express* wrote that "Hitchcock leaps once again into the front rank of British directors." Hitchcock concurred, stating on one occasion that "I think you'll find the real start of my career was *The*

Man Who Knew Too Much." He also said later that the popularity of the film "re-established my creative prestige." At the beginning of 1935 he received a gold medal from the Institute of Amateur Cinematographers for the best English film of the previous twelve months.

.　.　.

So the "Hitchcock thriller" was fully born. It defined him, sometimes to his dismay. He once said that if he made a film out of *Cinderella*, a corpse would have to roll out of the golden coach. Yet this had become the genre of his choice and, buoyed by his success, he set to work almost immediately on a thriller by John Buchan entitled *The Thirty-Nine Steps*. He collaborated once more with Charles Bennett on a script which began as a half-page scenario and concluded as a seventy-page outline of the film, scene by scene. This visual emphasis was deepened as Hitchcock began to produce the drawings or storyboards that helped the cameraman and the set designers. The dialogue could come later, a task for which other writers were employed. Hitchcock and Buchan had broadly similar sensibilities. Both compared the thriller to the fairy tale, conflating an atmosphere of fantasy and wish-fulfilment with the essential narrative of good and evil. Hitchcock remembered reading *The Thirty-Nine Steps* in his teenage years, and said that it once more impressed upon him his "fear of policemen." He said also that "what I find appealing in Buchan's work is his understatement of highly dramatic ideas."

He wanted to build on the strengths of his previous film by creating a fast pace of humour and suspense, charting the perils of the world when order breaks down. So scene follows scene, and climax follows climax, in quick succession. There is no opportunity for the characters, or for the audience, to pause for breath. As he said in an interview, "you use one idea after another and eliminate anything that interferes with the swift pace." Logic and plausibility are not to be considered. The audience did not expect to see a documentary. The hero, Richard Hannay, becomes unintentionally involved in the murder of a strange woman and in the theft of national secrets by a ring of foreign spies. He has to clear his name of the former and thwart the latter. The narrative moves from London to the North, leaving the murdered woman behind, from a jump off the Forth Bridge to a crofter's cottage, from the mansion of the leader of the spy ring to a small town where Hannay tries to evade his pursuers by twice changing his identity; he is handcuffed to Pamela, his initially unwilling fellow traveller, but they flee across the moors and find a remote inn. And then back to London where the conspiracy is unravelled.

It may be baffling in cold print but on the screen it is pure flight and pursuit, rapid changes and fleeting moments. If it needed a composer it would be Mozart with his high spirits and extraordinary technical virtuosity. One "switch" follows another with such speed that the audience registers only panic and excitement. An innocent man is being hunted to his death. That is all they need to know. Hitchcock adopted the technique of cutting to a second person while the first person is still speaking, and explained that it was "one of the devices which help the talkies tell a story faster than a silent film could tell it." Once the narrative is set in motion it never for a moment stops. That is the true music of Alfred Hitchcock.

Yet he always said that audiences should see his films at least twice, simply because on the first occasion they are swallowed up in a delirium of images and scenes, surprises and disasters. He wanted them to look carefully at what was being projected on the screen. If the film were to be slowed down, for example, scene gradually dissolving into scene, they would become aware of the craft and care that fill every frame. A shot taken from a high angle communicates fate or doom; a rapid montage suggests a subjective point of view; shots down a train corridor are signals of anxiety or panic; the camera itself is part of the action, a good or bad companion to the players who themselves are trying to express what it is like to be trapped in a Hitchcock film.

The 39 Steps (Hitchcock deliberately used the numerals, perhaps to distinguish it from the novel) begins and ends in the same London music hall, as ornate and shabby as anything painted by Sickert, and it never once loses its serio-comic tone or its reliance on a series of variety acts or performances for the delectation of the audience. Hannay himself leads the dance, since he is caught in a trap and must escape it. So he takes on a number of roles, impersonating in turn a milkman, a car mechanic, a member of the Salvation Army, a professional politician, a murderer and a devoted husband. In the fifth chapter of the novel Hannay is told "that the secret of playing a part was to think yourself into it. You could never keep it up . . . unless you could manage to convince yourself that you were it." It was Hitchcock's habit to read aloud to his actors. He may have read this passage.

Robert Donat and Madeleine Carroll, the two leaders of the ensemble, were distinguished film actors; but Hitchcock did not care much for actors' distinction. On the first day of shooting the scene obliged the two of them to be handcuffed together, one of the most intimate of all possible unions with just the mildest hint of sex and pain. At some stage in the proceedings Hitchcock professed to have lost the key. It was one of his practical jokes. Exaggerated reports circulated that they had been locked together for hours, but Hitchcock would never have allowed filming to be delayed for so long. Perhaps a few minutes interposed, long enough for Donat and Carroll to become used to one another's company. In another scene Robert Donat and Peggy Ashcroft began to giggle uncontrollably; Hitchcock walked to the side of the stage and smashed a lamp with his fist. The actors recovered themselves and gave a sterling performance.

When he was once asked if he would like to film the *Titanic* disaster he replied, "Oh yes, I've had experience with icebergs. Don't forget, I directed Madeleine Carroll." It seems that he decided to break down, or at least roughen, her conventionally cool demeanour. The episode with the handcuffs is one example. He also explained to Donat that he must really drag his co-star through the briars and heather and rocks of the moorland set. Carroll's father was a professor at Birmingham University, from which she graduated, and Hitchcock would call out, "Bring on the Birmingham tart." But these were not privately motivated jibes. He wanted to make sure that the actress came as close as possible to her role. "Nothing gives me more pleasure," he said, "than to knock the lady-likeness out." But she took it well, and her part was more fully developed as filming continued.

When *The 39 Steps* opened in June 1935, it was at once a huge success. This seemed to be what the cinema was made for. The *Sunday Times* reviewer pointed out that "In *The 39 Steps* the identity and mind of Alfred Hitchcock are continuously discernible, in fact supreme. There is no doubt that Hitchcock is a genius. He is the real star of the film."

.   .   .

After the film was released Hitchcock took his wife and young daughter on a holiday or, rather, "we did manage a few weekends at our summer cottage." By this time, however, he had acquired another member of his more extended film family. He had advertised for a secretary and, perhaps to his surprise, a chic blonde graduate by the name of Joan Harrison arrived at his door. He seems to have put her through his usual tests of humour and unshockability—he read out to her, for example, the more obscene passages of James Joyce's *Ulysses*—and she passed the audition.

After *The 39 Steps* Hitchcock was looking for a project on a grander and more adventurous scale. Instead Balcon offered him another spy story, *Secret Agent*, which he felt obliged to accept. There was not much to it. Based on two of W. Somerset Maugham's "Ashenden" stories, it is set in Switzerland and the Alps at the time of the First World War. Ashenden is a British agent despatched to kill a German spy; by misadventure he follows the track of the wrong man, who is duly pushed off an Alpine cliff. The wrong man is always on hand in a Hitchcock plot. So Ashenden must dust himself down and find the right victim until a convenient train crash solves the problem for him.

John Gielgud was chosen to play Ashenden, although he was not in any way suited to the role. Hitchcock had given him the impression that he would be portrayed in the mould of a modern Hamlet, divided over his dilemmas, but this was only to tempt him into the part. The actor soon discovered as much himself.

Hitchcock may have divined the fact that Gielgud believed himself to be slumming by selling himself to film; it was for the actor, at this stage in his career, a decidedly inferior medium. In his memoirs he says that Hitchcock made him "feel like a jelly and . . . nearly sick with nervousness." Hitchcock said in turn of Gielgud that "his stage experience is of no use to him here. I've had to make him rub out everything and start blank." This may have been good advice, but Gielgud could not so readily unlearn what he had been taught to do. Hitchcock then began to treat him with indifference. "My performance was taken for granted," Gielgud recalled, "and I was unaccustomed to being taken for granted."

Gielgud also resented the fact that the director seemed to pay far more interest to his co-stars, Madeleine Carroll and Peter Lorre. They enjoyed his practical jokes, which Gielgud did not. Hitchcock seemed to adore Carroll, even though he sometimes treated her with scant respect. The icing on the cake was Lorre, who played the role of Ashenden's sly and shady assistant with a luscious lasciviousness that could only have been helped by his regular injections of morphine by a Harley Street doctor. He was sometimes permitted to improvise his own dialogue, which took the more subdued Gielgud completely by surprise. In the theatre the script was sacrosanct. It was like a mad pantomime in the tradition of *Harlequin Jack Frost*.

The only memorable aspect of *Secret Agent* lies in its sound—of a dead man's head pressing against an organ and sending forth a prolonged and eerie note, and of a dog howling at the precise moment when his master is pushed over a cliff. These episodes demonstrate Hitchcock's extraordinarily intuitive use of sound, but the film itself is awkward and uneasy. It is impossible to like Ashenden, the supposed hero, and impossible not to marvel, albeit from a distance, at Lorre. The only convincing character is the true villain of the piece, played by Robert Young as a handsome all-American college boy who turns out to be the real German agent.

It is all too contrived and overburdened, compared with the light symmetries of *The 39 Steps*. The characters perform as if they are on an invisible stage; they are a bundle of striking attributes or a repertoire of effects. They do not cohere. The reviewers, and the public, were disappointed after the triumph of the previous film; Hitchcock himself admitted that "I'm sorry it wasn't a success."

. . .

By the summer of 1936 he decided, after this relative failure, to follow his natural grain. He would leave Switzerland and the Alps behind to return to the lower-class streets of London. He said in the *Kinematograph and Lantern Weekly* that English film-makers "ignore the people who jump on to moving buses, the women squeezed together in the Underground, travelling salesmen . . . the typist and her boyfriend. Queues outside cinemas, music-hall girls, doctors, car salesmen, traffic cops and schoolmasters. It is in them that the spirit of England lies." This represented in part his documentary ambitions, but it also harboured memories of his own earlier life.

Sabotage was a reworking of Joseph Conrad's *The Secret Agent*, the story of a clandestine bombing by an enemy agent called Adolf Verloc. In the film he is a proprietor of a small cinema, living in a flat with his wife, Winnie, and her younger brother, Stevie. In Conrad's novel Verloc owned a shop but Hitchcock wanted to bring life to the London he had known as a young boy haunting "the flicks." The cinema is also located next to a greengrocery, which would convey the atmosphere of London streets at a crucial time of his life. Hitchcock himself confessed that "I have a penchant for including scenes of London in my films." And why not? It is the landscape of his imagination. Michael Balcon had announced in advance that the film would "feature more of the real London than any film yet made." That may in fact be an accurate account of its power. It depicts the movements of crowds and of the great waves of fear or enthusiasm that animate them; it portrays the shadows cast by money and power which agents like Verloc are determined to exploit. The fear of war that pervaded the late 1930s also adds its own shadow to a narrative concerned with the impending devastation of London.

All the nostalgia and fantasy of Hitchcock's nature go into his remaking of the urban landscape, from the open-air markets to the crowd lining up in front of the box office, from the pageantry of a lord mayor's procession to the fusty interior of a bird shop in Islington. It is an alembic of London's raucous mystery, with its own attendant darkness and shadows. When in a note to the novel Conrad describes London as "a cruel devourer of the world's light," Hitchcock knew precisely what he meant. One of the scenes shows an audience reacting with delight to Walt Disney's short animated film, *Who Killed Cock Robin?*; but the point is that the young Hitchcock might also have been among them.

He bears some similarity to another great London visionary, Charles Dickens. Although the outward circumstances of their lives differed very greatly, they shared a similar imagination. They were both fantasists who insisted upon meticulous detail in the unravelling of their plots; they were both poised between art and commerce, with a keen taste for the making of money. They were also great showmen in front of their respective audiences. Neither of them liked to discuss their work in detail. Hitchcock said to one interviewer that "I am not a realist at all. I am drawn to the fantastic. I see things 'larger than life.'"

"Metaphysically?"

"Thank you. That's why I love melodrama."

That is as close as Hitchcock ever came to delivering an artistic credo. He and Dickens were both poets and visionaries who posed as practical men of the world.

He seems therefore to have envisaged *Sabotage* as an efficient thriller, and to that end he disembowelled Conrad's novel for the sake of suspense and entertainment. He professed to have discarded all of his previous experimental techniques, with cuts and dissolves and wipes fighting for pre-eminence on the screen. "I have stopped all that today," he wrote. "I have not the film time to throw away on fancy stuff." He added in another interview that "I have become more commercially minded; afraid that anything at all subtle may be missed." But we must trust the tale and not the teller. There is enough "fancy stuff" in *Sabotage* to fill an experimental art cinema, not least with the subtext of the cinema itself as a cover for deceit and illusion.

Hitchcock set the scene for filming. "Out in a field near Harrow 'London' stands," he wrote in the *New York Times*. "It is a complete replica of a London street scene, built for my new Gaumont British thriller, *Sabotage*. Fully equipped shops, trams, buses, traffic lights, beacons, overhead railway, and hundreds of pedestrians are there, but nothing is happening. The cameras are covered up, the microphone is shrouded, the crowds stand huddled against the shops." There had in fact been three nights of cold and intense rain.

The weather was not the only problem. There were disputes over money, at which point Ivor Montagu left the production on the grounds of excessive expenditure. There were arguments with the leading lady, Sylvia Sidney playing Winnie, about the exact nature of her part. In a climactic scene, when Winnie murders her husband, Sylvia wished to say some words to motivate her act; but Hitchcock intervened. She must kill him in silence. He just told her to "look to the right. Not so much. Less. Look away." This reduced her to tears but, viewing the scene later, she confessed that it represented an act of genius. "Hollywood must hear of this," she is supposed to have said.

The fate of the younger brother Stevie, played by Desmond Tester—always called "Testicles" by Hitchcock, much to the young actor's embarrassment—was tendentious. Tester was part of the biggest mistake that Hitchcock ever made with his audience. Towards the close of the film Verloc persuades Stevie to take some film canisters packed with explosives into the heart of London. The boy agrees, believing that he is going on a simple errand, but the clock has already begun ticking. It will not be long before the fatal explosion. He dallies and is diverted on the streets of London. The clock is still ticking. Eventually he jumps on to a tram, and begins petting a puppy, but the moment has come. The bomb explodes, along with child, puppy and all.

One critic, with a small child of her own, belaboured Hitchcock and asked him how he could allow such a thing. She had a point. Hitchcock had miscalculated the nature of the suspense. He had written in that year that "I am out to give the public good, healthy, mental shake-ups. Civilisation has become so screening and sheltering that we cannot experience sufficient thrills at first hand." But in this instance he may have miscalculated. The blowing to bits of a small boy hardly counts as a thrill, as the events of coming years would testify.

That is perhaps why the English critics and English audiences were not greatly impressed by the film. Nevertheless *Sabotage* was risky enough, or adventurous enough, to find an appreciative audience in the United States; a critic of the American periodical *The Nation* was perceptive enough to note that "a live wire seems to run backward from any of his films to all the best films one can remember." It was enough to say that Hitchcock had assimilated all the virtues of the cinematic art. As T. S. Eliot said of the work of Wilkie Collins, a great influence upon Hitchcock, "it has no merit beyond melodrama, and it has every merit that melodrama can have."

The relative failure of *Sabotage* only enhanced the financial difficulties of Gaumont British, and shortly after the shooting of the film its studio at Lime Grove was closed down. Hitchcock's once close associates, Michael Balcon and Ivor Montagu, moved elsewhere, while the director himself returned to Gainsborough Pictures where he had once worked with Balcon. Hitchcock's producer at Gainsborough, Ted Black, was experienced in the business of entertainment and soon proved himself to be thoroughly capable.

. . .

Meanwhile Hitchcock's next contracted film, *Young and Innocent*, was waiting to be born. It was once more an adaptation, based upon Josephine Tey's novel *A Shilling for Candles*, concerning a fugitive pursued by police for a murder he did not commit; with the help of a young woman, who happens to be the daughter of the local chief constable, he must track down the real killer. This may all sound vaguely familiar. It is. Charles Bennett was the natural writer for the script, and Hitchcock recalled that "we went into a huddle, and slowly from discussions, arguments, random suggestions, casual, desultory talk, and furious intellectual quarrels as to what such and such a character in such and such a situation would or would not do, the scenario began to take shape." But the huddle was cut short; even while Bennett was preparing his treatment he received a telegram from Hollywood requesting his presence for *The Adventures of Marco Polo*. His name and skill had gone before him. There seemed to be no earthly reason to refuse, given the precarious state of the film industry at home, and Bennett crossed the ocean.

This made Hitchcock pause. The moment might now have come to follow his scriptwriter across the water, in order to redeploy his considerable reputation in the United States. He had become perhaps too large for the English film industry alone; he felt technically constrained and undervalued. Yet he had also constructed for himself a comfortable and agreeable life in London; he appreciated the restaurants and the theatres; he had his immediate family still close to him, having moved his mother to a flat in Kensington. He had even started collecting art. He was also a highly anxious and fearful man terrified of novelty and of change. These were the arguments for staying.

Yet he was also extremely ambitious, driven, as it were, by the cinematic Fates. The opportunities in America were vast, and the rewards much higher. He would be nearer the sun in every sense. He once told a colleague that in England "the sky was always grey, the rain was grey, the mud was grey, and I was grey." Soon enough he would be obliged to come to a decision.

Young and Innocent was a popular film both in England and in the United States, even though *Film Weekly* described it as a "typically English picture." It did have one remarkable innovation. Hitchcock devised a "travelling shot" or "crane shot" during which in one unbroken movement the camera crosses a large dance floor and closes on the face of a drummer with trembling eyes; the eyes give him away as the real murderer. The camera moved 145 feet and stopped four inches in front of the eyes; the filming lasted two days. It was the high point of

Young and Innocent and emphasised Hitchcock's gifts as a virtuoso of the camera. But what else might he achieve with the resources of Hollywood behind him?

Hitchcock was growing ever more restless. In the summer of 1937, just before editing the picture, he paid a visit to New York with his family on the understanding that it was merely a brief holiday. But he was in fact spying out the new territory. His presence was noted at the time, even though it was partly because of his portliness and apparently endless appetite. He is reported to have ordered in one restaurant three courses of steak and ice cream. But work also beckoned. The American producer David O. Selznick, the head of the newly established Selznick International Pictures, sent a telegram to his New York agent stating that "I am definitely interested in meeting Hitchcock as director, and think it might be wise for you to meet and chat with him." She duly achieved this mission and, by the time the Hitchcocks left, connections had been made with Selznick and with other studios. Eight months after *Young and Innocent* was released in England, and five months after it was first shown in America, Hitchcock returned to New York in search of a definite contract. In the spring of 1938 he had said that "the matter is still in the air but, if I do go to Hollywood, I'd only work for Selznick."

The wish was father to the deed. He had already taken the precaution of hiring Selznick's brother, Myron, as his agent. He sailed with his family at the beginning of June, on the *Queen Mary*, and soon enough arrived in Hollywood for the final negotiations. Hitchcock and Selznick seem to have got the measure of each other in the most cordial manner. They were both professionals, passionately devoted to the art of film. But they could both be stubborn and intent upon getting their own way; Hitchcock himself would find it impossible to avert Selznick's dominant will. There were differences between them: Selznick was extrovert, even explosive, with a propensity for sending long memoranda with complicated instructions to members of the production team; Hitchcock was subdued and secretive, preferring to get what he wanted by devious rather than open means.

The American producer David O. Selznick,
Hitchcock's longtime collaborator.

Courtesy of J.T. Vintage/Bridgeman Images

And how did he now appear to Selznick and to the world? His girth was the first impression he made upon strangers. He told one interviewer that he was of an "adrenal type," which apparently meant that "I'm all body and only vestigial legs." He may have been mistaken in his diagnosis, but he did look decidedly different; he once lamented "my odd, misshapen corporeal presence." He felt his fatness keenly, more so in Hollywood than in England. In the city of dreams portliness was perhaps out of place. He had no illusions about the matter. He once told an art director, Robert Boyle, that "I have all the feelings of everyone encased in an armour of fat." It is as well that he professed to be celibate all of his life, and that his attraction to his leading ladies did not go further than the adjustment of camera lighting. Or so he claimed. He had a large head and, at a height of five feet and seven inches, must have reminded some acquaintances of Humpty Dumpty. He was in fact very agile on his feet, with the daintiness sometimes associated with fat men; "Fatty" Arbuckle was another example.

He explained the matter further to a biographer, Charlotte Chandler. "I have always been uncommonly unattractive. Worse yet, I have always known it. The feeling has been with me so long, I cannot imagine what it would be like not to feel that way." This points the path towards a life filled with anger, sorrow, dismay, despair, anxiety and loneliness; these emotions must have been most acutely felt in his younger years, but their shadow would have followed him everywhere. That is why he came to require the "armour" of fat to protect himself against life's depredations. He also wore a uniform with almost military precision. He had a wardrobe of six dark suits, all of the same cut but subtly different in size to mark his changing form. They were all numbered, so that trousers and jackets could be matched. It is commonly claimed that they were black, but both Hitchcock and his wife confirmed that they were dark blue in colour. He also possessed six identical pairs of shoes, ten identical ties, and fifteen identical pairs of socks and underwear. They gave him a formal, and calculated, appearance. He appreciated the restraint, the external order and discipline that they imposed. Photographs reveal, however, that he often allowed one of the shirt collars to curl up, perhaps as a sign of a yearning to be free.

For a man filled with fears the uniform represented the triumph of artificiality and disguise, draping in stern cloth the "poor bare forked animal." He was capable of seeming motionless on the set, with a preternatural calm and silence. In an interview in 1938 he declared that "if someone came into this room now, and said, 'Mr. Hitchcock, there's a policeman waiting for you outside,' my expression would change very slightly and become almost dead for a second." It was as if he were playing dead to divert a predator.

He hated conflict and disagreement. He would suppress his anger or resentment and walk away. A harsh or unkind word would leave him anxious and depressed all day. There are references in his early life to the fact that he sometimes berated actors for bad performances, but those references soon stop. In conversation he was calm and even, almost softly spoken, with the firm but controlled voice that hypnotists use. He was courteous and gentlemanly, relying upon elaborate diction and perfectly enunciated words. Sometimes he affected a slight drawl, and would stick out his lower lip to register disappointment or disapproval; he had very expressive hands to tell a story or make an argument. "Precisely," he might say. "Exactly." He had a fondness for understatement which, in his films, became an aesthetic device. "Nothing amuses me so much," he once said, "as understatement." He had a fund of anecdotes and aphorisms that he would bring out for almost any occasion. In televised interviews he would repeat the same lines and stories endlessly; it was part of his carapace. He would never say anything out of turn, or surprising, or revelatory. The secret was that he could, or would, never reveal himself. He was often sly or subtle in his dealings with other people. He was a great calculator, ever watchful of himself and of others.

5

AT HOME

The Hitchcocks returned to England at the beginning of September 1937, and were at once faced with unfinished business. Another film was needed to fulfil the contract with Gainsborough Pictures before they could consider moving to the United States. Ted Black, the producer, offered him a once abandoned project, *The Lost Lady*, which had the prior advantage of being almost completely scripted by Sidney Gilliat and Frank Launder. Hitchcock saw its possibilities. It was his kind of film. A young and attractive English woman adopts as her travelling companion, on a train through central Europe, a rather dowdy middle-aged spinster. The journey has hardly begun when the older woman vanishes. None of the other travellers seem to have noticed her; some of them claim that she never existed. It is time for the romantic lead to take up the cause of the young lady and find the missing party.

Hitchcock loved trains. The corridors invoke panic, and urgency, and speed; the compartments offer only the illusion of safety and privacy. All is in suspense as the train hurtles through an unfamiliar landscape. It soon becomes clear that a conspiracy is under way, in which the English and the foreigners are on different sides. *The Lady Vanishes*, as it was eventually entitled, could only have been made in the fraught and fragile years before the outbreak of war.

It was filmed at Islington Studios where Hitchcock was reunited with his favourite cameraman, Jack Cox. Islington was a charmed place; he had first started in the film industry there, and had met his wife there. He had begun work with Michael Balcon there. So everything was coming together. Dame May Whitty was chosen as the vanishing lady, with an accompanying cast of Margaret Lockwood and Michael Redgrave as the romantic leads. Lockwood revealed later that Hitchcock "didn't seem to direct us at all. He was a dozing, nodding Buddha with an enigmatic smile on his face." She did notice one idiosyncrasy, however. After morning or afternoon tea, Hitchcock would throw his cup over his shoulder and wait for it to crash and splinter. It was a habit he continued for much of his life, saying that it was "good for the nerves. Relieves the tension. Much better than scolding the players." Or it may have been a small way of showing the symbolic order of the world to be as brittle as porcelain.

He may have had some cause to "scold" his male lead, however, since Michael Redgrave shared the common assumption of fellow actors that film was somehow inferior to theatre. The attitude infuriated Hitchcock, who took every opportunity of removing it or, as Redgrave put it, "he decided to cut me down to size." Redgrave had said of one scene that in the theatre he would have three weeks to prepare for it. Hitchcock told him that, in front of the camera, he had precisely three minutes. It was in Redgrave's presence that Hitchcock is supposed to have said that "actors are cattle"; Hitchcock never wholly disowned the remark, adding only that he said that "actors should be treated like cattle." It is therefore understandable that Redgrave also said of him that "he wasn't really an actor's director." He added that "he knew where he wanted to put his camera, he knew which mood he wanted to effect. He had the whole thing visualised ahead of time and, once we got to the set, it could all be done very quickly and painlessly." He seemed bored, perhaps, so that he might relax them. Ted Black recalled that there was "no larking about, wasting time and stupidities. He was quite a disciplinarian, but he didn't emphasise it at all; he just *was* it." *The Lady Vanishes* was completed within the cramped studio at Islington within five weeks.

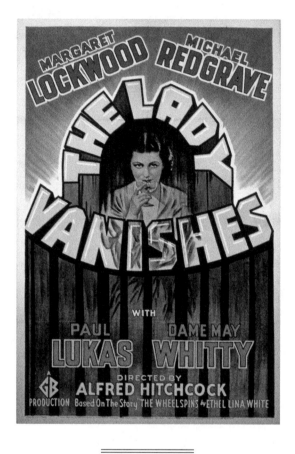

The film poster for *The Lady Vanishes,* Hitchcock's last major
motion picture with Gainsborough Pictures, 1937.

Courtesy of Movie Poster Art/Getty Images

The film has long been described as one of Hitchcock's finest. It shares some of the qualities of its immediate predecessors, with its emphasis on a couple who become united through a series of trials. This is in fact the great theme of Hitchcock's last British films. But *The Lady Vanishes* transcends its boundaries as a mild British thriller, complete with happy ending, by the simple expedient of the mysterious vanishing lady. She is the hole around which the whole is constructed. The film compounds the realism of the setting with the vertiginous mystery of disappearance; the theatricality of the plot has mystical implications, also, with the sudden erasure of a name outlined in steam on a train window and with a stray tea label blown against a corridor window.

The world is not ruled by chance, however, but by fatality. The characters of *The Lady Vanishes* come together by ones and twos, converging from widely different quarters, drawing slowly together in a sphere of suspicion where they are all eventually assembled. The surprises, the reversals, the disassociation from routine during the journey, the psychic claustrophobia of the train ride, the near hysteria of the heroine looking for the lady, the malign presence of enemy agents amongst ordinary English people, the threat of murderous violence towards the end, all contribute to the unique Hitchcock effect.

While making *The Lady Vanishes* Hitchcock received a telegram from Myron Selznick intimating that the first picture he would make in Hollywood might be based on the fate of the *Titanic*. This was an opportunity which Hitchcock eagerly grasped. The possibilities were tremendous. He already had several scenes in mind. The whisky in a tumbler might begin to tremble. As his pilgrimage to America grew ever closer, his ambitions increased. He had visions of building an entire ocean-going vessel for the climactic scenes. He and Alma returned to Hollywood at the end of May 1938, having just completed filming *The Lady Vanishes*.

By the middle of July, Hitchcock and David Selznick had signed a contract that guaranteed him one film with four one-picture-a-year options; he would earn $50,000 for the first production, with incremental increases over the next three years. It was not gold dust by Hollywood standards but it was a substantial rise after his period in England. The contract was modified and rewritten, with two pictures instead of one in the first year, but in the end it satisfied both parties.

But he had to return to England for one last film. For reasons known only to himself—perhaps for money or for fear of nothing to do—he had signed a contract to direct a film entitled *Jamaica Inn*, based on the novel by Daphne du Maurier. He had agreed to the project with the Mayflower Company, which existed primarily for the making and distribution of films starring Charles Laughton. In effect Hitchcock was working for, and with, the celebrated actor. It was to be an everyday story of wreckers enticing ships on to the shore, together with a sinister landlord who is more or less than he appears to be. Laughton played the landlord with a braggadocio that swept the other players from the screen. To say that he was difficult would be an understatement; Hitchcock joked that he was hired not to be a director but to be a referee, judging the bouts in which Laughton wrestled with himself. Hitchcock was used to actors being on time and in command of their lines; Laughton would hesitate, and delay, and improvise where he deemed it necessary. It took him days to perform the right walk for a certain sequence. It was to be Laughton's picture, not Hitchcock's. It was wall-to-wall ham, and Graham Greene commented that "the whole set of the sinister inn creaks like its own signboard."

· · ·

It was at last time to leave England. He sublet the flat on Cromwell Road, and locked the door on the cottage at Shamley Green. On 1 March 1939, the Hitchcock family sailed from Southampton on the *Queen Mary*. The party included a cook, a maid, Hitchcock's secretary Joan Harrison, and two dogs; they were arriving en masse. In England he had made twenty-four films in thirteen years, and he was in a sense eager to leave. One of his later screenwriters, Samuel Taylor, reported that "he felt that he was not really respected in England" and that "Brit-

Hitchcock, Alma and Patricia on their way to the United States, 1939.

Courtesy of AFP/Getty Images

ish critics regarded him as the house-clown." Alma was happy to leave, and for their daughter it was one big adventure.

And so, too, for her father. Hitchcock said that he anticipated "working under new conditions with an entirely fresh crowd of people," but he was not unnerved by the challenge. "There is scarcely a star in Hollywood," he said, "whose appeal I would not try to alter or develop." He put it more plainly in the same interview with a reporter, J. Danvers Williams, when he remarked that "I am itching to get my hands on these American stars." For him Hollywood was one vast laboratory, with all the latest equipment available. He had also been buoyed by the news that he had just been named Best Director of 1938 by the New York critics.

He would be introduced to a film system that had developed on unfamiliar lines. Hollywood was dominated by its producers rather than its directors, and was reliant on its star system in ways which were not customary in England. He would now be part of a much larger and more elaborate world, where he could not expect to be a dominant player as he had at Elstree.

He had agreed with Selznick to direct *Rebecca*, the novel by Daphne du Maurier which introduced the naïve Mrs. de Winter and the calculating Mrs. Danvers to the world; Hitchcock did not need much persuasion since he had previously expressed great interest in filming the book. Daphne du Maurier might have had some misgivings, however, since she profoundly disliked his version of *Jamaica Inn*. Hitchcock never had a high opinion of du Maurier's fiction, despite filming these two novels and a short story (*The Birds*); she in turn had no great admiration for his work and was concerned only with the financial rewards it gave her. Theirs was a thoroughly practical arrangement.

As soon as Hitchcock and Alma arrived in New York they were in the hands of the publicity department. Hitchcock gave a lecture on English theatre at Yale and on film at Columbia; he was asked to preside over a newspaper dinner. Then, on 16 March, the Hitchcock entourage decamped for a vacation in Florida and the Caribbean. At the end of the month, on their return to New York, they took the train to Pasadena. Their new home was in view. They were met on 5 April at the train station by Myron Selznick, and were at once driven to a newly leased apartment in the Wilshire Palms on Wilshire Boulevard. Joan Harrison, now seen as indispensable, was given an apartment close by.

Everything in the apartment was white, as bright as the sun and the air, while the complex included a pool and a tennis court. Alma was delighted by her new surroundings, and the atmosphere of freedom that they conveyed; she came to love America almost at once, as the perfect antidote to the stuffiness and mustiness of England. Hitchcock hardly seemed to notice the change. He said that he was not at all interested in Hollywood except as a place to work. One of the maids left soon after; she may not have objected to the American way of life as such, since she stayed and became a chiropractor. She was in any case replaced by a German cook who specialised in pastries. Within five days Hitchcock had reported to the studio in order to begin, with Joan Harrison, the script of *Rebecca*. Their standard of comfort at this studio was considerably higher than that at Islington; they were given a suite with a kitchen and bathroom.

Hitchcock and his team produced an outline of *Rebecca*. He knew it would have to be reworked by the studio, but was nevertheless disconcerted when at the beginning of June he despatched a draft of the screenplay to David Selznick. The producer professed himself to be "shocked and disappointed beyond words"; he did not enjoy Hitchcock's attempts to inject humour into what was essentially a sober melodrama. The lightness of touch that had characterised *The Lady Vanishes* was not considered suitable for *Rebecca*. "We bought *Rebecca*, and we intend to make *Rebecca*," Selznick wrote, "not a distorted and vulgarised version of a provenly successful work." He may have had a point, as the more faithful final version suggests, but it must have come as a serious setback in the relationship between the two men. It would not be unrealistic to believe that they both now questioned the contract they had agreed between them.

Hitchcock said later that "David insisted that we followed the book exactly. He decided that with so many readers who had their own favourite scenes, they'd be disappointed if they weren't included in the film." What Selznick also wanted was lushness on the screen, that thick velvety quality lavished on romances and melodramas of the period. The stars should be sparkling in their places, the photography should be all gloss and shimmer, while the music should sweep up the audience and leave it breathless. In this same period Selznick was also producing *Gone With the Wind*, which had that quality *in excelsis*. He had the reputation for creating "women's pictures."

Hitchcock, nothing if not professional, bowed to the inevitable and with Harrison and assorted American writers completed a composite script by the end of July which closely followed the original novel. Selznick responded with detailed comments, making it plain that this was to be his film, with his editing, his characters and his treatment. A reporter from the *New York Times* noted that in an interview Hitchcock "smiled a little cynically when he discussed producers"; the director, however, refused to be quoted.

The script was finally completed at the beginning of September, by which time shooting was about to begin. This was the story of a nervous young girl suddenly married to a rich man; she is soon plagued by the delusion that he still loves his dead wife, Rebecca, a fatal error which is reinforced by the serpentine suggestions and actions of the housekeeper Mrs. Danvers.

The casting had been completed with some difficulties. Laurence Olivier played the male lead, as Maxim de Winter, and had wanted his partner, Vivien Leigh, to play the second Mrs. de Winter. Vivien Leigh was brave and beautiful; the unnamed heroine of *Rebecca* is mousy and full of terrors. Eventually Joan Fontaine gained the part. Olivier took against her from the start, and broadcast his aversion; he also seemed, while filming, to take every opportunity of whispering obscenities into her ear.

Fontaine herself was experiencing moments of severe anxiety. Hitchcock had decided that she should become as fearful and as uneasy as her screen persona; he constantly told her that the rest of the cast did not like or appreciate her, and that only he would be able to give her the

A still from *Rebecca*, Hitchcock's first film with Selznick, during which they grappled for control of the picture.

Courtesy of Silver Screen Collection/Hulton Archive/Getty Images

security she required. "He wanted total control over me," she recalled, "and seemed to relish the cast not liking one another, actor for actor, by the end of the film." The trick worked. The apprehension on her face, as she walks around Manderley as an under-appreciated second wife, is real. There was one of many weeping scenes when Fontaine confessed that she had run out of tears. "I asked her what it would take to make her resume crying," Hitchcock said later. "She said, 'Well, maybe if you slapped me.' I did, and she instantly started bawling."

The atmosphere on the set was strained for international reasons. In the first week of filming in September 1939, war was declared against Germany, leaving the largely English cast and Hitchcock himself in disarray. Olivier stated that "we felt blighted right through, careers, lives, hopes." Hitchcock sent constant cables to London enquiring about his mother and the rest of his family, but a continent and ocean divided them.

·   ·   ·

He had no thought of returning to England, however, since in the following month he moved out of Wilshire Palms into what he might have called his first proper home in America. They rented 609 St. Cloud Road in Bel Air from Carole Lombard, a large and comfortable house on what still looks like a well-manicured country road. It is in what estate agents describe as a French–Norman style, and it is suitably gated and secluded. They immediately began to anglicise it with furniture from Cromwell Road and Shamley Green. They removed the ubiquitous white paint of California, and replaced the tile floors with parquet. The place was known as "The Farm" but it might as easily have been called "The Cottage." He had said that "what I want is a *home*, not a movie set with a heating plant added. All I need is a snug little house with a good kitchen, and the devil with a swimming pool." The census of 1940 shows them living with an English maid, Gladys Faulkner, and the German cook, Erna Graff.

Hitchcock slipped into his role as an Englishman abroad. He had soon enough created a routine in which he could hide himself. He wore his dark blue suit and kept his hours like any office manager; he imported English bacon and Dover sole, and tried to keep up with the London papers. On Sundays he or Alma drove with Patricia to the local Catholic church, the Good Shepherd, otherwise known as "Our Lady of the Cadillacs" due to the number of rich parishioners; the other fixed event of the week was the drive of three miles for dinner at a restaurant on Beverly Boulevard, Chasen's, on Thursday evening. Here he ordered steak, together with a champagne cocktail of his own devising. Their daughter was enrolled at a private school, Marymount, supervised by nuns. Everything became orderly; everything became familiar.

There was one thing, however, which some people considered to be odd. He would close his eyes, or fall asleep, at inopportune moments. If he was not the centre of conversation or attention at a dinner table, he would often doze off. In his own home, the moment he fell asleep was the signal for guests to depart. At a private party for a recent arrival, the author Thomas Mann, Hitchcock began to talk to him about fiction and film before closing his eyes. He invited Carole Lombard and her husband Clark Gable to dinner at Chasen's; Alma recalled that "before the salad was served, Hitch slept." When his wife woke him after a prolonged slumber at another dinner party he asked her, "Wouldn't it be rude to leave so soon?"

This may in part have been the consequence of his growing size, but there may have been another reason. He was a man filled with constant dread of the world, and it is reasonable and plausible to assume that he took medication to alleviate the anxiety he suffered. Before the arrival of antidepressant drugs in the 1950s, opioids or opiates were readily available to treat depression and high anxiety. In a culture of drugs such as that of Hollywood it would not have been difficult for Hitchcock to obtain them; David Selznick, for example, was addicted to Benzedrine. If Hitchcock were indeed prescribed an opiate, its reaction with alcohol, which he drank in larger and larger quantities, would induce slumber. This is mere speculation, without evidence, but it is a natural and indeed likely circumstance to account for his somnolent interludes.

Hitchcock's world of fear, however, is not in doubt. By his own account he was afraid of everything; he always imagined the worst, and prepared for it. He still did not like to cross the studio floor in case a stranger came up to him. François Truffaut said of him after a series of exhaustive interviews that he was a "neurotic" and "a fearful person"; he was "deeply vulnerable" but as a result became "an artist of anxiety." That was the secret. Hitchcock projected his anxiety into his films, in which fear becomes an intrinsic aspect of daily life. He was aware of the innate and uncontrollable terror that can suddenly afflict a human being, and in that instant the outer world becomes unreal. This is also the awareness of his films.

The business of filming itself, for an essentially timid man, was formidable and frightening. How could he control the restless life of the studio that was insidiously threatening to him? That was why he sought all the time to render himself invulnerable by total control, routine, neatness, quietness. His daughter testifies that he was afflicted by migraines if things did not go to plan. There is an anecdote told by the screenwriter of *Psycho*, Joseph Stefano, who agreed to drop off Hitchcock at a cab rank in front of a hotel; but the last cab was driving off as Stefano pulled away. He saw Hitchcock standing alone with a look of abject terror upon his face at this abandonment.

Hitchcock suffered from vertigo and the fear of falling; in many of his films there are sequences of vertiginous falls into the abyss. The hanging man is one of his central motifs with the unspoken assumption from Edgar Allan Poe that "my whole soul was pervaded with a *longing to fall*; a desire, a yearning, a passion utterly uncontrollable." Hitchcock was a superb fantasist of fear. So like a tuning fork he finds the hidden fears and anxieties of his audience; as an artist he had access to the collective unconscious. He had such an intimate connection with his own anxieties that he was able instinctively to stir those of the public.

· · ·

Hitchcock and Selznick still did not seem to be working as a partnership. It was customary in America for the producer to make all the important decisions; he would expect to be given long stretches of film, "master shots" of the action, as well as close-ups, shots from different angles, which he could mix until he found the version he preferred. But Hitchcock did not work in that way. He had so designed the film in his imagination that he used precisely the camerawork he had envisaged; the completed film would fit like pieces of a puzzle. In his world there was no room for second-guessing or interference from anyone else. His first shock came quickly. After the rehearsal of a scene he had said "Well, let's go." The script girl intervened. "Oh, wait a minute—I have to send for Mr. Selznick."

Despite the director's displeasure, the producer persevered. He ordered retakes, and changed the script; he continued to supervise the costumes of the leading players and saw the daily rushes. Fortunately for Hitchcock, perhaps, he was becoming increasingly preoccupied with the problems of completing *Gone With the Wind*, and after a few weeks his interventions in *Rebecca* became less frequent. It is hard to say, with *Rebecca*, where the director ends and the producer begins, but it hardly matters.

The director himself said later that "it's not a Hitchcock picture," but he was only half right. The lighting is still conveyed with his expressionistic use of darkness and shadow, while the vast and gloomy house takes on all the characteristics of a Gothic prison where the heroine is alone and vulnerable. The house is a living thing that in the end must be destroyed by fire. Fear is once more the key. Yet *Rebecca* has a purely cinematic depth that had eluded him in the past; he was learning from Selznick even as he was resisting him. In the last weeks of post-production, for example, Selznick supervised the editing of the film until it reached the tempo and atmosphere which he desired.

The production went over budget, and over time, but it did what it was meant to do: it made a large profit. It delighted audiences and went on to win the Oscar for Best Picture of 1940. It was an undeniable achievement for a foreign director's first film in the United States, even if Selznick himself picked up the statuette.

Hitchcock had made an auspicious start, even if in not quite the way he had anticipated, but by the autumn of 1939 Selznick had already decided to "loan out" his British director to an independent producer. Selznick made a profit on the deal, charging $5,000 a week for Hitchcock's services while still paying the director his stipulated weekly fee of $2,500; Hitchcock, always aware of deals and finances even as he pretended not to understand them, was furious. The producer was making a hundred per cent profit out of him. In the end he could do nothing; yet he was at least free from Selznick's immediate control. Hitchcock said in an interview that "as soon as I was working for someone I wasn't under contract to, the supervision was lessened." The result was *Foreign Correspondent*, a film much closer to Hitchcock's British thrillers than to Hollywood melodrama.

The producer, Walter Wanger, had bought the rights to a memoir of an American foreign correspondent. Vincent Sheean's *Personal History* concerned his journalistic adventures in Europe and Asia while working for the *Chicago Tribune* in the late 1920s and '30s, but Wanger wanted to employ it to create a film about the war only recently begun. Hitchcock seemed genuinely excited at the opportunity, but his mind was already working in the direction of *The 39 Steps*; he wanted to mix once more the ingredients of international espionage, assassination and pursuit with the war as a convenient backdrop.

Hitchcock persuaded Wanger to hire Charles Bennett as the principal scriptwriter; much to his delight his old colleague, now resident in Hollywood, was available. Through the month of February 1940 he and Bennett, together with Alma and Joan Harrison, worked on the screenplay. It was largely to be set in Holland, already under threat from the German forces. "We'll have the hero see a windmill turning against the wind," Hitchcock told them. "He'll know that's some kind of enemy signal." That was pure Hitchcock—a visual conceit, remarkable in itself, that would somehow be welded to the plot. An American reporter is sent to London where he promptly falls in love with the heroine; the girl in question, however, is the daughter of a prominent peace campaigner who turns out to be the chief of the enemy spy-ring in England. It was worthy of Buchan himself. Wanger said of Hitchcock that he is "fat, forty and full of fire." An observer noted of the filming that "Hitchcock's full lips move with the words of the performer, his round face grimaces with every emotion, he sways with their action. He is each character in turn, enacting each part silently, without rising from his chair. He is like a child participating in a Saturday afternoon thriller."

This energy and inventiveness forced the pace of the film, with Hitchcock dreaming of and then devising spectacular set scenes to maintain the momentum of the narrative. A prominent statesman is apparently assassinated in the large public square of Amsterdam, and for that purpose Hitchcock arranged for the building of an elaborate facsimile that covered ten acres; the Colorado river had to be diverted, and a sewer system built, to provide and accommodate endless rain. In another Hitchcock fancy a hundred umbrellas fill the square. The hero, played by Joel McCrea, chases the assassin to a large windmill in the fields outside the city; it is a vaguely Gothic construction of ladders and beams and wooden sails, where Hitchcock can once more indulge his love of shadows, steps and silhouettes. In a later scene a complete aircraft was crashed into a vast water tank to splendidly realistic effect.

At a total cost of $1.5 million, *Foreign Correspondent* was the most expensive film Hitchcock had ever made, yet it was also one of his most successful, considered by some to be superior even to *Rebecca*. The critic of the *New Republic* considered that it provided "a seminar in how to make a movie travel the lightest and fastest way, in a kind of beauty that is peculiar to movies alone."

He shot the film from March to May, even as events in Europe left him more apprehensive by the day. Norway and Denmark had gone by April; Belgium and Holland followed with Paris about to fall. London's turn could only be days or weeks away. At the last minute he added a codicil to the film, when the foreign correspondent delivers a broadcast speech to America from a BBC studio. "All that noise you hear isn't static. It's death, coming to London. Yes, they're coming here now! You can hear the bombs falling on the streets and homes!"

As soon as filming was complete, he and Joan Harrison decided to return to England in order to pick up their respective parents. (Alma had already returned to take her mother and her sister to California.) Theirs was not a comfortable journey; they took ship in a convoy under crowded conditions with a shortage of bathrooms. This was not Hitchcock's idea of travel. It was a fruitless expedition. Emma Hitchcock flatly refused to travel back to the United States with her famous son. She had survived the First World War without a scratch, and had no wish to run for cover now. She was persuaded, however, to remove permanently to "Winter's Grace" at Shamley Green, the Hitchcocks' country home, which might be considered safer; she was later joined there by Hitchcock's older brother William, as well as their sister, Nellie. Hitchcock did not travel back empty-handed, however; he brought for his daughter an empty incendiary bomb case, which she put by her bed.

In this period, he came under sustained assault from some of his English colleagues who effectively accused him of deserting England at a time of peril. He should not have been swanning around Hollywood, but fighting the war on the home front. This of course did not mean that he should be "called up"; he was too old and too fat and had already been considered unfit for combat during the First World War. Instead it was believed that he should have become involved in the film propaganda in England. Michael Balcon, his former friend and colleague, led the charge with an unmistakeable attack. "I had a plump young junior technician in my studios whom I promoted from department to department. Today he is one of our most famous directors and he is in Hollywood while we who are left behind short-handed are trying to harness the films to our great national effort . . . I do not give this man's name, as I have decided not to mention any of the deserters by name." Yet everyone knew whom he meant. One satirist imagined a film, *Gone With the Wind Up*, directed by Alfred Hitchcock.

Hitchcock was terribly hurt by the criticism, particularly by the reference to him as a "deserter," to the extent that he broke the habit of a lifetime and replied very sharply in public to Balcon's criticism. He attributed it to envy at his success. He wrote that "Balcon's view is coloured by his own personal experiences with Hollywood, which have invariably wound up unfortunately for Balcon. He's a permanent Donald Duck . . . The manner in which I am helping my country is not Mr. Balcon's business and has nothing to do with patriotic ideals. Mr. Balcon apparently hates Hollywood. I can only put his remarks down as personal jealousy. How else could he be so unintelligent?" He could have added that he had in fact agreed to make films with the Ministry of Information in London, and had already made unpublicised contributions to the war effort. He edited, for example, American versions of two British documentaries concerning the war.

The episode harmed him in another sense, because it marked a sea change in the attitude of certain English critics and pundits. They decided that Hitchcock's American films were below his best, and that his departure from London had been at the expense of his cinematic imagination. He was no longer the Hitchcock of *The 39 Steps* and *The Lady Vanishes*; he had become a component of the Hollywood machine, churning out glossy and vulgar artefacts for the sake of profit. This was of course a vindictive and mistaken argument, but it was not until the 1960s and '70s that it was finally overturned.

. . .

On his return he was once more loaned out by David Selznick, on this occasion to RKO for two successive pictures. RKO—or Radio-Keith-Orpheum—had already gained a reputation for musicals and light comedies to which at this point Hitchcock was not necessarily averse. He always ascribed the first of the two pictures, *Mr. & Mrs. Smith*, to a sense of obligation. Carole Lombard had rented out her house to him, and they had found each other agreeably abrasive company. That was the reason why he agreed with RKO to direct a comic vehicle for the star. It was perhaps not quite so simple. He had in fact expressed a wish to work with her for some time, and he enjoyed the opportunity of directing a comedy in an American landscape with what he called "typical Americans."

Lombard herself was hardly typical. When on set he was discussing the rushes with her, she told him that "I don't give a fuck about that. How did my new tits look?" She knew about Hitchcock's supposed remark to Michael Redgrave that "actors are cattle," so on the first day of filming he was surprised to find three stalls on the set. Each one contained a calf, with the names of Carole Lombard, Robert Montgomery and Gene Raymond around their necks. These were the three principal actors.

As a cinematic team they worked well, and Hitchcock completed filming within six weeks. It was, all in all, a success as a Hollywood comedy in the tradition of It Happened One Night and My Man Godfrey. Lombard was the queen of screwball, effortlessly able to become the dominant female in comedies of courtship and marriage. It was light, amusing and eminently forgettable. It was also a huge success at the time, confirming Hitchcock's growing reputation as a director for American themes.

His second film for RKO was a very different matter. It had its comedic moments but the comedy was black. He began shooting Suspicion in February 1941. It is a psychological thriller in which the heroine comes to believe that her husband is trying to kill her. In the novel from which the film is derived, Before the Fact, the wife willingly drinks the poison she is offered; she is carrying her husband's baby, and does not wish to give birth to the murderer's child. It is all somewhat contrived, but the macabre situation appealed to Hitchcock. Joan Fontaine and Cary Grant took the lead roles, although Hitchcock seems to have become obsessed by the amounts they were paid in comparison with his own standard salary.

By the time shooting began, the script was still in pieces. No one as yet had a title for the film, and endless rewrites on differently coloured pages were ordered. Hitchcock fell sick from the tension and indecision, while his principal actress complained that he was not giving her performance enough attention. Fontaine had been ceaselessly coached in *Rebecca*, and now believed that the director was losing interest in her. He had in fact become more confident of her abilities. She and Grant also had difficulties, with both complaining of the other's subtle attempts to steal scenes. This was not an uncommon rivalry, and Hitchcock would have done his best to exacerbate it to increase the necessary tension on the screen.

Hitchcock admired Grant's abilities as an actor. The actor eventually performed in four of the director's films, and would be considered for another six which time and circumstance denied him. It has been said that Grant was the man who Hitchcock in his fantasies wished to be. It is possible but not likely. "Cary Grant" was in any case a fiction, an invention designed for the public. He was actually an English circus performer, Archie Leach, who had by various methods vaulted from the trapeze into stardom. His secret was to do little or nothing; his face was in many respects a blank, on to which the audience could read any and every emotion. There were occasions when his eyes moved very slightly to register that something had happened, even if he himself was not prepared to say what it was. A single phrase, or a single gesture, was enough. That was his style. In the famous scene when he brings up to his ailing wife a glass of milk, in which Hitchcock had placed an electric bulb to increase its luminescence, he might have been carrying a sleeping potion or a dose of poison. The accompanying music is that of a waltz by Strauss entitled "Vienna Blood." Grant's posture, and his expression, fulfil Hitchcock's familiar advice to actors: "Do *nothing*." This is not as simple as it sounds.

One of Grant's fellow actors in another Hitchcock film, James Mason, recalled that "Cary was a very serious person, not the character he played. He would be there waiting, clutching his script as though his life depended on it until the last possible second. Then he would step into his part, confident, flippant, and casual, appearing to be making it up as he went along." He managed at the same time to convey intimacy and distance, the sort of strangeness that accompanied his creation of "Cary Grant."

Three different conclusions were prepared for the film, a sign of the

A press shot for *Suspicion*, 1941. Cary Grant, left, was to become
a favourite actor of Hitchcock. In 1942, Joan Fontaine won an Oscar
for her role in the film.

Courtesy of Hulton Archive/Getty Images

confusion that bedevilled the entire process of filming. In one of them Grant's character is in fact the murderer. The studio rejected that ending, on the grounds that the romantic star could not be the villain. The second, in which the wife drinks the milk to no ill effect but saves her husband from poisoning himself, was derided by a preview audience. Hitchcock had to settle for an ambiguous close, in which the ill-starred couple drive away in a show of apparent amity after the wife realises that her own fears had clouded her judgement. This ending, with its hint of menace to come, seemed to satisfy the director.

To general surprise, however, there was a happy ending in another sense. When the film was released in November 1941, it quickly became a success, with one critic believing that it was "far finer" than *Rebecca*. The audiences agreed, and *Suspicion* became the most popular and profitable film of that year for RKO. The president of RKO, George Schaefer, cabled to Hitchcock that "ORCHIDS TO YOU AGAIN REVIEWS EXCELLENT AND PICTURE DOING OUTSTANDING BUSINESS WE ARE ALL VERY HAPPY AND KNOW YOU MUST BE TOO." The public approval was sealed in February 1942 when Joan Fontaine won the Oscar for Best Actress.

It is in fact a film that displays some of the director's characteristic themes; unease bubbles quietly beneath the surface, the darkness hidden from view in familiar and even homely surroundings. Strong horizontal shadows cross the innocent participants, like the mark of Cain. There are shadows everywhere, encouraging perpetual suspense and unjustified suspicion. The tension is almost palpable.

It is a film about legibility and readability. In one scene a detective is seen looking momentarily at a work of abstract art; but his glance tells you nothing. Does he understand it or does it pass his comprehension? In similar fashion the camera will pause upon Cary Grant's face. Is he a hapless playboy or a sociopath? It is impossible to tell. All is inscrutable and ambiguous, which is perhaps why the ambivalent ending perfectly suits the tone and manner of the film. Yet the film has the strange power of drawing the spectator forward, in a state of constant anticipation.

.   .   .

Even while filming *Suspicion* Hitchcock had begun working on his next picture. *Saboteur* was primarily of his own devising. With the assistance of Alma and Joan Harrison he developed a scenario for a film in which a munitions worker is falsely accused of sabotage. With the help of an attractive young woman the suspect must pursue the real criminal. If this sounds like *The 39 Steps* transposed to American soil, that is exactly what it is. In some ways he liked to look back. Vague ideas of remaking *The Lodger* and *The Man Who Knew Too Much* were considered before being shelved.

He delivered the treatment of the proposed film to Selznick, who was intrigued but not convinced. Selznick wrote to Hitchcock that he should "try to get something instead of [a] dam being blown up. This is not very new for a picture catastrophe." He also took the precaution of sending one of his senior colleagues, John Houseman, to supervise the process of turning the treatment into a viable film. Even at this early stage Selznick planned to sell the film and director to another studio, and naturally wanted to protect his investment. He hoped that Houseman, another Englishman, might be able to work more easily with Hitchcock. Houseman had spent previous years working with Orson Welles, and so had perhaps acquired a reputation for dealing with difficult characters.

Houseman was immediately taken with his compatriot. "I had heard of him as a fat man given to scabrous jokes, a gourmet and an ostentatious connoisseur of fine wines. What I was unprepared for was a man of exaggeratedly delicate sensibilities, marked by a harsh Catholic education and the scars from a social system against which he was in perpetual revolt and which had left him suspicious and vulnerable, alternatively docile and defiant." This is, perhaps, overstressing the point; whether by Hitchcock or by Houseman is not clear.

He went on to say that "his passion was for his work, which he approached with an intelligence and almost scientific clarity to which I was unaccustomed." He worked with Hitchcock by means of long conversations, concerning "anecdotes, situations, characters, revelations and reversals, which he would think up at night and try out on us during the day." Hitchcock had images and scenes in his head, quite unconnected with one another, but, as Houseman says, "the surviving elements were finally strung together into some sort of story in accordance with carefully calculated and elaborately plotted rhythms." This was the origin of *Saboteur*, where certain notable set scenes and conflicts are held together by the slenderest of threads.

In the course of planning and writing the film, one of the essential members of his team left. Joan Harrison had decided that she wanted to further her career in Hollywood by striking out alone. Hitchcock asked Selznick to increase her salary but, when the producer declined to do so, Hitchcock left the office in a rage. Harrison and Hitchcock managed to remain on friendly terms, however, and eventually they were reunited.

Her replacement at the time was a young man, Peter Viertel, who had never written a script before. Hitchcock promised that he would teach him how to do so in twenty minutes. When Viertel questioned him about a problematic piece of action Hitchcock replied that "they'll never ask"—"they" being what he described to Viertel as "the great masses" and "the moron millions." He needed to sell them tickets, to furnish his own livelihood, but he did not have to admire them. This was the paradox of his position. He needed to consult the tastes of his audience, and to a certain extent pander to them, while at the same time he believed himself to be an artist rather than a mere entertainer; this would encourage odd contortions on his part. It may have been a sign of self-hatred, however, that he was willing to belittle his own achievements.

The filming of *Saboteur* was given an additional impetus by the bombing of Pearl Harbor by the Japanese on the morning of 7 December 1941. American neutrality in the larger war was no longer an option, and it allowed Viertel (and his eventual co-writer, Dorothy Parker) to pepper the script with remarks about those rich American socialites and industrialists who sympathised with the fascist cause.

Selznick sold the film and its director to an independent producer, Frank Lloyd, who in turn supervised the film for Universal Pictures. Universal was not at that time as formidable as it became, and Hitchcock was given a modest budget. But he also enjoyed the minimum of interference, which compensated for everything. He went to work with a will. The production designer, Robert Boyle, remarked that "everything we did had to be short cuts." A storage facility became an aircraft factory. Mattes and miniatures formed the backdrops. When anyone questioned him, Hitchcock would say, "Well, I know it can be done." Out of these sometimes makeshift elements Hitchcock re-created the look and atmosphere of contemporary America—the large ranch of a fascist agent, a ghost town, a Manhattan town house, the Boulder Dam, the Brooklyn Navy Yard, the Radio City Music Hall and, most astonishing of all, the upper part of the Statue of Liberty from which the real saboteur falls to his death. Some of it was actual footage, some of it was painting, and some of it reconstruction. When a French liner caught fire in the Brooklyn Navy Yard, Hitchcock sent a camera unit to film the disaster which he then incorporated into the film.

He proceeded with the filming very quickly, as if the pace of events in the outer world had quickened him; he began in October 1941, and finished in January 1942. The speed showed. It has some remarkable moments, such as the fall from the Statue of Liberty, but it is a little ramshackle in its construction. It is fast, and it is furious. It has the power of raw drama that involves the audience, conveying an extraordinary intensity and excitement. Hitchcock relies upon the sudden surprise, the unlikely connection, the satirical twist in the plot. As one critic pointed out, "this is Hitchcock at his most Hitchcock, which does not necessarily mean at his best." Hitchcock himself later seemed to agree, citing the script and the actors for being less than perfect. More importantly, however, it is the villain rather than the hero who is in imminent danger of falling to his death. That was an aesthetic mistake. Yet the film was a popular, if not necessarily a critical, success. Hitchcock had at last managed to create a properly American thriller set entirely in the United States, and the audiences responded. This was also the first film in which his name surmounted the credits, with "Alfred Hitchcock's *Saboteur*" across the posters; he never lost that position.

. . .

He had now finally decided to settle in his adopted country. The sudden death of Carole Lombard in a plane crash, in the same month he had finished filming, required him to leave the house he rented from her. The Hitchcocks (predominantly Alma) began looking for a home of their own. They found one in the same neighbourhood of Bel Air, at 10957 Bellagio Road, where they remained for the rest of their lives. It was just a few miles from St. Cloud Road but it was newly built in what was called the "colonial style"; Hitchcock was probably the first owner. It was spacious, with seven bedrooms and five bathrooms, comfortable, and entirely hidden by trees. He had homely, if increasingly expensive, tastes. He was across the road from the fifteenth hole of the golf course owned by the Bel Air Country Club, and Alma would pick up the stray balls that landed on their lawns. They also had two terriers who helped in the chase. They were at home.

He had already put down roots when, in the summer of 1940, he had purchased a weekend retreat among the redwoods of California. "Heart o' the Mountain" was high up in the Scotts Valley on the slope of the Santa Cruz mountains; it commanded an eighty-five-acre estate, complete with orange groves and grapefruit trees. It was a large house built in the "California–Spanish" style of the 1930s with red-tiled roofs, white walls, arched doorways and wooden beams. It had the advantage of a panoramic view of Monterey Bay, and the Hitchcocks built an outside dining room of glass with heated floor. The front door was made out of a wine cask. In its walled rose garden Alma grew white roses, her favourite flower, and on a whitewashed stone wall hung a mosaic of *Les oiseaux* by Georges Braque. In a cupboard Hitchcock kept a gramophone and his collection of classical records.

It soon became known as "The Ranch" but, with baskets of hanging flowers, it also summoned up memories of Shamley Green and

England. Robert Boyle said that "I think northern California always reminded Hitch of England. There was something about the weather, which was very unpredictable. It was fog and rain and then sunshine. It was a moody strange area both forbidding and foreboding and I believe that's what intrigued him. It had a kind of mystical quality." It possessed an unmysterious vineyard, too, and Hitchcock's caretaker made wine from the grapes. Hitchcock served it to a range of guests, among them in later years Ingrid Bergman and James Stewart (not to mention Princess Grace and Prince Rainier) and was known to fly in Dover sole or steak and kidney pie from his favoured suppliers in London for these occasions. One of his actors, Hume Cronyn, once said that he "took a marvellous, malicious delight in seeing his guests fall apart with all those vintage wines and liquor."

6

FAKE IT

He was already thinking of his next film. He had so much enjoyed the freedom of Universal Pictures that he was more than happy to continue working with the studio. He was happier still when David Selznick increased fees all round as a result of the success of *Saboteur*. Hitchcock himself received $50,000, which poured a little balm over his resentment of the producer's exploitation of him. The idea for his next project came over lunch at the beginning of May 1942, when Gordon McDonell, the husband of one of the story editors at the studio, outlined the narrative of a true event. This was the beginning of *Shadow of a Doubt*. McDonell sent Hitchcock the story as he envisaged it; Hitchcock, taken with the idea, outlined a screenplay and took it to the studio. It was irresistible. Evil comes to a small town. A sociopathic murderer takes refuge from the attentions of the police by being ostensibly reunited with his long-lost family in a provincial town; they welcome him, but his niece soon finds reasons to doubt the intentions and even the sanity of "Uncle Charlie."

That was to be the name of the film. Hitchcock wanted Thornton Wilder to write the script, since Wilder had written the play *Our Town*, a drama of everyday people in the fictional setting of "Grover's Corners" in New Hampshire. Wilder, perhaps to Hitchcock's surprise, accepted the assignment. The director was accustomed to eminent writers turning him down with sometimes ill-disguised contempt.

The two men were intent upon fidelity to American experience, and settled on the town of Santa Rosa in California for its exploration. They found the right public square, they found the right library, they found the right street and they found the right house (partially reconstructed on the studio set). They talked to the residents, looking for certain characteristics or turns of phrase that they might use. When they returned to Hollywood, stimulated by their visit, they began work at once. They talked in the morning about the coming day's work and Wilder wrote to a friend that "in long story conferences we think up new twists to the plot and gaze at each other in appalled silence, as much to say 'Do you think an audience can bear it?'" Wilder would then spend the afternoon writing the scenes in a notebook, animated by what he described as "that old Wilder poignance about family life." They both had such a clear idea of the narrative that they did not need to work chronologically; the film already had an organic shape that did not need cultivating.

Nothing could have been more congenial to Hitchcock than the character of Uncle Charlie, on the surface a humorous and likeable companion but in truth a man who has a manic grudge against conventional society. Hitchcock also took pleasure in setting up an orthodox small-town family into which this all-American Nosferatu insinuates himself. All of Hitchcock's preoccupations, of the fear and trembling just below the surface of ordinary life, came to the surface. Joseph Cotten, chosen to play Uncle Charlie, professed some anxiety about his role. "Just be yourself," Hitchcock told him. That accounted for the realistic triumph of the film; everyone was simply "themselves"—the scatter-brained but sympathetic mother, the slow but steady father, the sharp-eyed niece—in what seems to be an authentic environment. After *Saboteur*, it was Hitchcock's second attempt at re-creating Americana.

The proposed title was changed to *Shadow of a Doubt*, perhaps in deference to the film's darker shades, but Hitchcock remained remarkably faithful to Thornton Wilder's original scenario. Teresa Wright, playing the niece who discovers the truth about her uncle, recalled that Hitchcock "saw the film completely in his mind before we began—it's as if he had a little projection room in his head." He would sit at his desk, his thumbs emerging above his folded arms, and go through every scene with his principal cameraman and other colleagues. With his cast complete, including Joseph Cotten and Hume Cronyn, he began filming in August 1942.

Shadow of a Doubt was meant to be realistic, yet Hitchcock always preferred the artifice of the set. His art director explained that "we would take a few shots on location, the minimum amount, and then he always liked to work in the controlled area of a stage . . . he would sacrifice many things to get that control." Occasionally, however, he was happy to improvise or extemporise. There is a photograph of him, on location in *Shadow of a Doubt*, actually looking through the lens of the camera. This was a practice in which he claimed never to indulge, but surely the camera does not lie? It was his custom, however, to position himself in a chair just to the right below the camera.

Timing was all. Teresa Wright reported that "if an actor was strumming his fingers it wasn't just an idle strumming, it had a beat, a musical pattern to it—it was like a sound refrain. Whether someone was walking or rustling a paper or tearing an envelope or whistling, whether it was a flutter of birds or an outside sound, it was carefully orchestrated by him. He really scored the sound effects the way a musician writes for instruments." Some of the effects were not intentional; when Uncle Charlie arrives at the railroad station of Santa Rosa, the sun providentially hides itself behind clouds.

The musical score was enhanced by his insistent use of a doubling effect—the niece Charlie and Uncle Charlie, two detectives, two children, two dinner scenes, the sequence at the "Till Two" bar where two double brandies are served, the figurines of couples dancing to "The Merry Widow" waltz, and so on. This is always assumed to be deliberately planned, as a way of emphasising the duality of the central character or even the ambiguity between comedy and suspense that suffuses the film. But it may simply be instinctive, a consequence of the musical pattern of the film. Much that has been attested about the director's use of symbolism, which in private at least he ridiculed, may be simply a forced interpretation of what was initially accidental or coincidental. His own interpretations of his films tended to be bland or hesitant, as if he did not want to scrutinise his intentions too carefully. He was happy enough for the more highbrow critics and scholars to supply their own analyses, since he knew very well that they would give him credit among the intellectuals and the college teachers, but he took it all *cum grano salis.*

He celebrated his forty-third birthday while beginning to film *Shadow of a Doubt* and, with his usual ghoulish sense of humour, picked up a long carving knife and put it to his throat; he was grinning and, of course, everybody laughed. Yet there was bad news on the way. His mother had been ailing for some time with acute renal and intestinal infections, and she died at the house in Shamley Green that autumn. Five months later his older brother, William, died from what seems to have been a self-administered dose of paraldehyde. His suicide might have been prompted by his mother's death, but it is impossible to say. He was a heavy drinker, and the fatal mixture of drugs and alcohol might have killed him in any case. The continuing strain of the war no doubt contributed its part.

Hitchcock's reactions to the two deaths are not recorded, but it is known that he began to lose a great deal of weight in the following months. Mortality beckoned. By the end of 1943 he had shed one hundred pounds, which was a cause of concern to David Selznick. He wrote that "I am sincerely and seriously worried about Hitch's fabulous loss of weight. I do hope he has a physician, as otherwise we are liable to get a shock one morning about a heart attack or something of the sort." After a medical examination for an insurance policy Hitchcock discovered that he had an enlarged heart, and a hernia. Such was his fear of treatment that he refused the operation on his abdomen, and so was obliged to wear a truss. His insurance was declined.

The loss of his mother might have affected him in another sense. Ever since he had been planning and filming *Shadow of a Doubt,*

Emma Hitchcock had been declining. The mother in the film is also called Emma, and she is played by Patricia Collinge as an endearing and benign figure; she seems to have shared some of Emma Hitchcock's characteristics, including the tendency to shout down the telephone as if her voice had to make up the distance. Hitchcock recalled later that "there was the constant danger from the war, as well as her own failing health. She was in my thoughts at the time. I suppose that if we think about a character who is a mother, it is natural to start with one's own. The character of the mother in *Shadow of a Doubt*, you might say, is a figment of my memory." That was perhaps the nearest he ever came to revealing his private thoughts. He did not want anyone to come too close.

He was similarly reticent about the film itself. One of its early admirers, Gordon McDonell, the man who had brought him the story in the first place, wrote to him that "you certainly did put the whole of yourself into that picture." Hitchcock might have declined the compliment. On some occasions he said that it was his "favourite," and on others that it was "one of my favourites" or that it was "a most satisfying picture." For most critics it remains one of the finest films he ever made. Such is the verdict of posterity. At the time it was treated as an intriguing crime thriller, and nothing more. It has been said that there are only two stories in the world; one of them concerns a journey, and the other documents the moment when a stranger comes to town. Hitchcock manages to convey all the suspicion and the anxiety, all the tension and even the terror, of the latter situation. We have already learned of his trick of throwing the empty teacup over his shoulder. Everything is brittle; everything can be shattered.

· · ·

The film was released at the beginning of 1943 but, two months before, he had been sold by Selznick to the highest bidder. That may be a harsh verdict, but it is one to which Hitchcock himself would fully subscribe. Joseph Cotten inverted Hitchcock's remark about actors and remarked to him that "I see they're selling directors like cattle." In November 1942, he moved into the sphere of the producer Darryl F. Zanuck, and into the offices of Twentieth Century Fox.

Hitchcock already had a proposal for his new employer. He had conceived the idea of a "lifeboat film" that might reveal some of the complexities of the wartime world. He was also intrigued by the technical challenge of shooting in the confined space of a small boat. The idea of incompatible survivors stranded together in the middle of a menacing sea, after their ship has been torpedoed by a U-boat, interested him; it might seem to be a metaphor for life as well as for war.

He began work on a treatment as soon as he joined Twentieth Century Fox. In the absence of Zanuck, who was on military duties as a colonel in the Army Signal Corps, he was assigned to the producer Kenneth Macgowan. He and Macgowan, together with Alma, worked on a rudimentary treatment but they needed a named and if possible famous author to lend credibility to the enterprise.

Hitchcock had first considered Ernest Hemingway for the script, but the novelist demurred. Macgowan and Hitchcock then turned to John Steinbeck, whose novel *The Grapes of Wrath* had been made into a film by Twentieth Century Fox only three years before. Steinbeck himself was between projects and had leased a house in Hollywood. It was considered to be a perfect opportunity. Steinbeck seemed to think so too, and even before his contract was signed he had completed what he called a "novelette" of a hundred pages. It was more like an omelette.

Steinbeck then flew to New York, ready to travel to the European theatre as a war correspondent for the *New York Herald Tribune*. The Hitchcocks followed him for what they considered to be important script conferences. Steinbeck was under the misapprehension that his work was almost done, but Hitchcock was naturally intent upon changes and revisions. The novelist had written the narrative from the perspective of one survivor, but this was not considered to be suitably cinematic. Steinbeck said later that Hitchcock "was one of those incredible middle-class English snobs who really and truly despise working people." The remark makes it clear that Steinbeck did not understand, or bother to understand, the motives of his director. He may have been misled by Hitchcock's manner, or accent, or both. Their collaboration was not a success.

The script then passed through several writers, the last of whom, Jo Swerling, did not care for Steinbeck's original version. He testified that "after the first reading that I gave to the Steinbeck story, I never again referred to it, nor did anybody else working on the picture." Nevertheless Steinbeck's name remained in the credits, perhaps for contractual reasons or perhaps to convince audiences of the film's essential seriousness. The guiding hand remained that of Hitchcock himself, who devised many of the scenes and incidents in collaboration with Swerling. In the summer of 1943 Zanuck unexpectedly returned from duty in the Army Signal Corps, and was irate at the length of time it had taken to produce a working script. He had the screenplay timed with a stopwatch, even as Hitchcock was filming the first scenes, and was astonished to discover that the finished picture might extend to two hours. He sent a memorandum to the director, asking him "to drop some element in its entirety."

Hitchcock was always sure of his timings. He could see the picture in front of him. He replied to Zanuck with the message that "I don't know who you employ to time your scripts, but whoever has done it is misleading you horribly. I will even go so far as to say disgracefully." He signed it, ironically, as "Your obedient servant, Alfred Hitchcock." He was right and, after a more accurate timing was made, the matter was dropped.

The making of the film was no less difficult than its preparation. The technical challenges may have interested him but they were less appealing to the performers who, for example, were obliged to climb a ladder to a small boat in a great water tank. Sometimes they fell in the water and had to be hauled out; sometimes they were drenched by the crew; sometimes they were rocked violently from side to side, making them seasick or, rather, tank-sick. Most of the cast came down with colds or fevers or worse. Tallulah Bankhead, who played the role of a socialite journalist, remembered that she was "black and blue from the downpours and the lurchings. Thanks to the heat, the lights, the fake fog and submersions followed by rapid dryings-out, I came up with pneumonia early in November."

It is interesting that she "came up" rather than "came down." She was always looking to the bright side. She even caused a minor scandal on the set with her habit of never wearing any underwear. As she climbed the ladder and entered the lifeboat the crew drew lots as to who should be able to peer up at her. Hitchcock, when told of the situation, said that it was a problem for a barber and not for a director. But he remained on the best of terms with the actress; she was a drinker with a caustic tongue, mischievous and dirty-minded. Hitchcock seems often to have been obsessed by beautiful blondes but the women he liked were feisty, witty—even foul-mouthed—characters such as Carole Lombard and Tallulah Bankhead.

Lifeboat was not well received. It was a year in filming and post-production, when it should have taken half the time, and was clumsily released by the company. It was treated as an allegory for the war even then being waged, when essentially it was an exercise in dramatic adventure and personal crisis with the war as its setting. The plot, such as it is, concerns a disparate and disorganised group of Americans who are deceived by the German officer they have hauled to safety; he turns out to have been the captain of the U-boat that had sunk their liner, and to be gradually steering the lifeboat towards enemy lines. Several notable episodes, such as an amputation and the suicide of a woman with her dead baby, are still very powerful; but contemporaneous critics believed that it had become a subtle celebration of unflinching Nazi character and a denunciation of weak and divided Americans. Hitchcock countered with his own quickly invented moral that it was a call for America to unite, but the damage had been done. He recalled that one critic gave *Lifeboat* "ten days to get out of town."

·   ·   ·

By the time the reviews appeared, Hitchcock had taken that advice. He had been preparing for a return to England in order to consult with his old friend from the London Film Society, Sidney Bernstein, about two films for the Ministry of Information, for which Bernstein now worked. These would be propaganda "shorts" which would help to assuage Hitchcock's guilt about playing no defined or prominent role in Britain's war. He told an interviewer later that "I knew that if I did nothing I'd regret it for the rest of my life." He was also eager to confer with Bernstein about their possible collaboration in the post-war period, when a new form of Anglo-American film company might have distinct benefits.

At the beginning of December 1943 he had the uncomfortable experience of flying across the Atlantic under wartime conditions. He recalled that "I flew over in a bomber, sitting on the floor, and when we got halfway across the Atlantic, the plane had to turn back. I took another one two days later." This would have been torture for someone of his nervous temperament.

When he arrived in London he was booked into Claridge's but the relatively luxurious venue did not conceal the privation and terror of the city at war. He managed to see some friends, and to visit his sister who had continued living at Shamley Green, but his main memories were of bombs, searchlights and anti-aircraft fire. "I used to be alone at Claridge's hotel, and the bombs would fall, and the guns, and I was alone and didn't know what to do."

Yet he did have work on hand. He had agreed with Sidney Bernstein to make two short films to be shown in the parts of France that had been recently liberated from German occupation. He worked on *Bon Voyage* and *Aventure Malgache* in the first two months of 1944, with French players. The films were of no great significance at the time, and there is some dispute whether they were actually distributed. Yet *Bon Voyage*, in particular, gave him the opportunity for strong drama as a German agent uses an escaped English prisoner to infiltrate a Resistance group in France. It was much closer to real war experience than either *Lifeboat* or *Saboteur*; it had all the makings of a grand *film noir*, and he even entertained the notion of turning it into a full-length picture.

He and Bernstein also continued their discussion about a partnership, a possible relationship about which David Selznick had already been informed. "I hope," Selznick wrote to his agent in England, "that one of the motives behind bringing Mr. Hitchcock back to England is not a desire to negotiate a private deal with him for the future." He did not wish to lose his most profitable investment. Even before he had left for London, however, Hitchcock had purchased the rights in what he considered to be appropriate material. *The House of Dr. Edwardes* is a novel concerning strange events in a Swiss lunatic asylum, and therefore highly congenial to Hitchcock's tastes. He thought that he had already found the perfect scriptwriter in England. Angus MacPhail had known Hitchcock in the days of the London Film Society and had become the head of Michael Balcon's story department at Lime Grove when Hitchcock was making *The Man Who Knew Too Much* and *The 39 Steps*. So there was a long association, compounded by a shared sense of humour and of mischief. He had also assisted in the writing of the two French propaganda films.

Yet MacPhail had become unable to write in any determined or continuous fashion. "He rewrote his own stuff wildly," said one of his colleagues, Sidney Gilliat, "and at all hours for sometimes no good reason." He also seems to have been a heavy drinker. Nevertheless he did manage to complete a seventeen-page treatment which was then revised and revised again. If it did nothing else, it prepared the ground for the subsequent film.

Selznick, who was himself undergoing psychoanalysis, was much taken by the proposal. "I'd like to stress," he wrote to his story editor, "that I'm almost desperately anxious to do this psychological or psychiatric story with Hitch." Hitchcock was also ready and prepared. He returned from London to Hollywood at the beginning of March, and began to work directly with David Selznick for only the second time. Their previous collaboration, *Rebecca*, was the occasion of mixed memories for both of them.

There might be further trouble ahead. Unlike Hitchcock, Selznick had a real enthusiasm for, and interest in, psychiatric matters. He had entered analysis during a severe bout of depression. Psychoanalysis was the fashion of the age in the United States, with those who could afford it treating it as the secular equivalent of the Catholic confessional. Freudianism had become the new orthodox faith. This may be the reason why Hitchcock had bought up the rights to *The House of Dr. Edwardes*, in the hope of catching a trend. The bait worked splendidly.

In the absence of MacPhail, Hitchcock asked to work with the redoubtable Ben Hecht. Hecht had been a crime reporter and war reporter on the *Chicago Daily News* before becoming a novelist and dramatist, but his real skill lay in scriptwriting and he became known as "the Shakespeare of Hollywood"; his hallmarks were speed and street-smart simplicity. Hitchcock reported later that Hecht told him, "Well, Hitchie, write the dialogue you want and then I'll correct it." Hecht himself applauded "the gentlemanly Alfred Hitchcock who gave off plot turns like a Roman candle." They visited mental hospitals and psychiatric wards seeking local colour; they interviewed doctors and nurses, looking for pertinent information. They were perfect collaborators and, in the end, they were composing twenty pages of script every day. Hecht stated that "Hitchcock was beaming amid his nightmares." Selznick asked his own analyst, May Romm, to go over the script; she set to work with a will and managed to excise many of the mistakes that the two men naturally made. She gave various mental conditions their right name and provenance.

The plot, concerning the director of an asylum who murders his putative successor before being unmasked by one of the psychiatrists working for him, is of no importance. The only matter of consequence was the casting of Ingrid Bergman and Gregory Peck in the two principal roles. Peck was a relative newcomer and was not at his ease in the part of an amnesiac. He made the mistake of asking Hitchcock a question about what his character was thinking. What was his motivation? The director's usual answer to such a question was "Your salary," and on this occasion he was only a little more helpful. "My dear boy," he said, "I couldn't care less what you're thinking. Just let your face drain of all expression." Peck's own description of his "soul-searching" and "lack of ready technique" was not helped by Hitchcock's characteristic lack of reaction to his performance, which Peck interpreted as lack of interest. Some of his hesitation and nervousness can be glimpsed on the screen.

Ingrid Bergman was another matter. She had arrived in the United States from Sweden five years before, under the tutelage of David Selznick who described her as "the most completely conscientious actress with whom I have ever worked." She had already starred in *Casablanca*, *For Whom the Bell Tolls* and *Gaslight*; so she was no novice. Hitchcock seems to have been enchanted with her, and an intense friendship grew up between them which remained sexually unfulfilled. They were just good companions. In later life he used to say that she had always loved him and that she had once made a pass at him, but this sounds like an old man's fantasy. In this first film together he was remarkably patient with her on the set, and the other members of the cast noticed that he seemed to approach her with a genuine shyness or nervousness. Peck recalled that "whenever he was with her, I had the feeling that something was ailing him, and it was difficult to know exactly the cause of his suffering, although some of us had our suspicions."

Hitchcock himself described her as "worried, miserable, high-strung, romantic, idealistic, sensitive, emotional." It is hard to think of another occasion when he was so sympathetic towards an actor, and it may be that Bergman helped him to think much harder about the projection of a female presence upon the screen. There had been memorable performances before, notably Joan Fontaine's in *Rebecca*, but none of them had the allure or intensity that he elicited from Bergman in a trio of films. He seems to have experienced an emotional sea change.

He was equally docile with her on the set. She recalled that "he would sit patiently" while she outlined her problems over a scene, or a line, or a gesture, and then "he would say very sweetly 'Fake it!'" She admitted that this was the best piece of filmic advice she had ever been given. Later in life, after she eloped with Roberto Rossellini and Hitchcock seems to have felt betrayed, he was less sentimental about her. He would say to associates "Ah, Ingrid. So beautiful. So *stupid.*"

Hitchcock began filming in the summer of 1944. He arrived on the set in his limousine at precisely nine o'clock, and shooting continued in a brisk but unhurried fashion; the film was completed on schedule within forty-eight days. Peck remembered that he gave very little direction at all. He was calm, and still, but Peck also recalled that "Hitchcock liked his actors and movements to be as much under his control as the camera movements or the props or the scenery." On occasion he seemed to be dozing, eyes closed, and Peck himself believed that there were times when he was "sound asleep" until woken by an assistant. He may have been asleep or he may have been, in a phrase of the time, "resting his eyes" for a further effort. He may even have been running through the scene in his head and, as Peck admitted, when he woke he seemed to know "exactly what was going on."

He had also learned how to deal with David Selznick, who had as much concern and involvement in the production as Hitchcock. When the producer wandered on to the set, the camera was suddenly halted by one technical problem or other, and did not begin working again until Selznick had left. He must have known, in the end, that he was being diverted; but by now he had such respect for Hitchcock's working methods that he refused to be annoyed. He told his production manager that "I have seldom seen so smooth running a crew, or as obviously efficient a company as the *Dr. Edwardes* unit." He may also have calculated that he would work his own way through the film in post-production.

There were some false starts. Hitchcock had asked Selznick to hire Salvador Dalí to create a startling dream sequence. Dalí arrived in Hollywood in the autumn, and created oil paintings and sketches to convey the essence of a disturbed dream. But his vision was too unsettling, and at Selznick's wish much of it landed on the cutting-room floor. Dalí was of course outraged, but Hitchcock himself accepted the cuts. There are times when he seemed not to care what happened to his films after he had finished with them. He was more interested in their commercial success.

Selznick did indeed manage the process of post-production. He changed the opening, he revised certain scenes, he altered some of the dialogue, and generally made the film shorter and snappier. He used to call the process, confusingly, "mogo on the gogo," which meant some form of love-sickness. Gregory Peck uses the phrase in *Spellbound*, as the film was titled, from where Selznick may have picked it up. When the film was released, however, it was widely believed to be another Hitchcock thriller but one without the intensity of previous successes.

Yet it was a public success; Selznick reported that, at a preview, "we could not keep the audience quiet from the time his [Gregory Peck's] name first came on the screen until we had shushed the audience through three or four sequences and stopped all the dames from 'ohing' and 'ahing' and gurgling." *Spellbound* gained one Oscar for its music and was nominated for six others, but Hitchcock professed indifference to such baubles. He may have received more satisfaction from the crowds surrounding him at the film's premiere at the London Tivoli, on the Strand.

Hitchcock later said of *Spellbound* that "it's just another manhunt story wrapped up in pseudo-psychoanalysis." Some critics did not disagree. Ingrid Bergman was disappointed with the finished product. But any interpretation of the completed film is as fraught with ambiguity as psychoanalysis itself. The image of the locked door, the motif of vertical bars, the theme of watchful eyes (including, of course, those of the audience), and all the complex visual distortions that Hitchcock devises, intimate the world as a prison from which there is no possibility of escape. Again the eyes are everywhere.

A special effects artist, Clarence Slifer, wrote of the Dalí sequence that "Hitchcock wanted some bloodshot eyeballs moving through the scene. I went down to Skid Row [in Los Angeles] on Christmas Eve to photograph these bleary-eyed fellows who'd been drinking heavily all their lives. We got more varieties of eyes than you can imagine, from bloodshot to weepy and then expressionless eyes." Yet the presence of Bergman in the film ensures an underlying tenderness and textural softness. The woman is, for the first time in a Hitchcock film, the healing agent. She is the blossom in the dust. *Spellbound* conveys an intimate and a claustrophobic world. Within these ambiguities, Hitchcock dwells.

. . .

Two days after the filming of *Spellbound* was complete, Hitchcock returned to England to renew his discussions with Sidney Bernstein on a possible collaboration. They wished to form Transatlantic Pictures, employing the best crews, scriptwriters and actors from both countries; but for this purpose they needed investors, who were notoriously nervous about any new ventures. Hitchcock remained in London for some ten weeks, but no startling progress was made in the search for finance. He was ready to return to the security of Hollywood, where he was contracted to make another picture for David Selznick.

While he was in London he had heard from Selznick's agent that the producer was ready to start work on one of Hitchcock's favoured projects. The popular and financial success of *Spellbound* was such that Selznick had begun preparations for another film with part of the same team: Ben Hecht would once more be scriptwriter, and Ingrid Bergman again the star. Selznick had found the perfect vehicle in a magazine serial, "The Song of the Dragon," that had been published more than twenty years before. It concerned an actress who is persuaded to seduce a suspected double agent and discover his secrets.

As soon as he returned to the United States, Hitchcock met Ben Hecht in New York where they discussed the new picture that had already been entitled *Notorious*. In December 1944, they met for most days of the week, from nine in the morning to six in the evening; when they were not together, Hecht would be at his typewriter. A reporter from the *New York Times* observed that "Mr. Hecht would stride about or drape himself over a chair or couch, or sprawl artistically on the floor. Mr. Hitchcock, a one-hundred-and-ninety-two-pound Buddha (reduced from two hundred and ninety-five) would sit primly on a straight-back chair, his hands clasped across his midriff, his round button eyes gleaming."

A second and third draft duly followed, with comments scribbled by Selznick; in the spring of 1945 Hitchcock and Hecht returned to Los Angeles for the final collaboration. The story had changed. The German double agent had a daughter (Ingrid Bergman) who is persuaded by an American agent (Cary Grant) to seduce and marry another prominent German (Claude Rains) in order to infiltrate his circle of conspirators. Her true identity is discovered by her new husband, and she becomes the victim of secret and stealthy poisoning. At the last minute the American comes to her rescue. At some point in this process Hecht, or Hitchcock, or both, hit upon the idea that the Germans were dealing with uranium, a remarkably prescient idea in the months before Hiroshima. The uranium was concealed in red wine bottles.

The months of writing and rewriting *Notorious* had been very costly. Hecht and Hitchcock had been given large weekly salaries, and Selznick was growing anxious over delays. Hitchcock was also hesitating over any new commitment to Selznick, since he was still waiting to sign the agreement with Bernstein for Transatlantic Pictures. As John Houseman pointed out, Hitchcock had "a lifelong and highly neurotic preoccupation with money."

Selznick decided to cut his losses, present and possibly future, by selling the entire project to RKO. Hitchcock was happy with the arrangement, since it afforded him independence; he had enjoyed his time at the studio, four years before, where he had made *Mr. & Mrs. Smith* as well as *Suspicion*. RKO provided the studio space and the distribution, but left the actual work to the director and producer. On this occasion, however, Hitchcock also managed to exclude Selznick from the process. One clause of the agreement stipulated that the producer would not have "any voice in the production, or the supervision of production, of the PHOTOPLAY." He was on his own.

He had one other, less happy, project to complete. He had agreed to

Sidney Bernstein's request to act as consultant on a documentary about
the Nazi concentration camps. He flew back to London in June 1945,
to scrutinise the raw footage shot in Belsen, Dachau and elsewhere. He
was so horrified by what he saw that it took him some days to be able
to work on the material. In a later interview Bernstein stated that "I
wanted somebody to compile it together . . . but I wanted the imaginative touch that somebody like Hitchcock could give." The contribution
that Hitchcock made is still unclear, but he seems to have insisted that
long travelling shots should be included to confirm that the sequences
had not been faked. It was important to show as many people as possible
in real situations.

He returned to Hollywood after a month in London, and immediately resumed work on *Notorious*. The filming was scheduled to begin
in October, and the revisions of Hecht's last script were made by Clif-
ford Odets. Odets was a noted playwright, and might be considered an
expert on dialogue; Hecht himself disagreed and wrote "this is really
loose crap" on the margin of one page, but Hecht was eventually persuaded to compose one more rewrite before filming began. He began
turning out material even as filming continued, and was sometimes
only a day ahead of the schedule. This was of no real concern to Hitchcock, despite his usual predilection for careful planning, because he
trusted Hecht. It is enough, in any case, to dispel the theory or fantasy—
conveyed by Hitchcock himself—that every element of his films was set
in place before the first camera rolled.

The process of filming itself, after a year's preparation, went
smoothly. The three stars of the film—Bergman, Grant and Rains—
were perfectly at ease with each other and with the director. Patricia Hitchcock recalled how intimate and yet authoritative her father
became on the set. "Now I think it might be . . ." he would say to one
actor, or "Why don't you try this?"

Hitchcock's principal concern was the relationship between Grant
and Bergman—Grant's character is secretly in love with the woman
he is about to sacrifice to the Germans, and she in turn is dismayed by
his apparent indifference to her plight. Hitchcock focused the camera

steadily upon them in close-up and medium close-up. He said, late in his life, that film "begins with the actor's face. It is to the features of this face that the eye of the spectator will be guided, and it is the organisation of these oval shapes within the rectangle of the screen, for a purpose, that exercises the director." This is Hitchcock as a master of aesthetics and formal artistry, but he also made the remark in particular relation to Ingrid Bergman whose face is frequently seen in close-up as if it were a form of pure cinema, intimate and pre-verbal.

With Hitchcock in sole charge of direction and production, *Notorious* differs markedly from its predecessor, *Spellbound*. For the first time he was able to control every aspect of post-production without the hindrance or interference of a producer. As a result, perhaps, the film has a much more sinister texture with the suspense mounting like a quickened pulse. It was also very much a film for its time; the revelation of the German death camps, and the explosion of the atomic bomb, gave the film a startling relevance beyond that of any thriller. That intensity of interest remains on the screen, like radioactivity, and conveys an atmosphere of menace and foreboding that can still possess a cinema audience. The film was a critical success at the time, with *The New Yorker* remarking that it was "a happy example of what Alfred Hitchcock can do when he is really bearing down."

He was not able to "bear down" on his next film, where he was once more accompanied by Selznick. *The Paradine Case* was the last film they made together. It was a project favoured by the producer ever since the novel of the same name had been published in 1933. It is essentially the story of a beautiful woman who hires a successful barrister to defend her against the charge of murdering her blind husband; inevitably, perhaps, the barrister (Gregory Peck) falls in love with his client and in a doomed attempt to prove her innocence alienates his wife and falls from his previous eminence.

Hitchcock was not at first averse to the proposal. He had as a child been fascinated by the Old Bailey and its adversarial duels, and had even nurtured the ambition of being a judge in just such a court. Now he had the opportunity of re-creating his interest, or passion, on a Hollywood set. In May 1946, he returned to London in order to survey the city for suitable backdrops. He and the production manager, Fred Ahern, visited police stations, Holloway Prison and the Old Bailey itself; these were the principal scenes of the drama, to be strengthened by what Hitchcock called "Dickensian backgrounds."

Another drama was unfolding elsewhere. In the previous month the partnership of Hitchcock and Bernstein in a new venture, Transatlantic Pictures, was announced with the news that their first film would star Ingrid Bergman. The report came as no surprise to Selznick; he had been monitoring events since the new partnership had first been suggested. He could scarcely complain. With *The Paradine Case* Hitchcock would have completed his contract with him. But he could not help but feel bruised and anxious, a situation that would only exacerbate his difficulties with the director on their last film.

Hitchcock had persuaded Selznick to hire James Bridie, a Scottish playwright, to turn *The Paradine Case* into a film. But at the same time he had also asked Bridie to start work on *Under Capricorn*, the film to be made by Transatlantic Pictures. This further irritated Selznick. Bridie had completed a script of *The Paradine Case* by the autumn, but Selznick wanted it shortened and sharpened. The results still did not satisfy the producer, who decided to sit down and write the screenplay himself. Hitchcock was by now thoroughly alarmed and despondent at the prospects for the new project. Selznick had chosen an Italian actress, Alida Valli, to play the mysterious Mrs. Paradine; she was twenty-five and had already earned considerable success in the Italian cinema. Selznick hoped that she might become another Bergman. Gregory Peck was to play the lovelorn barrister but, as had been the case in *Spellbound*, he received very little instruction or praise from the director. Hitchcock had already told Valli "to do nothing well," and the same attitude was once more conveyed to Peck.

But Peck was not trained to do nothing; he had been trained to act, and his discomfiture is evident on the screen. Gregory Peck was an experienced actor whose stage career had begun in 1941; Cary Grant, as has been observed, came from the circus. But the difference

Hitchcock with Alida Valli on the set of *The Paradine Case*, 1947.
This was his last film with Selznick.

Courtesy of Ralph Crane/The LIFE Images Collection/Getty Images

endeared Grant to Hitchcock, who had more than a touch of the circus in his own style. He did not warm to Peck in the same manner; he always distrusted pure actors.

In this fraught period Hitchcock himself seemed to fall ill or, at least, he believed that he was ill. Hypochondria had always been one of his many neuroses, and he began to tell the people closest to him that "something is wrong, something is very wrong." The ills of the body, if such they were, were the consequence of the ills of the mind. Anxiety was the problem. He was anxious about the film. He was anxious about his future after Selznick and Hollywood. He was anxious about Transatlantic Pictures. He was anxious about everything. Gregory Peck remarked that "he was obviously suffering terribly about something during the shooting of *The Paradine Case.*"

He had decided to construct a replica of Central Criminal Court Number One at the Old Bailey; it took eighty days to build and was reputedly exact in every detail, including the scratches on the tables left by bored or impatient barristers. To the cost of construction must be added the cost of production; since the scenes in the courtroom are necessarily static, Hitchcock employed four cameras simultaneously during the filming so that he could create a tapestry of looks, gestures and effects.

Even as filming continued Selznick sent down pages of script he had just completed; these of course had to be incorporated into the shooting schedule at the last minute, causing enormous complications for the director. Peck also recalled that "Selznick was totally disorganised but essentially a lovable man, while Hitchcock, whose manner was not quite so lovable, was totally organised. This created an unavoidable tension, and it clearly affected Hitchcock's attitude during production." Sometimes he seemed bored; sometimes he slept, or pretended to sleep, in his chair. He had planned and orchestrated a continuous take of some five minutes for an important episode in the film, but Selznick came down on to the set and countermanded Hitchcock's direction. Selznick told him that "we're not doing a theatre piece." So there was anger, and frustration, throughout the filming. It did not bode well for the finished article.

Ann Todd, who played the barrister's increasingly desperate wife, furnished another and more familiar aspect of Hitchcock during the filming. She said that he was "a very complex man—an overgrown schoolboy, really, who never grew up and lived in his own special fantasy world. He had a schoolboy's obsession with sex that went on and on in a very peculiar way. He had an endless supply of very nasty, vulgar and naughty stories and jokes. These amused him more than they amused anyone else, but I think he was really a very sad person." She attributed this sadness to his dismay at the shape and size of his body.

The delays in filming continued, with Selznick complaining to his staff that Hitchcock had "slowed down unaccountably" and that he was "out of hand." When the director heard of these complaints he replied that the equipment he was obliged to use was twenty years out of date. The filming ground to a finish in the spring of 1947. Hitchcock had scored a record in his own career by filming for ninety-two days, and producing a film that was three hours in length, at a cost of $4.25 million. It was the most expensive he had ever made. He then abandoned it to Selznick who in post-production managed to cut fifty minutes out of the finished film, complete with retakes and redubbing. The producer was concerned about "Hitch's sloppiness about story points," and tried every means he could to remedy them.

The film was not a disaster; it was a disappointment. It did not flow, largely because of the wooden performances from most of the cast. The critic of the *New York Times* described it as "a slick piece of static entertainment." It did not succeed at the box office, and lost money. When asked which film he would most readily burn, Gregory Peck replied, without a beat, *"The Paradine Case."* Hitchcock never worked with Selznick again.

Yet in retrospect the film has virtues which were not readily discernible at the time. The fluid and luxuriant camerawork, a sort of golden rhetorical prose written by the camera, is everywhere apparent. Hitchcock has once again explored his fascination for shadows, barred windows, strips of darkness, corridors, staircases and mirrors so that all of the participants seem to be trapped in his artificial world where all the forces of passion and disorder spread like a stain over the well upholstered surface. This is perhaps what Ann Todd meant by "his own special fantasy world."

. . .

It was time to move on. The first fruit of the collaboration between Hitchcock and Sidney Bernstein, at Transatlantic Pictures, came as a surprise to many. It did not star Ingrid Bergman, as had been previously announced, but instead derived its inspiration from a sordid murder that had occurred twenty-three years before. Two wealthy and homosexual law students, Nathan Leopold and Richard Loeb, kidnapped and murdered a fourteen-year-old boy in order to demonstrate that they could commit the perfect crime; five years later, in 1929, the notorious episode was dramatised by Patrick Hamilton in his play *Rope*. In the late months of 1947, and the early months of 1948, it was reconstructed by Hitchcock in his film of the same name.

The point of the film was indeed reconstruction. The scenario never left the young men's Manhattan penthouse, as if it were a stage, and was elaborately orchestrated from first shot to last in the Warner Brothers studio at Burbank rented for the occasion. It could be said that, in this instance, the director gained his inspiration from his technique. He had decreed that the entire action would be filmed in segments of uninterrupted ten-minute takes when the camera would roam freely across the set; props and furniture were built on rollers so that they could be moved effortlessly out of the way. Hitchcock wrote later that "every movement of the camera and the actors was worked out first in sessions with a blackboard . . . even the floor was marked and plotted with numbered circles for the twenty-five to thirty camera moves in each ten-minute reel. Whole walls of the apartment had to slide away to allow the camera to follow the actors through narrow doors, then swing back noiselessly to show a solid room." Chairs and tables were pulled back by prop-men before being replaced in exactly the same position. Everything was "wild," which simply means that everything could be moved at a moment's notice. If an actor had to put down a glass on a table that was no longer there, an unseen member of the crew would take it from them.

Further technical problems had to be solved. Through the windows of the apartment could be seen, according to Hitchcock, "an exact miniature reproduction of nearly thirty-five miles of New York skyline lighted by eight thousand incandescent bulbs and two hundred neon signs requiring one hundred and fifty transformers." He insisted that the light should fade from that of day to night quite naturally and fluently. This of course required a degree of subtlety not usually required of lighting men.

This was the first film that Hitchcock made in colour or, as it was known, "the Technicolor process." He was not particularly interested in colour for its own sake; he wanted it to play a role in the unfolding drama as a kind of background music. It was a device rather than an effect. After the natural glow of sunset the apartment captures the variously coloured lights of neon signs and street lights, reflecting and helping to create the increasingly dramatic nature of the action.

Hitchcock himself handed the task of adaptation of the play to Hume Cronyn, the actor with whom he had worked before; he sensed in him literary ability. Cronyn later revealed that the director seemed as interested in the innovative technique of filming as in the drama itself. It was a unique technical challenge that might, at the same time, take some of the emphasis away from the controversial sexual material. Their conversations would become intense, and even heated, but then Hitchcock would change the tempo by telling a story or a dirty joke. "We're pressing too hard," he would say, and would wait until the moment when the words or themes presented themselves naturally.

Casting had been completed by the autumn of 1947; many actors were named but few were chosen. Some of the stalwarts of Hollywood, such as Cary Grant and Montgomery Clift, declined on the grounds that they did not wish to play the parts of homosexuals. So the roles of the two young men went to relatively unknown actors, John Dall and Farley Granger, who were in life homosexual or at least bisexual. The subject was never formally mentioned, of course, and nor was the homosexuality of the story itself; but it was always in the air. One of the other writers brought in by Hitchcock, Arthur Laurents, recalled that "homosexuality was the unmentionable, known only as 'it.'"

His most surprising choice of player was, perhaps, James Stewart as the presumably homosexual teacher whose principles of the Nietz-schean *übermensch* or "superman" the two men had imbibed as students. It was a very difficult part, and one not entirely suited to Stewart's screen persona. He had already created the character of the "average guy," dry and folksy at the same time, which was not necessarily consistent with that of a repressed homosexual. Yet Hitchcock saw the possibilities. "Stewart is a perfect Hitchcock hero," the director once said, "because he is Everyman in bizarre situations." In *Rope* Stewart does manage to convey the nervousness and harshness of a man perpetually on the edge; his voice sometimes trembles under the strain, and the terrified panic he displays in a later film, *Vertigo*, is already on the screen in *Rope*. The director admired his style of acting; Stewart seemed to make thought visible, in a barely perceptible movement or change of tone.

Stewart vowed never to work with Hitchcock again, after his frustrating and demanding performance in *Rope*; he said that the real presence on the set was the camera. But in fact the actor and director remained occasional dinner companions and went on to work together on *Rear Window* and *The Man Who Knew Too Much* as well as *Vertigo*. Stewart once confessed that "*Rope* wasn't my favourite picture. I think I was miscast, though not terribly so. So many people could have played that part, probably better." It may have been Hitchcock, however, more than any other director, who rescued Stewart's screen image from ordinariness.

The rehearsals were lengthy and difficult. Stewart complained that he could not sleep at night. He said that "if the rest of the cast is perfect and I fluff a line at, say, 895 feet [of film], it becomes the most colos-

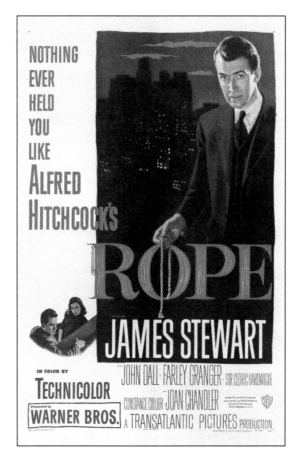

Film poster for *Rope*, Hitchcock's first film in Technicolor
and his first with Sidney Bernstein. Hitchcock later dismissed the film,
which was adapted from the Patrick Hamilton play of the
same name, as a "stunt."

Courtesy of Movie Poster Art/Getty Images

sal fluff in screen history." The entire and uninterrupted ten-minute sequence would have to begin again. Constance Collier, another player, was terrified of going on to the set. Towards the end of each long take the actors became visibly more tense. Hitchcock said that "I was so scared that something would go wrong that I couldn't even look during the first take." All this of course contributed to the atmosphere of tension and anxiety that was an integral part of the story itself.

The story was in essence simple. The two young men have strangled their victim and then placed his body in a *cassone* or wooden chest in their apartment. They then invite guests, including the victim's father, to a party for the murdered young man, where the food is served off the wooden chest itself. Their psychotic drollery is gradually realised, and then unmasked, by the teacher.

The filming took place over the first two months of 1948 and was completed in eighteen days. Hitchcock once declared it to be "my most exciting picture," and the excitement is visible in a photograph of him half rising from his director's chair at the moment when the two young men begin to strangle their victim. He would later change his mind and dismiss *Rope* as a "stunt," claiming that "I really don't know how I came to indulge in it." This was often his reaction to films that had been less than successful.

The ten-minute takes, which in fact varied slightly in length, really contribute nothing to the picture except an example of Hitchcock's virtuosity. But far from creating the illusion of a seamless reality, they only add to the formality and theatricality of the narrative. It was an example of the genre he always said that he hated most—people simply talking. *Rope* was altogether a very self-conscious exercise which did not prove a success with the critics or the public. It made a triflingly small profit, thus undoing much of the previous enthusiasm for the prospects of Transatlantic Pictures.

Hitchcock told Truffaut that "when I look back, I realise that it was quite nonsensical because I was breaking with my own theories on the importance of cutting and montage for the visual narration of a story." He had even written, twelve years before, that "if I have to shoot a long scene continuously I always feel I am losing grip on it, from a cinematic point of view." But the combination of technical experiment and artistic self-assertion proved more powerful at the time.

It is safe to assume that David Selznick would not have countenanced such an approach to filming, and leads to the question whether Hitchcock owed as much to his producer as he owed to his writers. It is impossible to answer. It is clear enough, however, that more than Hitchcock was needed to create a "Hitchcock film."

7

OH DEAR

Ah yes," one of the characters in *Rope* exclaims, "Ingrid Bergman! She's the Virgo type—I think she's just lovely!" This may also have been Hitchcock's reaction, since he had already determined to make the actress the central figure of his second film for Transatlantic. *Under Capricorn* could not have been more different from *Rope*. It was a historical melodrama set in Australia in 1831. He had always said that he hated costume dramas because he could never visualise how the characters went to the lavatory or earned their money, but he swallowed his objections on this occasion for the greater glory of Bergman. She would play the drunken wife of a man (played by Joseph Cotten) who had climbed his way up from convict to landowner. It transpires, of course, that their relationship is more complex. And, in the old tradition of *Rebecca*, a malevolent housekeeper is at work.

Even while finishing *Rope* Hitchcock, characteristically, began work on the first treatment of the new film in February 1948, in California; he had completed it by the end of March, and then travelled to England where he had arranged filming at Elstree Studios. His chosen scriptwriter, Hume Cronyn, recalled how they met for story conferences at Sidney Bernstein's offices in Golden Square in Soho. Yet problems were already emerging. Hitchcock had announced that he wished to use the techniques of long continuous takes that he had employed in

Rope; Cronyn believed this to be a mistake, but did not wish or dare to challenge him on the matter. Cronyn also echoed others in recalling that Hitchcock often planned the narrative image by image, without considering the line that would connect them; he was interested in the arresting detail or scene rather than the completed story.

Yet Hitchcock had his own doubts about the script. He said later that he had asked Cronyn to work with him "because he's a very articulate man who knows how to voice his ideas. But as a scriptwriter he hadn't really sufficient experience." On one morning, according to Cronyn, Hitchcock "suddenly reared back in his chair, scowling like an angry baby, and announced 'This film is going to be a flop. I'm going to lunch.' And he stalked out of the room, pouting." His apparently imperturbable exterior had cracks and flaws; in the preparatory work for a film, in particular, his mood could veer wildly from one extreme to another.

Ingrid Bergman was still the principal element, however, and at a later date he insisted that he had made the film on her behalf. "I was looking for a subject that suited her," he said, "rather than myself." He even claimed that she had persuaded him to embark upon the project. "From that," he said, "I learned that it was better to look at Ingrid than to listen to her." But this may have been just a convenient excuse; he had a habit of blaming others for his own mistakes. Certainly he had been thrilled by the prospect of stealing her from the Hollywood studios and bringing her to England as *his* star; he visualised them coming down the steps of the aeroplane together to meet the flashbulbs of the waiting cameramen. He later characterised his behaviour as "stupid and juvenile"; he had not properly assessed the cost of hiring Bergman, with a salary that completely unbalanced the budget, and had in general concentrated upon her rather than the other players.

The reality was in any case less appealing than his vision. From the beginning the actress had reservations about the technique of long takes; she had seen *Rope*, and did not like it. The fatigue and anxiety that had affected the players in *Rope* now began to beset her. Moments of strain were inevitable. Hitchcock and Bergman argued for half an hour over a particular scene. "Very well, Hitch," she said, "we'll do it your way." "It's not my way, Ingrid," he replied, "it's the *right* way." On one occasion she broke into tears for the first and only time in her career. Director and actor also had another long and apparently bitter dispute on the set, which Hitchcock ended by simply walking away. Bergman had her back towards him at this moment and, not realising that he had gone, continued the argument.

Bergman had her own version of the incident. She wrote to a friend that "the camera was supposed to follow me around for eleven whole minutes, which meant that we had to rehearse a whole day with the walls or furniture falling backwards as the camera went through, and of course that couldn't be done fast enough. So I told Hitch off. How I hate this new technique of his. How I suffer and loathe every moment on the set . . . Little Hitch just left. Never said a word. Just went home . . . oh dear." At other moments of exasperation he would say to her "Ingrid, it's only a movie!" It was not so much an expression of his opinion as an attempt to calm her down. Patricia Hitchcock, recalling the period of dispute, remarked that "frankly, with Daddy, there was no room for discussion."

Other problems beset the production. The Elstree crew went on strike just as filming was about to begin and, although the dispute was settled, it left a difficult atmosphere. A speeding camera made a large dent in one of the stage walls of the set. The director of photography, Jack Cardiff, recalled that "we would rehearse one whole day and shoot the next. Good recorded sound was impossible; the noise was indescribable. The electric crane lumbered through the set like a tank at Sebastopol." So the dialogue had to be added by the cast without cameras being present. On another occasion the camera rolled over Hitchcock's foot and broke his big toe. Cotten wrote home that the most favoured expression on the set was "Now what?" The actor himself had a moment worthy of Mrs. Malaprop when he once called the film, in the presence of Hitchcock, "Under Cornycrap."

Hitchcock told Truffaut in an interview that the completed film "didn't amount to anything." But he was wrong. It is a beautifully executed picture with the tracking shots of Ingrid Bergman, in particular, giving the narrative an additional power and resonance. She herself admitted, in retrospect, that the technique had served her performance very well. Hitchcock was right to have faith in her, even if that faith drained away when she began a love affair with Roberto Rossellini. His later disparaging comments about her are likely to have been prompted by hurt and anger.

Under Capricorn was released in September 1949, to general dismay. The reviews were tepid, and the box-office receipts were dire. The *Guardian*, in England, complained of "intolerable dullness on the screen" while the *Hollywood Reporter* described Hitchcock's direction as "crude, obvious, and frequently silly." It was remarked that, without David Selznick to guide him, the director often lost his way. The effect of the reviews on Alma, who had played some part in writing the script, was devastating. It is reported that she wept uncontrollably.

The failure of the film effectively bankrupted Transatlantic Pictures, which soon went into receivership. Hitchcock, sensing danger, ran for cover. He had already come to an agreement with Jack Warner and, at the beginning of 1949, had signed a contract for four films over a period of six and a half years; his total salary was likely to be $1 million. Warner was apparently a hard man to like but he left his new acquisition to do his job, and Hitchcock responded favourably.

. . .

Hitchcock decided, for his next picture, to play safe. There were to be no long takes, and no colour. That particular period of experimentation had come to an end. *Stage Fright* was, as its name suggests, an ironic thriller; it was to be set in London. It also had the incalculable advantage of a cast that included Joyce Grenfell, Alastair Sim, Miles Malleson and Sybil Thorndike in what seems to have been a deliberate echo of the then popular Ealing Comedies. The "stars" of the film, Richard Todd, Michael Wilding and Jane Wyman, have not survived so well in popular film mythology; but Marlene Dietrich, in her characteristic role of femme fatale, made an enduring impression upon Hitchcock and his audience.

The film was based upon Selwyn Jepson's story *Man Running,* which had been published two years before and had been justly or unjustly nominated as ideal "Hitchcock material." A young actress is enlisted to help a male friend who has been accused of murdering the husband of a glamorous entertainer with whom he has been having an affair. So far, so good. An accused man on the run was always grist to the Hitchcock mill.

The Hitchcocks, returning to Bellagio Road in Bel Air suitably chastened after their experience at Elstree Studios, worked together on the preliminary treatment of *Stage Fright.* They also enlisted the help of a short-story writer and dramatist, Whitfield Cook, whose drama *Violet* had starred Patricia Hitchcock on the Broadway stage for a run of twenty-three days. Pat would also play a small part in *Stage Fright* itself. There have been rumours and reports of a clandestine romance between Cook and Alma but, if so, it has been well concealed. They were good companions and collaborators, but perhaps nothing more.

In the spring of 1949 the Hitchcocks and Cook sailed to London in order to work, as it were, at the coal face. They had already finished a treatment of 113 pages, together with dialogue and accompanying camera angles. Richard Todd recalled being invited to the Savoy hotel, where the Hitchcocks were staying, and he was struck by the enthusiasm of the couple. Hitchcock had said to him, "You see, we do this, and then we do that and this happens, and then that happens," while Alma "kept piping up as well."

On the set, however, Hitchcock was his usual disciplined and determined self. He asked the first assistant director to set the actors in position for their moves; he would then disappear into his office, and only return to the set when the cameras were about to roll. "Hitchcock," Todd said, "was a very distant man—cold and professional." Dietrich said of him that "he frightened the daylights out of me. He knew exactly what he wanted, a fact that I adore, but I was never quite sure if I did it right." She need not have worried. She was a woman with whom he immediately felt at ease—outspoken and sometimes foul-mouthed, unafraid of her sexuality to the point of sporting with it. She insisted on having her astrologer with her at all times, and conducted an amorous relationship with the leading man—Michael Wilding—off and on the set. The noise from the dressing rooms was sometimes unignorable. "Marlene was a professional star," Hitchcock remarked. "She was also a professional cameraman, art director, editor, costume designer, hair dresser, make-up woman, composer, producer and director." In a less guarded moment Dietrich described the director to her daughter as "a strange little man. I don't like him. Why they all think he is so great, I don't know. The film is bad—maybe in the cutting he does all his famous 'suspense' but he certainly didn't do it in the shooting."

Hitchcock was in any case feeling ill at ease at Elstree Studios. He wrote to Jack Warner, ensconced at Burbank, that "they have some pretty crude people . . . I don't want to bother you with the sordid details . . . They are my affair, really, and all I have to do is deliver you a picture . . . Well, Jack, that's about all . . . As soon as I'm finished shooting and I have the picture rough cut I'm going to pack all the dubbing tracks into tins and get the hell out of here."

Stage Fright does have the air of a wasted opportunity. It has no natural or even pace. As well as being set in the world of London theatre, under Hitchcock's guidance it becomes theatrical both in tone and execution. The characters wear various disguises and adopt various roles, many of the scenes are melodramatic in intent, the landscape of London resembles a set, and nothing is truly what it seems. The innocence of the accused man, as narrated in the first scenes, turns out to be false. This confuses the audience, and acts as a check upon suspense until the end. A succession of virtuoso performances, from Alastair Sim and Joyce Grenfell among others, does not cohere.

The dialogue is always drawing attention to its own artificiality. "This is not real, this is a piece of theatre . . . the curtains, Johnny, draw the curtains . . . you are an actress, you are playing a part." Despite the fact that it is a comedy or farce rather than a thriller, it is a little heavy-handed. The reviews were neither hot nor cold, and one critic described it as "rambling." It was generally considered, however, to be an expression of the "real" Hitchcock after the experiments of *Rope* and *Under Capricorn*.

Although he had been only too eager to return to California, he came back to discover that he had very little to do. Between September 1949 and the spring of 1950 he spent seven months in a state of suspended animation; there were no stories to consider, no treatments to contemplate, and no stars to pursue. This was for him a form of torture.

Though agonised by this idle period, he was, at any rate, comfortable financially. He was by any standard a wealthy man. He owned two properties, one of them very large. He possessed land and stocks, with an interest in oil and cattle. He checked on his investments almost every day. He had also decided to put his vineyards in Santa Cruz into proper shape with the help of viticulturalists. He travelled between his house in Bel Air and his estate above Monterey Bay; he dined at the most celebrated restaurants in their respective neighbourhoods.

He held dinner parties for his closest associates, in which drinking seems to have been a large part of the proceedings. He was sometimes persuaded to do his "breast ballet" in a primitive form of striptease, as well as other stunts and pranks that suggest a reserved nature ready to burst out of control. He built a wine cellar for his house in Bellagio Road, as well as a "walk-in" refrigerator for his range of delicacies. A film critic, Penelope Gilliatt, recalled that "I remember that he was once showing me his kitchen in Bel Air. Everything was spick and span. Not a cornflake visible. A desert for cockroaches. He opened a door, and icy air steamed out. The freezer locker: a whole room. I saw hams and sides of beef hanging from hooks like rich women's fur coats in summer storage. Hitchcock courteously bowed me in first. I hesitated and looked back, imagining the door clanging shut behind me. He knew what I was thinking, and I knew that he knew."

He had been a serious, if not professional, collector of art for some years. He preferred early twentieth-century French art, and in Bellagio Road hung the work of Utrillo, Dufy and Modigliani as well as three paintings by the German–Swiss artist Paul Klee. "I'm not self-indulgent where content is concerned," he said. "I'm only self-indulgent about treatment. I'd compare myself to an abstract painter. My favourite painter is Klee." In the house above Monterey Bay he hung the prints and etchings of Thomas Rowlandson. Rowlandson epitomised a London vision of grotesquerie and farce, of which Hitchcock himself might be described as a prominent twentieth-century exponent. The fact that he hung the eighteenth-century prints in northern California suggests the direction in which some of his deepest loyalties lay.

There was, at last, the chance of a script. In the spring of 1950 he had read a recently published novel, *Strangers on a Train* by Patricia Highsmith, and saw its possibilities. He instructed his agents to keep his name out of the negotiations and to bid for the rights in what was, after all, a first novel. They acquired them for $7,500, much to Highsmith's subsequent chagrin. He had been attracted by the dual charge of the fiction. On the train, there are two men who exchange two murders—and it was this "two" that Hitchcock emphasises, on the understanding that "nothing could be without its opposite that was bound up with it . . . there's also a person exactly the opposite of you, like the unseen part of you, somewhere in the world, and he waits in ambush." All Hitchcock's reading of Poe and Wilkie Collins could have brought him to the point. In his filmic world he was always contemplating the possibilities of doubles, of dualities, of dichotomies.

He noted that at first "I couldn't find anyone to work on it. They all felt my first draft was so flat and factual that they couldn't see one iota of quality in it." His agents approached Dashiell Hammett, but nothing happened. But then a story editor at Warner Brothers, Finlay McDermid, came up with an equally enticing name. Raymond Chandler was the one to be enticed. The writer was intrigued by the prospect of working with Hitchcock, and no doubt by a salary of $2,500 a week. He met his director briefly and then set off for his home in La Jolla with Highsmith's novel, Hitchcock's treatment, a bundle of writing paper and a secretary.

It was not a happy collaboration. Chandler's contract had stipulated that he would not travel, so Hitchcock had to come to him. On one occasion, as Hitchcock struggled to emerge from his limousine, Chandler could be heard saying, "Look at the fat bastard trying to get out of his car." Chandler resented all the meandering discussions of script meetings, or what he called the "god-awful jabber sessions," and disliked the suggestions that Hitchcock would throw in his direction. "If you can go it alone," Chandler told him, "why the hell do you need me?" He also considered *Strangers on a Train* to be "a silly enough story."

The author did complete a second draft, however, but he was now complaining about the director's invisibility. Chandler wrote to Finlay McDermid that "this screenplay was written without a single consultation with Mr. Hitchcock . . . not even a phone call. Not one word of criticism or appreciation. Silence. Blank silence then and since . . . I find it rather strange. I find it rather ruthless. I find it almost incomparably rude." He also expressed a complaint that other writers had articulated. "He is always ready to sacrifice dramatic logic (in so far as it exists) for the sake of a camera effect or mood effect." The disparate shots had then to be shoehorned into the existing narrative. Sometimes it simply could not be done, and the storyline degenerated into a string of actions or scenes into which anything could be added at the last minute.

By late September 1950, Chandler had left the process of writing altogether. He had realised in the end that, as he put it, "a Hitchcock picture must be all Hitchcock." But his departure came at the last minute and, just weeks before filming was due to begin, the studio threatened to close down the whole production. Hitchcock enlisted the help of one of Ben Hecht's co-writers, Czenzi Ormonde, to rewrite. He consigned the Chandler script to a waste-paper basket, and told her that they would begin again "with page one." She worked quickly and efficiently, even as Hitchcock was in the middle of filming, and produced the ending just one week before the scene was shot.

When Hitchcock began work at the end of October, he seemed to be full of confidence. He announced on the first day of filming that this was the true start of his American career, and he remained on the set from seven in the morning until nine in the evening. Yet he seemed hardly to direct at all and one of the principal players, Laura Elliot, remarked that he never praised her. It was always "Cut, next shot." Or it was "Walk here . . . walk there."

The filming was completed by the end of December, and for its speed and efficiency he owed much to the production team that he had assembled. He was indebted in particular to his director of photography, Robert Burks, who worked with him on twelve films over the next fourteen years. A scriptwriter remarked that Burks "gave Hitchcock marvellous ideas" but that he also "had a very tense time . . . by the end of each picture he was emotionally worn out." Burks merely stated that "you never have any trouble with him as long as you know your job and do it. Hitchcock insists on perfection." By the end of their relationship Hitchcock trusted his cameraman so completely that he did not bother to look at the rushes after each day's filming.

Hitchcock once said of *Strangers on a Train*, "Isn't it a fascinating design? You could study it forever." It has been reported that towards the end of his preparation of the script with Czenzi Ormonde he gave her an inspired account of all the "doubles" and "pairs" that could be included in the narrative; he was perhaps prompted by the tennis match that occurs at a crucial moment in the story, but it is more likely that he was moved by the cinematic possibilities of two men exchanging roles. In the opening sequence we see them wearing shoes that distinguish their characters immediately, and the effect of duality works its way through the entire film. For his own characteristic entry in a cameo role, Hitchcock carries a "double" of himself in the bulky shape of a double bass.

Truffaut once noted that Hitchcock filmed scenes of murder as if they were love scenes, and scenes of love as if they were scenes of murder. This is nowhere more evident than in *Strangers on a Train* when the putative strangler, with his hands around the neck of an old lady, falls back in a romantic swoon. Hitchcock liked the concept of strangulation. Most of his murderers, and victims, are part of the same game. He himself was photographed many times rehearsing the method. It appears so many times in his films, most particularly in *Dial M for Murder* and *Frenzy*, that it is plausible to claim that it holds some especial significance for him. He told one screenwriter that "I can kill a man, you know, with a swift press of the thumb." But women are usually the victims, and in some prolonged scenes of strangulation we can hardly distinguish between love and death.

Patricia Hitchcock was given a part in *Strangers on a Train*, and it is indeed her chubby bespectacled face that prompts the strangler's swoon. Quite by chance a photographic sequence by Philippe Halsman shows the director with his hands around the neck of Jacob Epstein's sculptured bust of his daughter. It is not by chance, however, that Patricia Hitchcock is wearing spectacles. The woman wearing glasses was also something of a Hitchcock speciality. Madeleine Carroll wears them in the first scene of *The 39 Steps*, Ingrid Bergman wears them in *Spellbound*, and Barbara Bel Geddes in *Vertigo*. There are many other examples. But Hitchcock's fascination for them was not limited to film. One of his permanent secretaries in Hollywood, Carol Stevens, recalled that he ordered four or five sets of spectacles for her from the studio optician. "If I came on the set without my glasses on, it irritated the devil out of Hitch. He had a fetish about glasses." There were times, also, when he asked her to take them off. Alma wore glasses when she was working but, in the fashion of the period, put them away when she was socialising. It might be construed that a woman wearing glasses is somehow more invulnerable, more knowledgeable, more scrutinising; the female gaze may be disruptive and even threatening. When she removes them she reveals a certain vulnerability, even isolation, which of all characteristics Hitchcock is most eager to convey on the screen. To be more vulnerable is, perhaps, to be more attractive.

So *Strangers on a Train* has the double charge of Hitchcock's own preoccupations in a film that is established upon guilt and thwarted desire. The two men are meant to exchange murders, but only the psychotic commits the crime. The other is possessed by the desire to reveal him and to protest his own innocence.

With the help of Robert Burks, Hitchcock created a shadow world of silhouettes and darkness; he became an artist of chiaroscuro which reflects the pervasive atmosphere of guilt and anxiety. Everyone seems to be guilty of something, partly concealed by an unspeakable pact with the forces of "order" that must in the end be triumphant. In such a dark setting objects are fraught with meaning and menace—a broken pair of spectacles, a cigarette lighter. Hitchcock selected the piece of orange peel, the crumpled paper and the chewing-gum wrapper that were to be seen in a storm drain. Jean-Luc Godard wrote that "perhaps there are ten thousand people who haven't forgotten Cezanne's apple, but there must be a billion spectators who will remember the lighter of the stranger on the train." Godard went on to celebrate Hitchcock as "the greatest creator of forms of the twentieth century." Careful construction and calculation are the twin accompaniments of obsession and wild fantasy.

8

I AM TYPED

And then he was quiet. He had finished work on *Strangers on a Train* two days before Christmas 1950, and the Hitchcock family spent the season at Santa Cruz before embarking on a long holiday in the spring and summer which took them through much of Europe. *Strangers on a Train* was a success when it was released in June, and his reputation as the "master of suspense" was reaffirmed at the box office and in the press. Yet he had no new project. He had often been told that he should take a break, but the long vacation of 1951 proved that he was not built for holidays. When he travelled to a Swiss ski resort he sat on the porch and read. He looked at the scenery but never ventured into it. He could look, but he could not act. Throughout the rest of the year, after the family had returned, he had very little to do except to deal with correspondence and search for ideas wherever he might find them. This inactivity prompted the usual sensations of panic and nervous fear as he sat and pondered in Bellagio Road or at Santa Cruz.

There was a diversion in January 1952, with the marriage of his daughter to a New England businessman. Hitchcock said later that "Alma and I were relieved, in a way, when our daughter decided that being a mother of sticky-fingered children required all her creative attention." Alma recalled that "when he gave the bride away, Hitch's face was so white that a member of the groom's family remarked that he must have just come out of a Hitchcock movie." He was "relieved," perhaps, because his daughter had turned her back on a career as an actress; that was perhaps too close to home.

He still had no firm project in mind, when it seems that Alma furnished her husband with the solution. He had long ago purchased the rights to a play by Paul Anthelme, *Nos deux consciences*. At the time it had intrigued him, but he had left it to one side. It concerned a Catholic priest who cannot disclose the true identity of a killer, since the man had revealed his secret in the sacred space of the confessional. The priest himself is then accused of the crime and goes to trial.

The Hitchcocks had actually written a treatment four years before, and Alma recalled the impression the screenplay had made on them at the time. Once more she sensed the possibilities, and she went over the old materials with an eye for their revival. Hitchcock himself seems to have been reinvigorated by the project and by February they had conjured a new treatment, called *I Confess*, out of the existing scripts. The drama was to be set in Quebec; it was a largely Catholic city, and the priests still wore cassocks rather than collars as they walked through what seem to be vertiginously steep streets. It was a city where the crucifix was dominant. The Hitchcocks travelled there and within a few days had found the necessary locations, including the most prominent churches; they also found suitable co-writers in two playwrights, William Archibald and George Tabori, who proceeded to fashion a deeper and darker film than that proposed by Hitchcock.

The leading actor, playing the troubled priest, was obviously the most crucial choice, and Hitchcock may have regretted preferring Montgomery Clift; Clift was in many respects a fine actor but the director admitted later that he had two disadvantages. "There are some actors I've felt uncomfortable with," he said, "and working with Montgomery Clift was difficult because he was a method actor and a neurotic as well." Clift was also a near-alcoholic and one of the other players, Anne Baxter, recalled that "poor Monty was drinking so heavily, virtually all the time. He was so confused and removed from what was going on around him that his eyes wouldn't focus . . . he was so disturbed and unhappy, but Hitchcock never talked to him. He had the assistant director, Don Page, handle everything."

Clift brought with him on to the set his acting coach, Mira Rostova, which added to the tension. Another of the actors, Karl Malden, recalled that "Monty depended on her, kept a distance from Hitchcock and from the rest of us to go over his lines with her, insisted on her approval before a scene could be shot. Naturally this created a deep division and tension." The actors were meant to defer to Hitchcock, not to some teacher. Yet the director remained calm and polite with her, knowing that anger or recrimination might jeopardise Clift's performance. Malden also noticed that Hitchcock was "never ruffled, never gave any sign of being worried, never shouted, was always in control. There was no unnecessary noise or talking or shouting on his set. It was a quiet set because that's the way he wanted it." The director himself was also noticeably silent, and Malden added that "I really can't remember *anything* he said to me." At a dinner party, when Malden had a little too much to drink, he complained to Hitchcock that "you never tell us what you want. I know the blocking and the lines, but what I don't know is what you expect from me." He replied immediately that "you're a professional, and I'm a professional. I simply expect you to do your job." Another actor, Henry Corden, noted that the director never once said a word to him.

Patricia Hitchcock, visiting the set, recalled that for one shot Clift was required to walk across a large ballroom—"and he just sat there to think and think about it. He was holding everybody up, and Daddy became very impatient." Hitchcock hated self-indulgence, but he managed to restrain himself from any open criticism of Clift. The walk was in any case important, and Truffaut once noted of I Confess that "Montgomery Clift is always seen walking; it's a forward motion that shapes the whole film. It also concretises the concept of his integrity."

The location filming began in August 1952, and lasted for three weeks. Quebec City, the old quarter of Upper Town surrounded by a high stone wall, turned out to be an inspired choice; on the screen at least, with the gifted cinematography of Robert Burks, it is a city of shadows. As the camera glides over the waters of the Saint Lawrence river the spectator slowly enters Hitchcock's forbidding world. It is a menacing place, full of arrows and steep streets sloping downward; the inhabitants look down from their windows as if they were in the balcony of a courtroom. The locations once more exude a deep sense of guilt and horror. Taking its cue from Clift's performance, perhaps, this is a film of people thinking and judging.

Three weeks of filming in Hollywood completed the process, and the premiere was held on 13 February 1953, in Quebec. It is in some respects an odd and awkward film, possibly reflecting the circumstances of its production, but it also possesses the virtues of dignity and restraint in handling the spiritual imperatives of Hitchcock's Catholic upbringing. It is not permissible for a priest to break the secret of the confessional, even if it leads to his own false condemnation. Clift's own restraint, which some described as woodenness, lends an authenticity and even, perhaps, sobriety to the narrative.

There was no post-production celebration, no customary "wrap party," and Hitchcock rarely spoke about I Confess. He did give a small dinner party at Bellagio Road for the cast, after the film was completed, but it was noticeable only for the fact that the host plied large quantities of drink upon Clift who eventually collapsed on to the carpet. That was not perhaps the best treatment for an alcoholic.

Hitchcock was once asked in an interview whether he actually liked the film. "So so. It lacks humour." It is indeed one of the few films Hitchcock made that wanted the necessary ingredient of comedy to balance the suspense. He was always aware of the defect but, in I Confess, where could comedy have been found? It was too slow, and austere, for the general public. The American critics were no more enthusiastic, at best respectful about what one of them called "a ponderous, equivocal situation." The London reception was a little warmer but Hitchcock complained to Sidney Bernstein that "by God I am typed, though, what with the label 'thriller' and the search for 'suspense.' "

Yet these were exactly the directions in which he chose to go. After the relative disappointment of I Confess he ran for cover, deciding to film a very successful play which had all the ingredients of the best melodrama. *Dial M for Murder* had started life as a black-and-white television drama before being transmuted into a cosy West End (and then Broadway) thriller. In Hitchcock's version an ex–tennis star, played by Ray Milland, blackmails a small-time villain into murdering his wife; it all goes wrong when the wife, played by Grace Kelly, kills the killer in an act of self-defence. How will the original crime be ascribed to the husband? That is the sum of a plot which dealt in suspense rather than mystery.

It was to be filmed on a single stage-bound set that represented a family apartment in Maida Vale, London, but of course Hitchcock was used to the constraints of a small space. He told Sidney Bernstein that he was going to use "a modified *Rope* style"; as a very successful play it already had all the "speed and 'tightness'" it required. If he broadened the narrative, "the holes might show."

However he was not accustomed to the technique of filming that Warner Brothers imposed upon him. The early 1950s was a time of cinema gimmicks, none more successful for a time than 3D, which brought such things as scissors and knives into the laps of the audience. Hitchcock did not like the process, because it offended his beliefs in verisimilitude, and he considered it to be a passing fashion. Yet he was obliged to proceed with a camera the size of a small room, and Grace Kelly recalled that "with this camera it was like going into a boxing ring with your hands tied. But he was so extraordinary. I never saw him lose his patience—he never became angry. I would get furious for him, when I saw the frustrations and the things he wanted to do, and the technicians said, 'Oh no, with the camera we can't do this and we can't do that.'"

He was perhaps mollified by the presence of Grace Kelly, who represented for him one of his types of ideal blonde beauty. She seemed to be austere and unapproachable, but Hitchcock was well aware of all the sexual gossip that surrounded her. As Gore Vidal said at a later date, "Grace almost always laid the leading man. She was famous for that in this town." Sure enough she had embarked on an affair with Ray

Milland while filming *Dial M for Murder* that almost cost the actor his marriage. She was also well known for her earthy sense of humour and a fund of dirty jokes that she had amassed while at a Catholic convent school. This was the kind of woman Hitchcock admired. He also appreciated the combination of apparent frigidity and lust. He once explained to a journalist that "she's sensitive, disciplined and very sexy. People think she's cold. Rubbish! She's a volcano covered with snow."

That is perhaps why he treated her very carefully on the set. He called her "Miss Kelly" and she called him "Mr. Hitchcock." She reported that "Hitch was always so decorous and dignified with me. He treated me like a porcelain doll." He liked to consider himself her Svengali, coaxing out of her a performance that she could not otherwise have given. She in turn was competent, controlled, and always on time. It soon became clear that she was his new ideal actress.

Nevertheless it took him five days to film the assault upon her by the small-time gangster hired by her husband; at the end of the experience she was covered with bruises, and at last Hitchcock deemed the sequence to be satisfactory. He had used 3D with care throughout the film, limiting its effect to incidents of high tension such as the moment when the wife grabs a pair of scissors to ward off her attacker. He believed that the sequence had been "nicely done but there wasn't enough gleam to the scissors, and a murder without gleaming scissors is like asparagus without the hollandaise sauce—tasteless." He believed that 3D would lose its appeal, and that the film would eventually be released as a "flattie." It would be a "nine-day wonder" and "I came in on the ninth day."

Hitchcock had a pronounced interest in Kelly's clothes and recalled that "I dressed her in very gay and bright colours at the beginning of the picture and, as the plot thickened, her clothes became gradually more sombre." These are not perhaps details that the audience assimilated on an immediate level, but his attention to them attests to the sensibility of an artist. The same care emerges in his decision to use the noise of London traffic on the soundtrack of the few street scenes. A memorandum was circulated that he "feels that English traffic noises are different from the American ones. He would also like a few English auto horns."

Hitchcock knew well enough that Warners wanted another *Strangers on a Train*, with which *Dial M for Murder* has certain similarities, and required a relatively quick return on their investment. He managed to complete filming in thirty-six days, and was glad to have finished in so short a time. He said later that "I could have phoned that one in," with an ironic obeisance to its title. He later dismissed the film as a "minor work," but as an exercise in construction and ingenuity, with an underlying ironic wit, it still repays attention. It was also a success with the public, no doubt because of the presence of Grace Kelly who was rapidly becoming the star of the moment.

He was in any case possessed by another vision even as he was filming *Dial M for Murder*, and was eager to begin work on an altogether more challenging and significant project. His preparation for the next film was, according to Grace Kelly, "the only way he could remain calm" on the set. She added that "he sat and talked to me about it all the time. He was very enthusiastic as he described all the details of a fabulous set while we were waiting for the camera to be pushed around. He talked to me about the people who would be seen in other apartments opposite the rear window, and their little stories, and how they would emerge as characters and what would be revealed." She must have known by this stage that she herself would be one of "the people who would be seen," albeit in a more prolonged and intimate way than the rest of the cast.

·　·　·

He had not enjoyed the experience of working at Warner studios, not simply because of the cumbersome 3D equipment imposed upon him. He told Sidney Bernstein that "the Warner lot is the deadest that anyone can remember." It was relinquishing staff and contract players in order to cut costs. Even before filming of *Dial M for Murder* began, he was making other arrangements. He had signed a contract with Paramount Pictures for nine films, five of which would revert to his ownership after a period of eight years. This arrangement would seal his reputation as well as his finances.

Rear Window was the first of his films for the company. Paramount had asked that he choose one of Cornell Woolrich's short stories, Woolrich being then regarded as one of the finest writers of "crime" or "suspense" in the country. Hitchcock finished *Dial M for Murder* at the end of September, and immediately turned his attention to the preparation of the new film at the new studio. Earlier in the year he had needed a writer and his choice fell upon a young man who had already gained a reputation in radio drama. John Michael Hayes recalled that "Hitchcock had his agents and my agent get together for lunch and they handed me this book which had the story in it of 'Rear Window.' They told me 'You're to meet Mr. Hitchcock on Friday night at the Beverly Hills Hotel for dinner. Read the story and be prepared to discuss it with him.'" The proposed dinner passed in an alcoholic fog, for both parties, but Hitchcock seems to have liked the young writer enough to propose a collaboration that began in spring 1953. It proved to be a notably successful partnership, with Hayes bringing light and shade to characterisation in scripts that were more buoyant and more revealing than those of previous films.

Hayes had prepared a treatment of seventy-six pages which was sent to Paramount at the beginning of September. But the treatment was only part of the process. Hayes recalled that Hitchcock "went to his office in Paramount and sat down with the script. We went over it line by line and page by page. What we did then was try to break it up into shots. Now Hitch wanted to set them up into actual camera angles. He had a large sketch pad on which he sketched out each camera set-up for each scene." The director did not wait for the set to be built or the script to be finished. He called in assistant directors as well as cameramen and, with the aid of his sketches, told them precisely what he wished them to do. When one assistant director was hired he entered Hitchcock's office to find "what seemed like cartoon panels covering three walls of the large room." This was the storyboard that Hitchcock had constructed.

Hitchcock's office was part of the Paramount Studios on Melrose Road, approximately twenty-five miles from his house on Bellagio Road; it was on the ground floor at the centre of the building, and a short walk from his limousine took him into his sanctum. From here Hitchcock planned and executed some of the finest films of his career, from *To Catch a Thief* and *The Trouble with Harry* to the remake of *The Man Who Knew Too Much* and *Vertigo*. It was here, also, that he assembled the team that instigated what has been described as "the golden age" of Hitchcock. Among them were Edith Head, the doyenne of costume designers, and Robert Burks as cinematographer; George Tomasini, editor, and assistant director Herbert Coleman joined them. Henry Bumstead became Hitchcock's production designer, Leonard South the camera operator, and Saul Bass the designer of film titles for *Vertigo* and others. Peggy Robertson had worked as a continuity editor on *Under Capricorn* but now returned to her old boss, after an absence of nine years, as script supervisor on *Vertigo*. She remained with him, as his personal assistant, until the last months of his life. And then there was Hitchcock's favoured composer, Bernard Herrmann, who worked on eight of Hitchcock's films beginning with *The Trouble with Harry*.

These men and women were his vital collaborators in the creation of the Hitchcock style. He hardly ever mentioned them, and rarely gave them any credit for their work with him. As far as he was concerned any Hitchcock film was the expression of Hitchcock, and all others were merely extras in the drama of his achievement. This was sometimes the cause of resentment and even of anger, just as his equivocal relationship with actors also provoked dismay.

The preparation of the set for *Rear Window* began on 12 October on stage eighteen of the Paramount lot. It represented the back of a residential block in Greenwich Village with thirty-one separate apartments, eight of them with fully furnished rooms. It also had to include

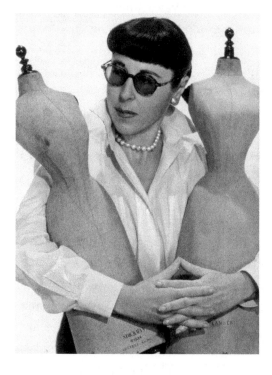

Edith Head, the renowned costume designer who worked on
several of Hitchcock's most iconic films,
including *Rear Window* and *To Catch a Thief.*

Courtesy of Hulton Archive/Getty Images

fire escapes and roof gardens, together with an alley leading to a street that can be fitfully glimpsed as a relic of the outside world. The huge and complex set took a month to construct, by the coordinated efforts of fifty men, and rose forty feet into the air at a length of 185 feet. One hundred arc lights and 2,000 smaller lamps were installed. A large console was created with a series of switches to control the lighting of each apartment. From here Hitchcock used a shortwave radio to communicate with all the actors. It was the biggest project on the Paramount lot since the heroic days of Cecil B. DeMille, and it shared the same theatricality. It was not real. It was bigger than reality.

The casting was not difficult. Although James Stewart had vowed never to work with Hitchcock again after the problems with *Rope*, he relented when he saw the script by Hayes and when told that his leading lady would be Grace Kelly. He plays a photographer, "Jeff" Jefferies, immobilised by a broken leg, who watches the events in the apartments opposite his own and concludes that a murder has taken place; his girlfriend, played by Kelly, is at first inclined to ignore his speculations for the sake of a little romance. But after he brushes off her advances, she herself becomes involved in the amateur investigation. Then the film becomes very tense indeed.

Hitchcock had asked John Michael Hayes to pay particular attention to Grace Kelly's character. Hayes simply found inspiration in the star herself. He recalled that "Hitchcock said of Grace Kelly, 'Look at her. She does everything well, but there's no fire in her.' So I spent a week with Grace Kelly, and got to know that she was whimsical and funny and humorous and teasing. She was like the girl next door, but she was very sexy and had all these attributes." This was the character, already almost fully formed, that he re-created. Hitchcock was also involved, and said once to a reporter that "I didn't discover Grace, but I saved her from a fate worse than death. I prevented her from being eternally cast as a cold woman." With Edith Head, he dressed her with minute attention to colour and to style. *Rear Window* was to be filmed in Technicolor in a widescreen format, so that it might provide a powerful entrance into Hitchcock's dream world.

The production, so carefully arranged from the command centre placed in Jeff's apartment, proceeded almost without incident. Hitchcock began filming at the end of November 1953, just two months after completing *Dial M for Murder*, and the production continued rapidly and smoothly until the middle of January. Very few problems were encountered. The telephoto lens had to be changed for heightened definition in certain sequences, and there was one occasion when the heat of the arc lights prompted a minor storm of water from the sensors, leaving everyone drenched; but that was nothing.

Hitchcock himself thoroughly enjoyed the direction, re-experiencing the energy and enthusiasm that he had felt on earlier films. "About this time," he said, "I felt that my batteries were really fully charged." James Stewart confirmed this mood of optimism. He recalled that "the set and every part of the film were so well designed, and he felt so comfortable with everyone associated with it, that we all felt confident about its success." The director was only occasionally discontented. "Every once in a while after shooting a scene," Stewart recalled, "Hitch would get out of his chair and come up to me. Then he would very quietly say, 'Jim, the scene is tired.' He would then go back to his chair and sit down, and you would know exactly what he meant, that the timing and the pace were wrong."

Hitchcock knew precisely the speed and tempo which he required. He once said that the film "was, structurally, satisfactory because it is the epitome of the subjective treatment. A man looks, he sees, he reacts—thus you construct a mental process. *Rear Window* is entirely about a mental process, done by use of the visual." He sees. He reacts. It is also a definition of the technique of montage that Hitchcock had learned many years before in Germany and, as Hitchcock told Truffaut, "Pudovkin dealt with this, as you know." It is one of the few occasions when Hitchcock betrayed any theoretical knowledge of what might be called cinematic aesthetics; his study of early European cinema was something he preferred to conceal. Much of *Rear Window* had also to be silent, in the sense that Jeff cannot hear what is being said in the opposite apartments. He must rely on the gestures and expressions

James Stewart, Grace Kelly and Hitchcock on the set of *Rear Window*, 1954.

Courtesy of Michael Ochs Archives/Getty Images

alone, and in the process Hitchcock revived his technique from the silent films of his early career. It has been estimated that thirty-five per cent of the film is silent. He was returning to the era of what he once called "pure cinema."

It was essentially a film about voyeurism, with the prolonged satisfaction of exposing or discovering what is usually secret and hidden. It is easy to recall here Hitchcock's own love of sexual gossip and innuendo. It could even be said that in fashioning Jeff he had created an image of himself—the man hiding behind the camera who creates a fantasy world out of observable reality, and who engages more fully with the women in front of his lens than with the women in his life. At certain moments Jeff is described as "abnormal" with a "problem" that "he can't discuss" and "too frightful to utter." This may be an allusion to repressed homosexuality, as some have suggested, but it may just be a piece of teasing by Hitchcock and Hayes. In the same spirit of teasing, Raymond Burr, who plays the part of the suspected murderer, is made up and coached to resemble David Selznick.

It is in many respects an unsettling film which presents an "ordinary" world which is anything but ordinary; it is a fragile place racked with nervous tensions, where the conventions of commonplace life conceal the burden of secrets and irregular relationships. It is a world of confused identities and thwarted desires, of loneliness and pain. A great deal of unstated tension exists between the central characters. The putative hero is ambiguous and difficult, self-absorbed, petulant and arrogant.

Hitchcock stated that "of all the films I have made, this to me is the most cinematic." The remark can be interpreted in more than one sense. Jeff's voyeuristic desires are no different from those of the spectators in the auditorium who are wrapped in the safe darkness where they can watch the actors unobserved. *Rear Window* is about the pleasures and penalties of the gaze. It is about the sheer act of seeing. But the gaze can be uncertain; it may come to unwarranted conclusions. Could everything that Jeff sees be a reflection of his fear of women? Even at the end of the film it is an open question. When asked once about the prurience of the film, Hitchcock remarked that "if anyone had mentioned that to me before I embarked on that picture, it certainly wouldn't have kept me from going ahead with it, because my love of film is far more important to me than any considerations of morality." Apart from confirming his belief in "pure cinema" the remark suggests that he was not necessarily aware of the implications of what he was creating. He was interested only in the tension and suspense.

Rear Window was eventually listed by the American Film Institute as one of the best one hundred American films, but even at the time it was considered a notable success. It premiered in Hollywood on 11 August 1954, and the critics variously described it as "exhilarating" and "roundly enjoyable." Within two years it had earned $10 million. No attention, however, was paid to the darker, more autobiographical aspects of the film. The American public demanded entertainment, and Hitchcock was ready to provide that innocent commodity with a smile. It was, after all, "only a movie."

·   ·   ·

By the beginning of 1954, even as he was putting his final touches to *Rear Window*, he was engaged upon another production. The managers of Paramount suggested to him that he might turn his attention to a novel, *To Catch a Thief*, the rights of which they had purchased two years before. The story concerned a cat burglar who returns to his old criminal haunts on the French Riviera in order to entrap a thief who copies his methods. Hitchcock loved France, as well as French food, and it may be that he took the assignment as a form of light relief after the arduous studio work on *Rear Window*. He had worked so well with John Michael Hayes on the film that he asked him to write the script for its successor. Hayes recalled that "when he found I'd never even been to the south of France, he arranged for me and my wife to go, at studio expense, so that I could research the locales. The trip was, of course, very welcome, and by the time I returned I had a good idea of what to do with the novel."

Hitchcock wanted Grace Kelly. She was to be his idealised female—perhaps he associated her from his Catholic schooldays with "the light of grace." Cary Grant, no doubt entranced by his large fee and the prospect of the leading lady, was also enrolled. Hitchcock and Hayes worked together upon the evolving script. "What made us a good team," Hayes said, "was that he had such brilliant technique and knowledge of the visual, and ego, and conviction; and I think I was able to bring him a warmth of characterisation." Hitchcock appreciated his contribution; he himself was notoriously unable to develop character as opposed to plot. Hayes went on to say that "we just discussed in general terms story and character, and he let me go on and write until I finished. We did have lunches together, and I'd tell him what I was doing, and he was patient enough to wait for it." Hayes said in another interview that "what I brought to Hitch was character, dialogue, movement and entertainment." But Hitchcock rarely complimented Hayes; as ever, he was of the opinion that if anyone did well, it was just part of the job. A subsequent screenwriter, Ernest Lehman, recalled that "he was very quiet, very unassuming, but everybody was afraid of his disapproval, and that's what made them do their best for him. You feared doing something that was below his standards." And of course in the end Hitchcock himself would take all the credit.

The script of *To Catch a Thief* was workmanlike enough, with occasional bursts of wit and sexual suggestiveness that enlivened the partnership of Grant and Kelly.

GRANT: Tell me, what do you get a thrill out of most?
KELLY: I'm still looking for that one.
 (*She offers him cold chicken.*)
KELLY: Do you want a leg or a breast?
GRANT: You make the choice.
KELLY: Tell me, how long has it been?
GRANT: Since what?
KELLY: Since you were in America last.

A glittering ball is arranged in the style of the seventeenth-century French court, and one of the American guests asks a waiter, *"Avez-vous bourbon?"* It may not be Oscar Wilde, but it was funny and daring enough for an American film in the 1950s. There are moments, in fact, when the film seems to become a parody of itself, a hollowed-out artifice with a gorgeous surface.

Filming began at the end of May, with rain or the threat of rain as the principal problem. Grant caused a few difficulties by walking off the set at six o'clock precisely; the timing was in his contract. Hitchcock also resented the fact that the actor received a percentage of the gross before any money was released to the director himself. Grant could also be demanding, at one moment ordering a limousine to drive him on to the set and at another moment asking for it to be replaced by a less extravagant automobile. He told a French actress in the film, Brigitte Auber, that Hitchcock "likes me a lot, but at the same time he detests me. He would like to be in my place." And who could deny it? Hitchcock, in the face of persistent complaints about the actor from the production manager, "Doc" Erickson, reassured Erickson that "I'll take good care of Mr. Cary Grant. On the last day of the picture, I intend to tell him off once and for all." Of course he did no such thing. He detested the strain of "telling off" anyone. When Erickson reminded him of his promise, Hitchcock replied "Well, I don't know. I might want him for another picture." Which indeed he did. Good relations on the set, however, were maintained. Hitchcock would entertain the actors and crew in a variety of restaurants where he would supervise all the details of eating and drinking with the air of a maestro or emperor.

Yet he was becoming tired with shooting on location; he always preferred to work in the safety of a studio set. Grace Kelly's current affair was also causing difficulties, with the presence of her lover, Jean-Pierre Aumont, on the set. Hitchcock excised some scenes that were meant to be shot in France and then, back in Hollywood, organised the most flamboyant sequences with all the proper technical equipment at his disposal.

Grace Kelly in *To Catch a Thief*, wearing a costume
designed by Edith Head, 1955.

Courtesy of Mondadori Portfolio/Getty Images

Work was finished at the beginning of September 1954, three weeks behind schedule. It had been filmed in VistaVision, with high-resolution images in widescreen, and some of the film's advertising claimed that "you'll feel that you're actually on the beautiful Riviera." Unfortunately this lent much of the picture the air of a travelogue, and reinforced the shallowness of the film itself. Hitchcock admitted as much at its premiere in London, where he confessed that "if sometimes you have to make corn, try at least to do it well."

To Catch a Thief had its moments, particularly those that combined the comedy of Grant and the sexuality of Kelly; but its light and almost frivolous tone did not please all of the critics. The reviewer from *Variety* said of Grace Kelly that she "clothes-horses through the footage in some fetching Edith Head creations." In truth Hitchcock created the film as a homage to his leading lady; he dressed her as a hierophant might dress a Madonna. But that did not mean he spared her some of the pain of a Magdalene. In one scene Cary Grant was meant to hold her wrists and push her against a wall. Hitchcock believed that he was being too gentle, and asked for the scene to be retaken again and again until the violence was more real. Grant recalled that "Grace went back alone behind the door where the scene started, and just by chance I happened to catch a glimpse of her massaging her wrists and grimacing in pain."

Grace Kelly herself had become a star, largely as a result of Hitchcock's direction, and *To Catch a Thief* was very popular with the public. Hayes was nominated by the Writers Guild for best comedy while the other salient points of the film were awarded with nominations for art direction and costume. It was a well-dressed film. Robert Burks, not a moment too soon, was given the Academy Award for cinematography.

While on location in Nice, at a flower market, Hitchcock was interviewed by André Bazin, the editor of the influential periodical *Cahiers du Cinéma* and considered to be one of the most prominent of French film theorists. He observed the shooting from the side of the set until Hitchcock was ready for him, and noted that "I had been watching for a good hour, during which Hitchcock did not have to intervene more

than twice; settled in his armchair, he gave the impression of being prodigiously bored and of musing about something completely different."
Their interview lasted some fifty or sixty minutes, during retakes, but
"Hitchcock did no more than throw one or two quick glances at what
was going on."

Bazin said that the director's answers were "disconcerting," by
which he meant that Hitchcock did not respond to his theoretical prob-
ings. Hitchcock seemed to be puzzled by the French critic's insistence
on the "meaning" or "message" of his films, and preferred instead to
talk of technical or practical matters. He told him, in Bazin's words, that
"it was easy to make an 'artistic' film but the real difficulty lay in making a good commercial film." It is no wonder that Bazin was disconcerted. The French theorists were characteristically interested in what
might be called the deep structures of everyday reality; when they were
confronted with the formal, methodical and highly organised nature of
Hitchcock's films, they found their ideal. American scholars and theorists, some in burgeoning film schools, picked up the habit of this form
of analysis. They were ready and willing to find meaning in anything.
Hitchcock's granddaughter entered a course on film at her school. She
asked him of one film, "Did you mean this in this scene? Because that's
what we were taught." Hitchcock rolled his eyes. "Where do they think
of these things?" On another occasion he helped her on an essay concerning one of his favourite films, *Shadow of a Doubt*. She earned only
a C grade. "Well, I'm sorry," he said. "That's the best I can do."

Bazin was also associated with the "auteur" theory, even then coming into prominence with the criticism of Truffaut and others, that
emphasised the importance of the director's personal vision and creative imagination in the making of a film. Hitchcock was by no means
opposed to this novel approach. He had always disseminated the myth
that he was the sole author of his films, principally by giving no public
credit to his collaborators. If the critics found something to detect and
to interpret, a symbol or a theme, he was not inclined to disillusion
them. For all his apparent pride and self-sufficiency he had a deep longing to be applauded and recognised. The "auteur" theory helped to

raise Hitchcock's reputation to levels that he had not so far reached, at least in French culture. No doubt he was also secretly delighted that a large portion of his European audience considered him to be an artist rather than a simple entertainer. He had always known as much but had preferred not to say so, for fear of frightening American producers and studio accountants.

· · ·

"I finished *To Catch a Thief* one afternoon at five thirty, and by seven thirty *Harry* was under way," claimed Hitchcock. This is in part self-admiring exaggeration; in truth he and John Michael Hayes had been working on the new film even when engaged on its predecessor.

Hitchcock had read *The Trouble with Harry* by Jack Trevor Story, and had been immediately struck by what might be called the novel's black pastoral comedy. It is the story of Harry, a corpse that will not stay buried but is constantly being dug up again by neighbours, each of whom believes for various reasons that he or she has killed him. The novel is set in an English village but the film was transposed to Vermont; autumn in New England might be the perfect setting for humorous melancholy. The comic and the macabre are set up side by side in an atmosphere of gentle understatement in what Hitchcock called "a strictly British genre." The tension heightens the comedy, and the comedy increases the tension. At the beginning of the film an elderly character known as "the Captain" is dragging the corpse of Harry through some undergrowth. A middle-aged lady, taking her constitutional, observes him. "What seems to be the trouble, Captain?" Hitchcock later claimed that this was his favourite line in all of his films. It captures perfectly the sweetness and insouciance of this study in death.

One of the principal delights of the film is the first appearance on screen of Shirley MacLaine; on her cinematic inexperience he commented merely that "I shall have fewer bad knots to untie." He actually had very little work to do with her. He wanted to retain her freshness and lack of guile, and had no interest in "directing" her. MacLaine recalled the first script-reading. "I didn't know how to act. I could hardly read the script. I was the dancer! I sort of played myself, or whatever." At the end of the reading Hitchcock turned to her and simply remarked, "My dear, you have the guts of a bank robber."

Certain phrases from Hitchcock during the filming have survived. "Let's move on! Spray the damned leaves! Move on." "It's only a movie, after all, and we're all grossly overpaid." "That's very good. But let's try it this way." The filming lasted only for a month in Vermont before the inclement rain and wind made the work impossible. In the middle of October Hitchcock and crew retired to the relative safety and comfort of the studio, bringing with them an ample stock of autumnal Vermont leaves to dress the set.

It may have been a very "British" film, as Hitchcock had suggested, yet it was admired in France, where it ran and ran, perhaps assisted by the new acclaim Hitchcock was enjoying with the younger French critics. It is an elaborately self-conscious and theatrical narrative that might have been set in the Forest of Arden; as Hitchcock remarked, "it's as if I had set up a murder alongside a rustling brook and spilled a drop of blood into the clear water." The playful and romantic music of Bernard Herrmann helps to create the appropriate mood. This was the first project on which Hitchcock and Herrmann worked together, and they collaborated for the next decade on the remake of *The Man Who Knew Too Much*, *The Wrong Man*, *Vertigo*, *North by Northwest*, *The Birds*, *Marnie* and, most sensationally, *Psycho*. Herrmann himself was sometimes difficult—excitable, nervous and prone to take offence—but they worked well together, principally by respecting each other's professionalism.

The film was released to an underwhelming reception in the United States, however, where audiences were generally bored or baffled by it. It may be the public did not respond well to the Britishness or, rather, Englishness of the film. Or it may be, as Hitchcock claimed, that the studio had not properly promoted it. "I'm afraid," he said, "that the people who run the cinemas, and those people who distribute films, my natural enemies, couldn't see it as an attraction for the public." At

Bernard Herrmann, who composed the music for eight Hitchcock films, starting with *The Trouble with Harry*, 1955.

Courtesy of Popperfoto/Getty Images

a later date he confessed that "the film has lost, I suppose, about half a million dollars. So that's an expensive self-indulgence."

. . .

Matters of finance may have been on his mind when he embarked on what was essentially a second career. After post-production on *The Trouble with Harry* was complete the Hitchcocks enjoyed a Christmas vacation in their favourite resort of St. Moritz. By the time they returned to Hollywood, Hitchcock was engaged in talks with Lew Wasserman, who had become president of MCA in 1946 and who had also been Hitchcock's agent for several years. In this dual role, therefore, he suggested that Hitchcock might like to make the transition from film to television.

The director had experimented before with different forms of broadcasting. He had acted as a host for a radio series, *Murder by Experts*, and had been a panel guest on a radio quiz show entitled *Information, Please*. On the latter programme, in 1943, he was asked, "In which famous case was the guilt fixed by the purchase of a hyacinth?" He had the answer exact to every detail. The moderator on the panel asked him, "How was the tide running at the time?"

Yet the transition to the small screen was a challenge. It is possible that at first he held back, out of genuine uncertainty, but all the forces of his nature propelled him forward. Television meant fame. Television meant success. Television meant money. He always needed more fame, more money, more success; these were just the laws of his being. In the mid-1950s, too, the Hollywood studios began to produce material for the small screen, having previously ignored it. Television dramas, each introduced by a celebrated performer, had also become more frequent since the late 1940s when the three major networks—ABC, NBC and CBS—began to provide full nightly schedules.

When Lew Wasserman made it clear that he would have to do very little in return for a very large fee, Hitchcock consented. He would be executive producer and script supervisor in name only, and his major role was as the presenter at the beginning and end of each instalment. For this he was to be paid $129,000 per episode. He would also own the rights to each programme after its first broadcast. It was money for nothing, or next to nothing. It was an offer that Hitchcock could not refuse.

Yet even as the negotiations continued he had another film on his mind. He had first considered a new version of *The Man Who Knew Too Much* in 1941. It is not at all clear why he returned to the idea fourteen years later. He said sometimes that he simply wanted to find an appropriate vehicle for the talents of James Stewart, but this does not seem plausible. It is more likely that he saw the commercial possibilities of what had always been one of his favourite films. The original had been released in 1934, and it might be seen as a quite new thing in the mid-1950s. It would be in colour, and have the benefit of a wide screen.

He began work with his old scriptwriter, Angus MacPhail, at the beginning of 1955 and two months later, John Michael Hayes joined them on the script. Hayes recalled that "I never saw the original script [of the film released in 1934] and never saw the original picture, except for the Albert Hall sequence at the end, which was pretty much the same as it was in the original. Hitch called me in and said, 'What I'm going to do is tell you the story, and you take notes and write the story I tell you, your way.'" The story was of a middle-class couple with a young son who witness the assassination of an agent in a foreign country; the assassins then kidnap their child to prevent them from revealing what they know and, when the setting changes to London, a series of bizarre confrontations ends with a climactic scene in the Albert Hall and an equally dramatic reunion of parents and child. In the new script the exotic location is changed from Switzerland to Morocco, the couple and child become American rather than English, the young girl becomes a young boy, and part of the action is transposed from a London dentist to a London taxidermist.

Hitchcock had chosen James Stewart and Doris Day for the principal parts. Stewart was an experienced actor who was accustomed to the role of an honest man in testing circumstances; Day was a musical star whose performance in a film about the Ku Klux Klan, *Storm Warning*,

Hitchcock had admired. She was, in life as well as in art, very much the American housewife abroad. She had never travelled out of the United States, and was nervous as the cast and crew flew to Marrakech for the opening sequences of the film. She was predictably dismayed by what she saw of the unsanitary conditions of the city, and horrified by what she considered to be the brutal treatment of animals. Hitchcock ensured that all the animals on set were well fed and properly managed.

But her problems did not end there. In his usual fashion Hitchcock kept his own counsel and did not comment upon her performance in front of the camera. She interpreted this formality and reticence as coldness and dislike. She commented later that "he never said anything to me, before or during or after a scene, and so I thought I was displeasing him, and I was crushed . . . I was convinced that I must have been the worst actress he had ever had." Eventually she arranged a meeting with him, in which she offered to resign and be replaced by someone else. Hitchcock was astonished. "He said it was quite the reverse, that he thought I was just doing everything right—and that if I hadn't been doing everything right he would have told me." It is an apt example of how he tended to disregard the reaction of his actors to his presence. Yet he had divined fear within her, and comforted her by explaining his own neuroses—how, for example, "he was afraid to walk across the Paramount lot to the commissary because he was so afraid of people."

Bernard Miles, who played the leader of the assassins, recalled his "very genial experience" with the director but he added that "he certainly did not annoy his cast with excessive attention." James Stewart had told him that "we're in the hands of an expert here. You can lean on him. Just do everything he tells you, and the whole thing will be okay." The filming in Marrakech was difficult, in part because some of it coincided with the observance of Ramadan; some of the extras were weak with hunger, while others were selling their food tickets and not returning to work.

The production report for 21 May records elliptically that it was "Overcast—delay caused by mob." The mob was in fact the extras, who had been angered by a rumour that they would not be paid if they could not see the camera. Hitchcock remained unmoved, sitting beneath a large umbrella; instead of his customary suit and tie, he had bowed to circumstances and wore a tightly buttoned shortsleeve shirt. He had a habit of blowing the flies off his face with his lower lip distended.

The furore confirmed his dislike of location shooting; it was disordered, uncomfortable and unpredictable. Now he began to enquire "who wrote all these sequences into the picture." He wanted to get out of Morocco. "Doc" Erickson wrote that "as usual he was ready to go home as soon as he arrived. He's not even keen about going to London, but he's committed himself to those damned interiors up there now." On 23 May the production report summarised, "Milling mobs in marketplace—had to move camera B out." That was the last day. They moved on to the "damned interiors" of London, and then with the scenes completed, cast and crew returned to the comfort of the Paramount set where Hitchcock felt most at home. The filming was complete by August, but it was thirty-four days over schedule.

Eight or ten pages of the script had been flown in by courier each day as they worked in Marrakech and, when they travelled on to London for the next stage of the film, John Michael Hayes was already at the Savoy hotel with his typewriter, delivering his material directly to the set. Everything was done, as Hayes put it, "on the rush." Hayes resented the fact that screen credit was given to "John Michael Hayes and Angus MacPhail" when in fact he believed that he had changed MacPhail's script out of all recognition. It was his script and his only. The complaint went to the official body who arbitrated such matters, and Hayes was given sole credit as writer. Hitchcock never worked with him again.

The Man Who Knew Too Much is very different from its predecessor. Hitchcock himself announced that "the first version is the work of a talented amateur, and the second was made by a professional." This was not at all fair on the original version, which is preferred by many, but in any case Hitchcock amended his opinion some years later when he said that "I think, actually, the difference would be in the original *The*

Man Who Knew Too Much. I wasn't audience conscious, whereas in the second one I was." This is closer to the point, since he had become highly sensitive to the expectations of the American public. At an even later date he changed his opinion again. He now believed that the earlier version "was more spontaneous—it had less logic. Logic is dull: you always lose the bizarre and spontaneous."

The second version is glossy. It has more elaborate set pieces. It is in colour. It pays regard to the psychological weight of the couple played by James Stewart and Doris Day. It is longer and, in certain respects, more various in atmosphere. It has a softer ending. The first version is not so well constructed but it has an energy and inventiveness that surmount all obstacles. Yet the American edition, if it can so be called, benefits from Hitchcock's longer experience of film. It is technically more accomplished, and with the technique comes the vision. They are not to be separated. *The Man Who Knew Too Much* is a fine example of a well-integrated filmic world, solid, brilliantly realised and fully detailed, which is exposed as frail and tissue-thin. Menace and tension flow through the film just as its music does. The clash of cymbals in the Albert Hall will signal an assassination. When Doris Day sings "Que Será Será," her voice creeps slowly and nervously up the staircase and along the hall of a foreign embassy to verify that her child is still alive. Adventure and melodrama, in the first version, have given way to psychological drama and the interpretation of character.

Hitchcock once summarised the difference between his English and American periods as one between spontaneity or instinct, and calculation. That element of caution is also related to the much larger financial risks involved in the American studio system where $1 million, or more, could be spent on one picture. It is the difference between a studio and a factory. It has also been observed that his English players are more solidly rooted in their social and cultural environment whereas the Americans tend to be more abstract, to float free from social ties and to exist in some large indefinite space. It is the measure of his response to the two nations.

The American reaction to the new film was not in doubt; it was an instant success and, within a week, had become the most profitable film of the year. Hitchcock had also made a decision in another sense. On 20 April 1955, before he set out for Marrakech and London, he had been driven to the federal court building in Los Angeles from which he emerged as an American citizen.

9

GOOD EVENING

At nine thirty on the evening of 2 October 1955, a portly figure appeared as a silhouette on the right edge of the television screen and, accompanied by the music of Gounod's "Funeral March of a Marionette," stepped into the shape of what would become a famous profile. "Good evening." So began a series of half-hour episodes, *Alfred Hitchcock Presents*, that lasted for seven years, followed by a further three years of extended programmes, guaranteeing the fame and fortune of the director in ways that he could not have imagined. He had always possessed a thirst for self-publicity, adduced by his cameo appearances in most of his films, but the power of television was such that his shape and visage became recognised all over the world.

The timing was propitious. The box-office proceeds from the American cinema had dropped markedly, while in the 1950s the number of American households with television had risen from 4 million to 48 million. He had a constant preoccupation with his audience's expectations, but now he had to give only himself. His role was suitably ambiguous. Although each episode had the hallmark of Hitchcock stamped upon it, he chose and directed relatively few of them; of the 335 television stories, Hitchcock directed approximately twenty, leaving the decisions to his staff or what he sometimes called "my own little family."

The television team were already old friends. Joan Harrison had been his assistant and adviser in the past, and she was now called upon to become executive producer. A little later Norman Lloyd, who had worked with him as an actor in *Saboteur* and *Spellbound*, became associate producer. They chose the stories and submitted them for Hitchcock's approval. The rest was up to them. They would develop the screenplay with a writer, they would cast it, choose a director, film it and edit it. Norman Lloyd related that "Hitchcock seldom spoke about how a script should be shot. He had nothing to do with the pictures until he saw a rough-cut. Then he would look at it and say, yes or no, and usually he'd say 'well maybe you need a close-up or an insert or something.' That was the extent he played in the actual making of it." He might say "good" or "very good" and, if he really did not like the material, he said simply "Well, thank you." His associates knew what to do next.

Hitchcock confirmed this relatively restrained role. "Miss Harrison does the casting, yes," he said, "and Norman Lloyd. I try to put out fatherly words of advice without trying to usurp their position." But he appreciated the speed of the procedure, which appealed to his sense of technical challenge. Most of the episodes were filmed and edited within three days, scarcely enough time to dress a set in the film studio. One day was allowed for rehearsal, and two days for filming. He stated in a press release just before the start of the series that "it annoys me, this notion that I cannot move around rapidly when the occasion demands."

His principal contribution was to lend his presence to the enterprise with what were known as "lead-ins" and "lead-outs." He introduced each episode, and provided a concluding paragraph to point the moral or adorn the tale with the shocking news that crime does not pay. This was necessary for the sake of the censor, and may have come as a surprise to the audience. It has been said that this was the first television series which adopted the point of view of the criminal rather than the victim.

He had a lugubriously jolly delivery, perfectly in keeping with the

A promotional picture for *Alfred Hitchcock Presents*, 1956.

Courtesy of CBS Photo Archive/Getty Images

manner of an English undertaker, but over the years there were occasions when he changed his appearance. He came on screen sitting in the stocks, or as a baby in a nappy, or with a hatchet in his head. He was once trapped within a bottle. He was found tied to a railway track from which horizontal position he announced to his television audience, "Good evening, fellow tourists. I think this proves that in some ways the airplane can never replace the railway." In another sequence he explained that the killer had been caught "because his dog Cassandra was really a detective in disguise and turned him in at the next town. It's getting so a man can't even trust his best friend."

It was generally assumed that he wrote his own scripts for these short appearances but in fact he had hired a television comedy writer. He had given Jim Allardice a screening of *The Trouble with Harry*, and asked the writer to provide scripts that could match the macabre humour of that film; he wanted something with an English twist of humour with understatement and menace. Allardice went further than that and provided material that might out-Hitchcock Hitchcock. "Here is the ever popular revolver. It is an excellent means of establishing credit in a strange city. It is equally useful in the removal of unwanted or unsightly persons." And "I was once arrested for indecent exposure when I removed a Halloween mask."

He also fought a running on-screen battle with the sponsors of the programme, whose advertisements began and concluded the narrative. "Naturally these remarks have nothing at all to do with tonight's story. They are only meant to divert your attention so that our sponsor can sneak up on you—and here he is, ready to pounce." "Now my sponsor would like to bring you an important message. I needn't tell you to whom it is important." The advertisers were at first ready to take umbrage at the presenter's droll or sarcastic remarks but, once they saw the viewing figures, they withdrew their objections.

His role as master of ceremonies was not unfamiliar or unusual. It may not have yet been exploited to the full on American television but for Hitchcock it had all the trappings of the "chairman" in the Edwardian music hall who would introduce each of the acts with a few ribald words. This light comedy routine was an essential part of his nature, spurred by some of his earliest memories of the London stage. His role has also been described as that of a jester or a dandy, with all the irony and distance those parts imply, but the most important duty of the chairman was to rustle up the "wet money" and increase the profits by persuading the audience to drink. He knew that his weekly appearance increased his ratings.

On a certain day each week he was driven to a studio on the lot of Universal Pictures where he filmed ten or more of these segments in sequence. The props were in place, his lines were fed to him, and he realised very soon that he enjoyed his position in front of a television camera. His company was called Shamley Productions, after Shamley Green in Surrey where the Hitchcocks had lived in the 1930s. It was another intimation of England from a new American citizen.

He tended to call the episodes "stories" and said that "I have always wanted to work in the short story. The small simple tale of a single idea building to a turn, a twist at the end." He had encountered this technique in the stories of Edgar Allan Poe which he had read as a child.

The first episode that he directed, "Breakdown," was a curious interpretation of Poe's "The Premature Burial." A callous and passionless businessman (played by Joseph Cotten) is caught within the wreckage of his car; he is believed to be dead until, as the coroner prepares the instruments of his trade, he sheds a tear in the morgue. It was also the first expression on television of one of Hitchcock's favoured images, that of a face motionless with rage, anger, fear or death itself. It is the quintessential Hitchcock visage, too traumatised to be able to react, stripped of all cultural referents, a bare blank stare. In his films, from *The Wrong Man* to *Frenzy*, that blind gaze is characteristically given to female victims.

He soon became acquainted with his popularity, on and off the set. One of his colleagues, Marshall Schlom, commented that "Mr. Hitchcock was the biggest thing around, especially on TV. To the studio, he was a hands-off client who got anything he wanted." Hitchcock told a reporter in 1956 that "before TV I'd get about a dozen letters per week. Now it's several hundred . . . Thirty years I've been directing pictures on the set. Just the other day I overheard a lady guest say 'There's Alfred Hitchcock of television.'" He was recognised everywhere, and accosted with imitations of his booming "Good evening." He had the most famous silhouette in America. And he now became engaged in what must have seemed like an everlasting process of self-promotion in which his screen "character" became in many respects the character that he projected on to the world. He loved it.

. . .

While he had been working in Marrakech on *The Man Who Knew Too Much*, he had been asked a question. "Hitch, what are you thinking about?"

"I'm thinking about my next movie."

He told a reporter in 1956 that "I've seen many stories about the arrest of an innocent man from the point of view of his champion—a lawyer, or reporter, and so on. But it is never told from the point of view of the person who underwent the ordeal." It was the perfect story for a director who had often created films out of the crisis of the innocent being mistaken for the guilty. It was one of the mainstays of Hitchcock's art.

The Wrong Man sprang out of some of his deepest preoccupations but was in fact based on a contemporary real-life episode. Due to his uncanny resemblance to another man, Christopher Emmanuel Balestrero had been mistaken for a thief. He was duly arrested and tried. In the process his wife suffered a nervous breakdown. The untoward words of a juror resulted in a mistrial, and in the interim the real thief was discovered and apprehended.

Hitchcock had often expressed a wish to film a documentary, and this was the closest he would ever come to it. He willingly parted company from the Technicolor and the scenic range of his most recent films, exchanging them for the black and white "realism" of a New York environment and a carefully subdued plot. This was also the period in which Italian neo-realism had become popular, at least in the art houses, and Hitchcock was always keenly aware of cinematic fashion.

He was determined upon accuracy of detail and fidelity to mood. His production team mapped out the footsteps of Balestrero on his way home from his work in a nightclub jazz band; they ate in the same diner as he used, and interviewed the judge and the attorneys of the case. They visited the gaol in which he had been detained, and the mental hospital to which his wife had been consigned. The New York police wanted nothing to do with the project, given that it concerned a false arrest, and instead Hitchcock hired retired officers as consultants. He had decided to film the events in the actual locations where they happened, as far as that were possible, and to re-enact the night scenes *at* night.

For the role of Balestrero he had chosen Henry Fonda, who seemed to be the epitome of grim endurance. He had tried to enlist him earlier, for *Foreign Correspondent* and *Saboteur,* but had not succeeded. Now in the part of the wrongly accused Balestrero forced to undergo the ritual penance of the custodial system, he became darkness made visible.

Hitchcock had already found his leading lady. He realised that Grace Kelly, now accompanying Prince Rainier of Monaco, was no longer available, so he determined to catch another possible star. He had seen Vera Miles during an episode on television of *The Pepsi-Cola Playhouse,* and was immediately taken with her. He glimpsed her possibilities. He negotiated a contract for three pictures over five years, and also gave her the leading role in the first televised episode of *Alfred Hitchcock Presents.* Hitchcock explained in an interview that "I feel the same way directing Vera that I did with Grace. She has a style, an intelligence and a quality of understatement." He went further with *Cosmopolitan* magazine by telling its editor that "Vera Miles is going to replace Grace Kelly." Hitchcock wanted to dress her as well as direct her. He told his costume designer, Edith Head, that "she's an extraordinarily good actress, but she doesn't dress in a way that gives her the distinction her acting warrants." She wore too much distracting colour. That was perhaps one of the reasons why *The Wrong Man* was filmed in black and white.

The filming itself was without incident. "He was funny all the time," Henry Fonda recalled. "Hitch would come in and tell a funny story just before he'd say 'Roll 'em' into a serious scene. I loved working with Hitch." The only hint of trouble came in the director's relationship with Vera Miles, who came to resent his overbearing and dominating manner. He would spend far more hours with her than any other actor on the set. He advised her how to smile, and how to walk, and how to speak; he counselled her on her diet and on the company she kept. He insisted upon "story conferences" in her dressing room, but, curiously enough, she complained that he had never once complimented her on her acting. His assistant producer, Herbert Coleman, remarked that "Hitch had an obsession with her, sure. But it never went beyond imagining." Nor was it likely to do so. She was about to marry her second husband, and already had two children. She was too spirited, and too resourceful. When she resisted his influence over her life, he began to lose interest in her. That is perhaps evident in the subdued role that she plays in *The Wrong Man*, in which she never really comes to life.

Despite Hitchcock's aspirations toward realism and objectivity, the film did not follow the real course of events when cinematic imperatives demanded otherwise. It was still a slice of cake, however little it was sweetened, rather than a slice of life; it was also obliged to conclude on an optimistic and even reassuring note whereas the "truth" was far more ambiguous. When Truffaut questioned him on this Hitchcock replied that "it seems to me that you want me to work for the art houses" which suggests that all along he had a populist and a commercial, rather than purely artistic, motive.

It was not a great success at the time. The script and the plot engaged some of the director's predilections and even fantasies, the most prominent of them being those of mistaken identity and false imprisonment, together with the appurtenances of shadows, bars and labyrinthine corridors. But the film did not enlist his imaginative verve. It gives no sign of creative liberation, the wild energy that manifests itself in his more obvious "entertainments." It is serious, and even solemn. It is neither mercurial nor comic. It has gravity but no lightness. Despite its pretence to realism it seems too schematic and laboured to carry it off. At a later date he told Truffaut that "I don't feel that strongly about it." It was to be placed among what he called "the indifferent Hitchcocks."

· · ·

In any case he was flying to more exotic locations. In the early summer of 1956 he and his wife, together with key members of the production team, flew to southern Africa in search of settings for a new project. He had decided to make a picture out of Laurens van der Post's *Flamingo Feather* which he described as "a sort of John Buchan real adventure" that he intended to populate with "good, sophisticated stars." He had already enlisted James Stewart for the enterprise and, against all the odds, hoped to coax Grace Kelly—now Princess Grace of Monaco—out of royal retirement. He said that he had travelled to Africa "for atmosphere, just atmosphere," but soon discovered that he did not really care for the atmosphere at all. Hot and sultry locations, forests and jungles, bush and track, were not for him. In any case the problem of extras would be as insupportable as it had been in Marrakech, and costs might be enormous. It was too risky a proposition, for Paramount as well as for Hitchcock, and so it was dropped. He had, at least, taken a long holiday.

The nature of his next project was therefore still undecided. He was considering a novel by Hammond Innes, *The Wreck of the Mary Deare*, that had been recently published; Metro-Goldwyn-Mayer had purchased the rights, and persuaded Hitchcock to take on the project in a one-film contract. The story concerned a ship found adrift but, when it is boarded for salvage, its first officer is found alive. When the first officer returns to shore, he is brought before a board of inquiry to determine what has happened. It fascinated Hitchcock, and he enlisted Ernest Lehman for a scenario. Lehman was respectful and courteous. Nevertheless neither of them could make much progress with the story, which was turning into a retrospective courtroom drama.

Hitchcock then came upon a novel which seems to have been, literally, made for him. Truffaut set the scene in his interview with him in the summer of 1962.

> TRUFFAUT: *Vertigo* is taken from the Boileau-Narcejac novel *D'entre les morts*, which was especially written that you might do a screen version of it.
> HITCHCOCK: No, it wasn't. The novel was out before we acquired the rights to the property.
> TRUFFAUT: Just the same, that book was especially written for you.
> HITCHCOCK: Do you really think so? What if I hadn't bought it?
> TRUFFAUT: In that case it would have been bought by some French director, on account of the success of *Diabolique*. As a matter of fact, Boileau and Narcejac did four or five novels on that theory. When they found out that you had been interested in acquiring the rights to *Diabolique*, they went to work and wrote *D'entre les morts*, which Paramount bought for you.

That was the truth of the matter. Hitchcock had expressed an interest in *Diabolique*, a 1955 thriller in which an apparently dead man comes to life in a most involved conspiracy, and it seems that the French co-writers Pierre Boileau and Thomas Narcejac concocted a story that bore a superficial resemblance to it. *D'entre les morts* is about romantic obsession: a man becomes so haunted by what he believes to be the image of a dead woman that he changes the appearance of another woman to resemble her in every detail. They are in fact the same person, and the revelation will eventually come close to destroying him. Hitchcock was fascinated with obsession, especially that of the male with the female, and it became fruitful territory for exploring some of the more dangerous aspects of sexual fantasy and attraction.

A first version of the script was completed by the playwright Maxwell Anderson. He had already worked on the first versions of *The Wrong Man*, although his script was considered too fanciful and allusive for an apparently realist film. But his highly charged poetic style might be the best vehicle for *Vertigo*, as *D'entre les morts* was to be called. Yet, however distinguished a playwright, Anderson did not have the peculiar gifts of a scriptwriter; he declined the offer. Hitchcock experimented with one or two other writers before coming upon Samuel Taylor. Taylor recalled that his agent, Kay Brown, "said to have a go at it because she'd like me to know Hitchcock. So I said all right and I studied the screenplay on the train going out, because in those days you almost always travelled by train. By the time I got there I had a pretty good idea what I could do with it." He told Hitchcock that the film had to shed its romantic mists and become real. Hitchcock replied "That's what Jimmy Stewart said." Stewart was to play Scottie, the retired police detective who is lured into a false pursuit.

It was fortunate that they came to an agreement so quickly because, on the day after Taylor signed his contract in the second week of January 1957, Hitchcock fell seriously ill. There is a theory that certain people become ill in order to prepare themselves, as if in a rite of passage, for some great enterprise. His medical records contain the more mundane truth that he was suffering from a hernia and colitis; his hernia was already an old friend, but it might have turned cantankerous. After some minor surgery at Cedars of Lebanon hospital in Los Angeles, he was allowed to return home. It was the first time that he had experienced an American hospital and he told a journalist that "the biggest shock was the indignities to which institutions of healing subject your person. I am not a squeamish man, but some of the things they do to you in hospitals are no less than obscene." When they tied a name tag to his wrist he thought, of course, of the morgue. He was much possessed by death.

In the enforced absence of Hitchcock, Samuel Taylor continued work on the script, and when the director returned from hospital they resumed their collaborative sessions at Bellagio Road. Clearly Hitchcock had less energy, and perhaps fewer powers of concentration, but Taylor recalled that "he was in good form and we were having a very happy time writing . . . We'd talk about the picture and there would be a long silence and we'd just sit and contemplate each other and Hitchcock would say, 'Well, the motor is still running.'" After lunch he would

Hitchcock in his office at Paramount Studios, 1957.

take a recuperative nap, and Taylor would return to the studio and his typewriter. Then Hitchcock's health grew worse.

On the morning of 9 March he started moaning and clutching his chest. He and Alma seemed at first to believe that he had suffered a heart attack but tests revealed a disease of the gall bladder together with two gallstones. Two days later he had a successful operation for the very painful condition. "I suffered two internal haemorrhages," he told a reporter. "I was told that this often happened to people and not to worry. So I wasn't alarmed. But they told my wife she had better see a priest." Although Hitchcock said he was not alarmed, his daughter recalled that he was "terrified." This is more likely. He took two months to recover after this second operation, and by the beginning of April Taylor had completed the first script for *Vertigo*. Hitchcock was in no state to concentrate upon the matter for another month. The shooting script was eventually ready by September.

While recuperating from the operation he received the news that Vera Miles had decided to leave the production for the very good reason that she was now pregnant. Hitchcock was not happy about this, and told a reporter from *Cosmopolitan* that "she cost me several hundred thousand dollars. I don't know what I'm going to do with her. Movie careers have a rhythm you know. She broke the rhythm and it means making a whole new start." It was clear enough that he had designed a career, or a path, for her. His resentment emerged in another interview. "I was offering her a big part," he said, "the chance to become a beautiful sophisticated blonde, a real actress. We'd have spent a heap of dollars on it, and she has the bad taste to get pregnant." Their relationship was resumed only when she was granted a subsidiary role in *Psycho*.

It is possible, however, that he was secretly relieved. He had no doubt about her abilities as an actress, but he was not sure that she had that mysterious and indefinable quality that would lend her a commanding presence on the screen. Could she ever be a star? She, too, might have been relieved when the burden of expectation was lifted from her.

So the search began for a replacement. After a series of deals and negotiations Kim Novak emerged as the new heroine. Novak was already a tested Hollywood asset and came to the studio complete with demands. She would not wear grey. She would not wear dark brown shoes. Hitchcock invited her to Bellagio Road where, according to his assistant producer Herbert Coleman, he began to discuss with her topics such as art and wine that she had never considered before. Coleman added that "he succeeded in making her feel like a helpless child, ignorant and untutored, and that's just what he wanted—to break down her resistance."

Hitchcock recalled the episode in more detail. "She had very definite opinions about herself; her hair always had to be lavender; she would never wear suits under any circumstances . . . I said 'Look, Miss Novak, you do your hair whatever colour you like, and you wear whatever you like, so long as it conforms to the story requirements.' And the story required her to be a brunette and to wear a grey suit. I used to say, 'Listen. You do whatever you like. There's always the cutting-room floor.' That stumps them. That's the end of that." In another interview he remarked that "I even managed to get her to act." Novak said that "I think he's one of the few directors who allowed me the most freedom as an actress."

Some early filming had already been completed in February 1957, with location work in San Francisco. In *Vertigo* San Francisco is the city of dreams. Scottie, the retired detective, has been hired to follow Madeleine by her husband. She seems to have become deeply obsessed with a figure from the nineteenth century, Carlotta Valdes, who had been "thrown away" on to the streets of San Francisco by her rich lover. Scottie in turn becomes passionately fixated on the woman he is shadowing. When Madeleine apparently falls to her death from a church tower Scottie begins his own gradual journey into obsession, seeking this now idealised woman in every face. Quite by chance he finds Judy Barton, also played by Novak, and persuades her to shed her identity and take on the role of Madeleine. The decision is literally fatal for her.

When Scottie dresses Judy in the same clothes as Madeleine, and arranges her hair style in precisely the same fashion, it was remarked

Kim Novak with Peggy Robertson on the set of *Vertigo*, 1957.
Robertson was Hitchcock's personal assistant for the rest of his life.

at the time that there was some resemblance, to put it no higher, with Hitchcock's own behaviour towards his favourite actresses. It was easy to see why he had chosen this novel. The fictional hero's obsessive pursuit of an ideal or idealised woman came very close to the trajectory of Hitchcock's cinematic career.

Samuel Taylor remarked that "Hitchcock knew exactly what he wanted to do in this film . . . and anyone who saw him during the making of this film could see, as I did, that he felt very deeply indeed." The atmosphere on the set was as strained and as intense as in the film itself. James Stewart commented that "I could tell it was a very personal film even while he was making it." Kim Novak said to a reporter from *Le Monde* that "it's as if he had wanted to put himself in the skin of the James Stewart character."

He began intense filming at the end of September 1957, and it was completed by 10 December. About two and a half minutes of film was shot each day, slowly accumulating into a magnificent threnody that lasts a little over two hours. He had prepared the way with his usual care. One of the rooms in a local hotel, the Empire, had to be reconstructed in minute detail. Even the ashtrays had to be authentic. The local florist, Podesta, was also reproduced in the studio. The flowers were their flowers. This concern with detail is somehow congruent with a great deal of visual experimentation, when the camera does a 360-degree turn or when a forward zoom with reverse tracking is used to mimic the sensation of vertigo. The spinning camera emphasises the extensive use of spiral images in the film. They are one of Hitchcock's favourite motifs, in any case, but here they serve the themes of fate and eternal recurrence.

He told Novak before shooting began, "You have got a lot of expression on your face. Don't want any of it." He instructed one of the other players, Barbara Bel Geddes, "Don't act." He did not need to tell James Stewart to do anything. Stewart was often expressionless, with only a flicker across his face to register discomfort or even nervous collapse. By indirection Hitchcock coaxed the actors to perform only to his instructions. Characteristically he never commented upon their performances.

As the leading man tries desperately to find, and then to alter, his idealised woman, the cameras come closer; the atmosphere becomes more menacing and haunted. The history of San Francisco drifts slowly past them like woodsmoke. The crucial scenes of death are set in the city's oldest building, the Mission Dolores, established with its chapel in 1776. The impression is given that the lonely and wandering Madeleine believes herself to be the reincarnation of Carlotta, and dresses in the same antique fashion. A necklace is a clue to the final mystery of love and death, time past and time future. Yet if *Vertigo* is a ghost history of San Francisco, it is also a meditation on fate itself. What is the appearance and what is the reality? What is hidden beneath the surface? A brooding sense of gloom, and a sense of impending calamity, suffuse the film. It is a film of coincidence and double identity, of fatality and suspense. In one of the novels of Wilkie Collins, a writer whom Hitchcock greatly admired, a character reveals that "I felt the ominous Future coming close; chilling me, with an unutterable awe; forcing on me the conviction of an unseen Design in the long series of complications which had now fastened around us." The unseen designer is on this occasion Hitchcock himself, and he was blessed by a particular art and singular imagination.

In one sequence Scottie and Madeleine venture into a great redwood forest at Big Basin where they wander among the ancient trees. Scottie says to her "Their true name is *Sequoia sempervirens*: always green, ever living . . . what are you thinking?"

"Of all the people who've been born and who died while the trees went on living . . . I don't like it, knowing I have to die," replies Madeleine.

It is an exercise in nostalgia as well as obsession, creating an atmosphere of eternal recurrence in which all of the participants are involved. Hitchcock said that "I made the film in order to present a man's dreamlike nature." It is in fact sometimes curiously somnolent,

A composite portrait of Kim Novak showing her two roles in *Vertigo*, 1958.

Courtesy of Silver Screen Collection/Getty Images

as if suspended in time; the twin agents of Technicolor and VistaVision themselves create a fantastically coloured world which is so vivid that it seems artificial. This is the paradox inherent in Hitchcock's often quoted remark that "it's only a movie." He is a wonderful colourist and there are moments in *Vertigo* when the image on the screen resembles a canvas by Bonnard or Vuillard. It could almost have been conceived as a silent film, with a sequence of hugely powerful visual images that are both artificial and exquisite.

The performance of Kim Novak, despite the fact that it was treated with some coolness by Hitchcock himself, is impressive. She had to play the roles of two different women, Madeleine and Judy, intimating their genuine resemblance while expressing their different personalities. She is in a sense the presiding image of the film, wraithlike and insubstantial. Her role might have been based upon the premise, adumbrated by Edgar Allan Poe, that "the death, then, of a beautiful woman is, unquestionably, the most poetical topic in the world."

All the poetry of Hitchcock's vision is poured into what at first glance is morbid and obsessional material, worked over with infinite finesse and susceptible to various interpretations psychic or psychotic. That is why it has endured. It is a reverie and a lament, a threnody and a hymn, with an ending so abrupt, so shocking, that it prolongs the mood of emptiness and anxiety. The last words of the film are spoken by a sepulchral nun. "I heard voices. God have mercy."

Vertigo has in recent years been considered to be the most profound and exquisite of all Hitchcock's films. It did not seem like that to anyone at the time. It was treated as another Hitchcock thriller with suspense and pursuit as its principal elements. Yet it was not a success. It was greeted with bemusement by the reviewers, and with boredom by the public. It was too odd. It was too vague and too remote. It was too long, with music often taking the place of words. Hitchcock professed to believe that its failure was largely due to James Stewart's ageing appearance. When the rights of the film reverted to him, according to his contract with Paramount, he buried it in the vaults and it was never again released during his lifetime. It did eventually re-emerge and in 2012 was voted in a ten-yearly poll in *Sight and Sound* as "the greatest film of all time."

He was asked once, "What do you think about the prominence that *Vertigo* has assumed for your European critics?"

"I think they understood the complexities of the situation."

. . .

As soon as filming was completed, and before the process of post-production had begun, the Hitchcocks flew to Jamaica for a month's vacation. He already had another project in mind. Even as he was filming *Vertigo* he was working with Ernest Lehman on a script that was tentatively entitled *In a Northwesterly Direction*. They had previously worked on *The Wreck of the Mary Deare*, but Lehman recalled that Hitchcock "went to a meeting and told them that it was taking too long to write *Mary Deare*, and that we were planning to do another script instead." The studio managers at MGM were delighted rather than dismayed; they assumed that he would now be working on two films instead of the single one for which he had been contracted.

Hitchcock and Lehman began to imagine, and to improvise, new stories and new settings. Hitchcock said that "I always wanted to do a chase across the faces of Mount Rushmore." It was an image, and no more, but it seems to have been enough to create a new mood in both director and writer. As Hitchcock immersed himself in the spiral of *Vertigo*, Lehman asked himself questions. Who is chasing whom over the famous faces? Why are pursuers and pursued in such a location? How did they get there? If he is on a train, where is he going? Should he meet someone? Perhaps it would be a young woman. And then what? One question followed another as Lehman slowly wrote the pages of the script which would eventually become *North by Northwest*. Lehman admitted that "in the end, the audience never knows what's coming next, because I didn't either." But Hitchcock approved of the work that Lehman had already done and began to work enthusiastically on the script, going through it page by page as the quixotic plot unfolded.

At some point the director told Lehman that "I've always wanted to do a scene in the middle of nowhere—where there's absolutely nothing. You're out in the open, and there's nothing all around you. The cameras can turn around 360 degrees, and there's nothing there but this one man standing alone—because the villains, who are out to kill him, have lured him out to this lonely spot. Suddenly a tornado comes along and—"

"But Hitch, how do the villains create a tornado?"

"I have no idea."

"What if a plane comes out of the sky?"

"Yes, it's a crop duster. We can plant some crops nearby."

This is Ernest Lehman's recollection of their conversation. Hitchcock had certainly noted the crop dusters working the fields near his ranch.

But then, suddenly, he became the man alone. In the middle of April 1958, Alma returned to Bellagio Road to tell him that some routine tests had revealed that she had contracted cervical cancer and that she would have to undergo very risky surgery. This was a time when cancer was generally pronounced to be fatal. Although Alma tried to keep up her spirits, no doubt for the sake of her husband rather than for herself, Hitchcock himself was struck with fear and trembling. He continued with his filming schedule, which included an episode for *Alfred Hitchcock Presents*, but according to his authorised biographer John Russell Taylor "he would drive straight to the hospital, weeping and shaking convulsively." He dined alone in a nearby restaurant, but could not bear to go near the place in later years. Alma herself said later, "He wants it blotted out of his life." The days of panic, and near hysteria, had to be eliminated from his memories.

Norman Lloyd, who still worked with him on *Alfred Hitchcock Presents*, recalled that he once drove home with him to Bellagio Road. It was a hot day, and they were both in their shirtsleeves. Hitchcock talked about Alma and then began to weep incessantly. He reverted to the oldest sentiments in the world. "What's it all about?" he asked Lloyd. "What would it all mean, without Alma? After all, everything

I do in film is secondary to what is really important." The pioneering surgery was a success, however, and Alma slowly recovered. Yet it had been a close-run thing. Alma said later that "for a man with Hitch's phobia about suspense, it was like being impaled on a torture rack." His daughter recalled that "Daddy was totally devastated." Even while Alma was making a complete recovery "Hitch remained a complete wreck and continued to believe she was going to die." He told Patricia that he could not live without Alma, and in her memoir Patricia remarks that "had anything happened to her, he probably couldn't have gone on."

Yet he did go on after the weeping had passed and, under the aegis of MGM, he continued work with Lehman on the script for what was still called *In a Northwesterly Direction*, or sometimes *The Man on Lincoln's Nose*. His contract had given him complete control of the picture, and it might be described as an independent Hitchcock production with all the resources of a film studio behind it. Lehman decided to investigate the route that his hero would cover to get all the way from New York to Mount Rushmore; he and Hitchcock had decided that it would be another case of an innocent man on the run. On this occasion he has been mistaken for a government agent by a group of unspecified spies, instigating a relentless and sometimes comic pursuit in which the usual complications occur in an auction house, in a hotel lobby, in a field of corn where he is pursued by the famous crop duster, and of course across the heads of the four presidents. Hitchcock had effectively given Lehman a series of startling locales and images, some of which he had conceived previously, and asked him to provide a script that tied them together. He was not at all interested in logic or in the objections of what he called "our friends the plausibilists." So it became as much a circus ride as a chase. Hitchcock had also wished to include an episode that he had long considered. On a Detroit car assembly line a finished automobile comes off at the end, and a corpse promptly tumbles out of it. But this proved too difficult to accommodate. Other episodes did not.

Cary Grant was Hitchcock's first choice as Roger O. Thornhill, the advertising executive who is mistaken for a spy; having once been a trapeze artist, the actor could bring a life of performance to the role.

194 · ALFRED HITCHCOCK

In any case James Stewart was now deemed too old; the film world could be unforgiving. For his first lady Hitchcock chose, against the advice of the studio, Eva Marie Saint who was invited to lunch at Bellagio Road. After the encounter, she believed that "one of his greatest gifts as a director was that he made you feel you were the only perfect person for the role and this gave you incredible confidence." In the absence of Edith Head on other duties, Marie Saint was allowed to dress herself under Hitchcock's instructions. He said that "I acted just like a rich man keeping a woman." And that, in part, was what he was. They visited Bergdorf Goodman department store on Fifth Avenue and together chose a classic black suit, a black silk cocktail dress, and a charcoal brown jersey complementing an orange burlap outfit. All of these colours had meaning for Hitchcock, even if they seemed at the time simply to be charming accessories.

When filming started Marie Saint was asked to sit on her hands and look directly at Cary Grant. The most important instruction, however, was to lower her voice. Hitchcock developed a repertoire of signals to her so that she remembered. "It's still low to this day," she once said. Grant was of a less amenable nature, as he had proved in *To Catch a Thief*. "All I have to do," he told a reporter, "is to disregard everything he says. But I guess what's in his mind, and then I do just the opposite. Works every time, and I find it very pleasant." But the fact that he always consulted his script right up to the last moment before a scene was shot suggests that his bravado was in part assumed.

A few difficulties emerged during filming. The film crew was not allowed to use Mount Rushmore, a sacred site, but of course Hitchcock was not at all dismayed; he simply built replicas in the studio which were in any case much more convenient for sound and lighting. No film could be shot in the United Nations building, in which a vital episode takes place, and so Hitchcock built a model of its entrance hall on set. Lehman recalled that "Cary Grant and I had a few fierce battles in the back seat of a limousine on location at Bakersfield during the crop-duster sequence . . . He would sit there and go over some of his scenes with me. 'This is ridiculous,' he'd say. 'You think you are writing a Cary Grant picture? This is a David Niven picture.'" Grant was a professional, however, who had worked in front of the camera for twenty-six years; Hitchcock usually listened to his advice. For one scene in the film Grant told him that "if you'll get Bob to move the camera over a few inches you'll catch me going down the corridor through the hinge of the door." It worked.

In a break between scenes, Hitchcock once spotted Marie Saint drinking coffee out of a disposable cup. He was horrified. "You are wearing," he told her, "a $3,000 dress, and I don't want the extras to see you quaffing from a Styrofoam cup." He ordered his staff to serve her in a porcelain cup with porcelain saucer. He wanted to maintain the illusion for her, for the crew, and above all for himself.

Filming began at the end of August 1958, and was completed on 24 December. The final version of *North by Northwest*, running over two hours, was considered by the studio executives to be too long and they asked him to cut it. He refused. He knew that he had in his contract a cast-iron guarantee that no one else could touch it. His instincts were in any case right. When it was given its premiere at the Radio City Music Hall on 6 August 1959, it was greeted with acclaim. Hitchcock sent a telegram to Lehman with the words "Reception f-blank [fucking] enormous." The critic of *Time* magazine described it as "smoothly trowelled and thoroughly entertaining," and it became one of Hitchcock's most profitable productions. It was generally believed that, after the morbid experimentalism of *Vertigo*, he had returned to the entertaining and extravagant suspense thriller of which he was the master.

In some respects it does furnish a "typical" Hitchcock package in which he reprises some of his favourite moments from earlier films and provides a slick, vivacious and engaging rehearsal of his most popular devices. It comes close to pastiche or parody at certain points, but it is too clever, and too witty, to fall into that easy trap. Like his protagonist in the film, he is always one step ahead.

There may be a sense in which he is always making the same film. As in many previous works, such as *The 39 Steps* and *Stage Fright*, all of the protagonists are literally or figuratively playing a part. Roger O.

Thornhill, for example, enacts a different role for every person he meets; he is continually involved in reinvention that gives the film its slightly manic and unreal air. When asked what the "O" stands for he replies, "Nothing." (This may of course also have been a sly dig at David O. Selznick.) There is no such geographical direction as north by north-west and so the film is racing towards an impossible destination. It is full of chases, of movement, of angular escapes, but they are going nowhere fast. Like the "O" in Roger O. Thornhill it becomes an intriguing improvisation on the themes of emptiness and absence. That is why it seems to leave audiences, after the initial euphoria of a successful entertainment, sometimes uncomfortable and dissatisfied.

. . .

The public and the critics may have believed that Hitchcock was about to continue his Technicolor vistas of beautiful people in impossible situations, but they were wrong. He had quite another vision in mind. He always had a keen eye for cinematic fashion and the prospect of profit, and he had noticed the recent emergence of cheap black-and-white films that made a habit of terrifying the public, among them *The Fly, The Blob, Dementia, Curse of the Undead* and *The Brain That Wouldn't Die*. What if someone good, perhaps someone as good as Hitchcock, were to make one of these bargain-basement horrors?

He had been prompted into a new project after the failure of one in which he had already invested some time and much money. *No Bail for the Judge,* a novel by Henry Cecil, brought together some of Hitchcock's key preoccupations. A judge is falsely accused of murdering a prostitute, but his daughter tries to discover the real murderer by her own private form of sleuthing in which at one point she must pose as a lady of the night. Audrey Hepburn was chosen to fill the principal role. A script was prepared by Samuel Taylor. But it all came to nothing. It has been suggested that Hepburn was in the early stages of pregnancy. It has also been surmised that she did not care for her role as a prostitute. Or, alternatively, there may have been problems with the censor.

Yet the withdrawal of Hepburn seems to have been the reason for his abandonment of the project. "I spent more than $200,000 on *No Bail for the Judge*," he said, "and then decided against doing it. They said to me 'But you can't just let all that money go.' And I said, 'If we go on you will lose $3 million,' and then they asked no further questions." Hitchcock always liked his recollections to end on a decisive and formal note.

He was perhaps more deeply interested now in the prospect of a cheaply made horror film. One literary agent, H. N. Swanson, recalled that "Hitch never casually looked for 'something different.' He was relentless." Any play, any novel, any short story, any piece of news was scrutinised for suitable content. Soon enough he found a book ripe for picking. Robert Bloch's *Psycho* had stirred his interest on the basis of a favourable review. He read the novel during a weekend at Bellagio Road, and realised that it was his kind of story. "I think that the thing that appealed to me and made me decide to do the picture was the suddenness of the murder in the shower, coming, as it were, out of the blue. That was about all." In fact the shower scene plays no very prominent part in the novel. But Hitchcock could already *see* it.

The film would be something quite different. It would not be one of his "glossy Technicolor baubles," as he called them. It would have no stars, and no exotic locations. Much of the action would take place in a cheap motel. In an interview with the *New York Times* he went so far as to say that "some very ordinary people meet other ordinary people and horror and death ensue."

Paramount was not at all happy about the prospect. The story of a demented maniac who dresses up as his dead mother in order to kill his victims did not fill the studio managers with enthusiasm. The title was wrong, no reputable actor would be seen dead, or alive, in it. "Well," Hitchcock is supposed to have said, "I'll make do." He did more than that, however. He effectively subsidised the project, while Paramount arranged its distribution. His agent Lew Wasserman even arranged for the film to be shot in the studios of Universal Pictures where he could work without any interference at all. He waived his salary in exchange for sixty per cent of the ownership of the film, and in fact never worked for Paramount again after *Psycho*. Under the guidance of Wasserman, he remained with Universal for the rest of his career.

He said that "with *Psycho* I think I managed to do what I like best in the world: controlling the audience." But what audience was he hoping to control? At all costs he wanted it to be a large one. He was interested in making a great deal of money from this project. That may have been his primary consideration. He knew that the market for films such as *The Blob* and *The Fly* was largely comprised of impressionable and immature young people wanting to be scared and even to become hysterical. They were obsessed with sex, even if it was primarily of a voyeuristic nature. Hitchcock fully understood their demands. They were his target together, of course, with the television audience he had attracted with *Alfred Hitchcock Presents*.

He wanted to make it as cheaply and as quickly as possible, so he decided to follow the model of his television series, where nine minutes of completed film could be shot in a day. He would use his television cameramen because, as he said, "they know how to work very quickly. And I want to shoot quickly: I don't want to make an expensive movie because, in all honesty, I don't know if it's going to be successful or not." The television crew were used to filming in black and white, and Hitchcock saw no reason to change. Colour would in any case be a distraction. He also had an aesthetic objection. He told one interviewer that "in colour, the blood flowing down the bathtub drain would have been *repulsive*."

As so often in the process of filming, the details of the production were running ahead of the script. He had hired a young writer, Joseph Stefano, on a weekly basis; he was not yet sure of his potential. But they worked together well, and soon fell into a routine of meeting at eleven o'clock in the morning before having lunch and then talking for some of the afternoon. Hitchcock, as always, talked about anything and everything except the film itself, but by means of hint and indirection, suggestion and counter-suggestion, the treatment went forward. Stefano was then directed to write the first scene, on which Hitchcock's comment was that "Alma liked the scene very much." This was the highest compliment possible. From that time forward he and Stefano rehearsed the dialogue verbally before Stefano wrote it down. The whole process took approximately eleven weeks. Hitchcock often acted out certain episodes for Stefano's benefit. He was carefully rehearsing the scene where the murderer wraps the stabbed body of the woman in the shower curtain, when Alma suddenly walked in. Both men screamed in shock.

Stefano said later that "he was not interested in characters or motivation at all. That was the writer's job." Hitchcock was always more interested in the technical challenges ahead of him, and in the visual impact of the story on the screen. He was, for example, extremely interested in the details of the murder in the shower. Stefano added in another interview that "I don't think at any time he was making it he was knowingly or unconsciously reflecting any particular darkness from within. He simply had a script and he was shooting it."

The casting was not difficult. When Stefano was outlining the problems of characterising Norman Bates, the troubled proprietor of the Bates Motel, Hitchcock suddenly interrupted him. "We can get Tony Perkins." Tony Perkins was got. Perkins was already an accomplished actor, on both stage and screen, but his profile was higher than his price. When on another occasion Stefano told Hitchcock that the film was really about the victim in the shower, Marion Crane, rather than Bates, he leaned forward. "We can get a star." A star was got. Janet Leigh was already well known and, in 1948, she had been named as "number one glamor girl of Hollywood." "I'm not going to direct every nuance," he told her at an early meeting. "But if you don't come up with what I need I'll bring it out of you—and if you give too much, I'll tone it down. What you do has to fit into my framework and within my camera angle." His camera was the focal point, and she would move with it. When she visited him at Bellagio Road he showed her his miniature version of every set he would use, complete with miniature furniture and little dolls for the characters. Everything had been carefully designed in advance.

He still had Vera Miles under contract, ever since her casting (or miscasting) in The Wrong Man, and now he gave her the relatively subdued role of the victim's sister; the costume designer, Rita Riggs (Edith Head now being so busy that she was not always available), remarked that "Mr. Hitchcock made her look like a dowdy, old-maid schoolteacher . . . for most of the film we saw a lot of the back of her head." Vera Miles's future career lay principally in television.

The preparations for filming went ahead very quickly in conditions of the utmost secrecy. He did not want anyone to know what he was doing. The film was given no title but was known as "production 9401"; Hitchcock was photographed next to a camera slate marked "Wimpy," to disguise his intentions. Wimpy was in fact the surname of the second-unit cameraman, but it was used as the title of the film in all communications. Vera Miles recalled that, before they began work, cast and crew had to raise their right hands and promise not to reveal any details of the story. This of course soon became common gossip and, as was intended, raised even more interest in the secret project.

The famous Bates mansion, the prototype for the location of many later horror films, was built on the set. Many supposed progenitors have been suggested, including the cartoons of Charles Addams and a painting by Edward Hopper, but Hitchcock explained that in northern California "that type of house is very common. They're either called 'California Gothic' or, when they're particularly awful, 'California gingerbread.'" The building was authentic. Everything in the film had to bear the stamp of reality—the billboards, the motel, the neon signs, the car dealership, the highway, all the persiflage of "small town" or suburban America that would encourage the audience's deep involvement.

The filming was supposed to be completed within thirty-six days in a smooth and carefully calculated fashion; in fact it took forty-two days. He said that he wanted to film it quickly and cheaply, and so he did. Rita Riggs observed that "*Psycho* was a very reserved set, very formal. The male crew all wore shirts and ties." Hitchcock never went beyond three or four takes so that he could retain the immediacy of the first encounters. Every move and every camera shot were carefully measured. The actor stood on the mark. An actress who played a small part recalled that "he staged scenes like blueprints. He told me 'If you move one inch either way, you'll be out of my light.'" He might say, "Now on that line you look down, you wait a beat, and then you look back up at him, and hold."

He arrived each morning at eight thirty. At five thirty he would glance at his watch and turn to the assistant director, Hilton Green.

"Are we finished?"

"Yes, Mr. Hitchcock."

"I think that will be all for today."

He reserved most of his attention for Anthony Perkins and Janet Leigh who were, of course, the principal performers. They were all soon on very good terms, and Leigh in particular became the object of his practical jokes. He was experimenting with the mummified body of Mrs. Bates and would put one grotesque model or another into Leigh's dressing room while she was at lunch, and then measure the quality of her scream when she returned. He wanted to get it right. She wrote that he "relished scaring me." In retrospect, however, she wondered whether it was "an effort to keep me a bit on edge, thus more in Marion's jittery state of mind." She also said that "he couldn't have been more considerate, or thoughtful, or respectful, or agreeable, or companionable." He would also regale her with his fund of dirty stories just before she went on camera.

He was perfectly at ease with Perkins also, and the actor advanced in confidence enough to suggest changes to his script. It was not the kind of behaviour Hitchcock generally accepted, but with Perkins he seemed more generous. Perkins recalled taking some rewritten passages to Hitchcock's dressing room, where the director was studiously reading *The Times* of London.

"Are they any good?"

"I don't know. Shouldn't we be saving time if you would go over them now?"

"I'm sure they'll be very good."

"Don't you want to see them now?"

"Enchant me later."

The most important episode in the film is that of the stabbing in the shower, and indeed it has some claim to being the most memorable scene in the history of cinema. The music helps with the screaming intensity of the violins, but the most powerful effects were achieved by minute and adroit editing. This was a sequence in which speed of execution was not the point. Instead of nine minutes a day, it took seven days to shoot forty-five seconds of screen time. More than seventy camera set-ups were employed and seventy-eight pieces of film were somehow to be assembled; Hitchcock stated that in the laborious process of editing "we tightened it up and got the tempo going" and, as he put it later, "all the excitement of the killing was done by the cutting."

The irony of "cutting" would not have been lost on him. Each thrust was filmed at a different angle. The repeated stabbing of the body was reproduced on the soundtrack by a knife being driven into a casaba melon; chocolate syrup was used for the blood. It was believed on the set that the sequence would not pass the censor, but in fact nothing was actually seen on the screen that required erasure. The victim was never shown nude because nudity was forbidden. He always claimed that the knife was never seen entering the body, but in one short segment of film the knife is seen to enter what must have been a dummy torso. It was effectively hidden in the frenzy of cutting in post-production.

He may, however, have been trying to provoke the censor by showing a toilet bowl, down which Marion flushes some scraps of paper. It is believed that this was the first time a lavatory had been shown on screen, and suggests the ingenuity which Hitchcock employed in trying to shock his audience.

No one was quite sure of the film's potential. His personal assistant, Peggy Robertson, had said to one of its editors, Terry Williams, "Oh it's just a filler. It's not a biggy like *North by Northwest*." At some point Hitchcock despaired of it and pronounced it to be a failure. The composer Bernard Herrmann recalled him "nervously pacing back and forth, saying it was awful and that he was going to cut it down for his television show. He was crazy. He didn't know what he had." Yet in part persuaded by Alma, who had consistently encouraged the making of the film, he persevered. It was Bernard Herrmann who suggested a score entirely for strings. As soon as Hitchcock heard what he called the "screaming violins" he was convinced. He doubled Herrmann's fee, and was reported as having said that "thirty-three per cent of the effect of *Psycho* was due to the music."

Yet the film also conveys the intimacy and unmediated directness of television. Hitchcock insisted upon using a 50 mm lens to convey the effect of ordinary human vision. The supervisor of the script, Marshall Schlom, explained that "he wanted the camera *being* the audience all the time, to see . . . as if with their own eyes." He also required mirrors to be placed everywhere, in order to convey the ambiguities of appearance and reality.

The film is remarkably faithful to the short novel from which it is adapted; the main outlines of the plot are in Robert Bloch's narrative of Norman Bates and his mother, but of course Hitchcock changed the killing out of all recognition. In the book it takes less than half a page, and the murderer beheads his victim. The shower scene was against all film protocol and all cinematic tradition; nor was it considered wise to dispose of the star actress before the picture was half over. The scene leaves the audience in doubt and suspense, as the comfort zone of watching a "movie" is suddenly taken away. They can look at the screen only with a mounting trepidation.

The principal character of *Psycho*, however, is undoubtedly Norman Bates as played by Anthony Perkins. Bates is a notable Hitchcock type, the slightly fey and neurasthenic male, excitable and sexually ambiguous, who is particularly troubled by women. Hitchcock's first exploration of this character had been with Ivor Novello in *The Lodger*, thirty-three years before, and he had continued it in successive films. Perkins played the role so brilliantly that he never quite managed to shake it off; he appeared in three separate remakes of the film over the next thirty years.

Psycho is in certain respects cold, even brutal. Hitchcock was once asked "What, then, is the deep logic of your films?" and he replied that it was "to make the spectator suffer." Yet in an interview on BBC television, four years after the film was released, he commented that "I once made a movie, rather tongue-in-cheek, called *Psycho*" and added that "the content was, I felt, rather amusing and it was a big joke. I was horrified to find that some people took it seriously." He went on to say that "towards the end I had no violence at all, but by this time the audience was screaming in agony thank goodness." Anthony Perkins confirmed that it had been conceived as a comedy, or at least a black comedy; but it is perhaps one in which the joke is on the audience.

It has no hidden meaning at all, apart from a generalised sense of the horror of life. It has no purpose other than to shock or scare an audience. That is why the manipulation of the public began some time before the release of the film itself. In the trailer, it becomes clear that Hitchcock is complicit in sharing a joke with the audience. "And in this house the most dire, horrible events took place. I think we can go inside, because the place is up for sale. Although I don't know who is going to buy it now . . . You should have seen the blood. The whole, the whole place was, well, it's too horrible to describe."

He borrowed a technique from the publicity for *Diabolique*, by refusing entrance to the cinema after the film had begun; he obliged the cinema managers to sign a contract to that effect. There may very well have been aesthetic grounds for this decision but its promotional worth was greater still. The decision generated enormous publicity. A pamphlet was written by Hitchcock or by the studio, "The Care and Handling of *Psycho*," suggesting to managers the most appropriate way of publicising and screening the film. Large cut-outs of Hitchcock's rotund figure were placed in the foyers, bearing the sign "Please Don't Spoil The Ending—It's The Only One We Have." Taped recordings of Hitchcock's voice were played to the spectators as they waited in line. "This queuing up is good for you. It will make you appreciate the seats inside. It will also make you appreciate *Psycho*." The whole purpose was to elicit intolerable anticipation. Something terrible was about to be shown. This in turn induced a certain camaraderie in the crowds who were instructed to line up and purchase their tickets well before screening time. This was a novelty for the American public who were accustomed to turn up at any time. But the new discipline helped to

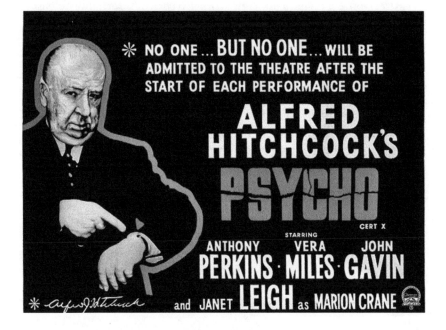

A promotional poster for *Psycho*, 1960. Taped recordings
of Hitchcock's voice were also played to queuing spectators as they waited,
to increase their anticipation for the film.

instil a common fear and susceptibility. The English director Thorold Dickinson once remarked that "no film ever frightens an audience. The audience frightens itself."

After some previews in New York *Psycho* was formally released in the late summer of 1960. After the ending, in which a glimmering skull is superimposed upon Perkins's smiling face, Hitchcock ordered that the lights in the cinema be kept low for another thirty seconds. The entire film created an immediate sensation for which Hitchcock and the rest of the team were not prepared. He told Perkins that "I've always been able to predict the audience's reaction. Here I haven't been able to."

The effect of the shower scene, in particular, reveals the extent to which Hitchcock had pierced the sensibilities of his audience. One teacher of film, Linda Williams, noted that "from the very first screenings, audience reaction, in the form of gasps, screams, yells, even running up and down the aisles, was unprecedented." The film-maker Peter Bogdanovich recalled that "*Psycho* is the moment in movies when for the first time movies weren't safe. I remember coming out of the screening and feeling I'd been raped or something, or mugged, it was absolutely terrifying, no one recovered from that shower scene, you couldn't hear the soundtrack because the audience was screaming through the entire forty-five seconds. I never heard those violins." Scriptwriter Joseph Stefano recalled that "I saw people grab each other, howling, screaming, reacting like six-year-olds at a Saturday matinee." The cinema had suffered a sea change. *Psycho* could not help but be a vast popular success, surmounting even Hitchcock's previous work. The critics, who had not been given a special screening, could not make up their minds about it. But the public had. Hitchcock told Truffaut that the film "caused audiences all over the world to react and become emotional."

It was also the best investment Hitchcock ever made. For an initial outlay of $800,000 he reaped millions. His initial cheque, for the first quarter's returns only, amounted to $2.5 million; he eventually earned approximately $15 million from the world release. He was now the richest, as well as the most famous, film director in the world. How had he done it? Stefano remembered meeting Hitchcock at a lunch just after the release of *Psycho*. "I walked in, seeing Hitch for the first time since all the rumpus and commotion started. He gave me this completely baffled look and just shrugged his shoulders."

10

BIRDS AND BEASTS

The morning after *Psycho*'s premiere Hitchcock's agent and head of studio, Lew Wasserman, sent him a telegram: "What will you do for an encore?" Hitchcock did not know. He was normally already busy on a new project or script but, as his script supervisor Marshall Schlom put it, "*Psycho* stopped everything else cold." Hitchcock needed time to digest the enormous reaction he had created and to assess his future. He was in a sense unsettled. His cheapest and perhaps quickest film had suddenly become his most successful. No one recalled *Vertigo* or *Shadow of a Doubt* or *Rebecca*. "Here's this bloody piece of crap," he told one of his cameramen, Leonard South, "and the money doesn't stop coming in." Suddenly he was being hailed as the great director for a work which he knew to be a modest exercise in Gothic. Could he trust his filmic judgement any more? (His unease was deepened the following spring by the fact that, at the Oscars ceremony, *Psycho* did not receive any awards. He could not interpret it as anything but a snub, a deliberate rejection of himself and his work by the film community.)

He decided to take a long vacation with Alma, which meant essentially that he spent many weekends on the estate on the slope of the Santa Cruz mountains. He planned a short promotional tour of *Psycho* in New York and other American cities before embarking on a world tour, later in 1960, that would include the major European cities as well as Sydney, Honolulu, Tokyo, Singapore and Hong Kong. It would be gruelling, but the health of both Hitchcocks seemed to have recovered from the ordeals of previous years.

The world tour confirmed that he had already become something of a legend, or a myth, to the general public. As his fame grew he appeared to become more remote, more reserved, more impassive; he now resembled the giant visage of Rameses the Great that he had used many years before in *Blackmail*. He had become what he aspired to be, imperturbable and indifferent; he was now enveloped in, and perhaps almost overwhelmed by, the persona that he had assiduously created on the screen and in interviews. It was a mask, of course, for a most anxious and fearful person; but it worked. He enjoyed being recognised in the street but he seemed also to be untouchable. On the set he spoke only to a few; he rarely attended parties or dinners, except those which he himself gave; most were afraid to approach him. Ernest Lehman suggested that as a "protective wall" "he projected the image of a snobbish, elitist, judgmental, critical, unpleasant, aloof, superior being—none of which he truly felt about himself."

Before he left for his grand tour, he had read accounts of a flock of 1,000 birds that plummeted down the chimney of a house in La Jolla, California, and wreaked havoc. They also attacked and injured the woman who lived there. It is likely that he was reminded of a short story by Daphne du Maurier, "The Birds," for which he had already purchased the film option. It was a story about sustained attacks by a variety of birds on an English farmer and his family, with an inconclusive but ominous ending. Yet it was, at this stage, nothing more than a reminder.

The tour itself was a great success, especially in Paris where he was celebrated and honoured. Joseph Stefano said later that "he loved the attention and the fuss and the fame, and if he didn't understand it, he didn't feel compelled to. It was good for business and good for his ego." Robert Boyle concurred by remarking that "Hitchcock appreciated other people's appreciation of him, and he did nothing to correct any impression they might have of his genius." When they compared him to Eisenstein, or Murnau, or Pudovkin, he knew as much as they did about the great directors; he had followed them avidly in his youth, as his early work in Germany testified.

On his return he had a number of possible projects on his desk. They included a film version of a French play about a missing wife suddenly returned, *Piège pour un Homme Seul* (*Trap for a Man Alone*), that had been staged in 1960. He was also interested in the cinematic possibilities of a novel, *Village of Stars*, about the complications of trying to jettison an atomic bomb. Daphne du Maurier's "The Birds" was still on his mind after the mysterious event in La Jolla, and he may already have been dreaming of a play by J. M. Barrie that he had seen in his youth. *Mary Rose* had been staged in London, in 1920, and is concerned with the mysterious disappearance and return of a young girl on a Scottish island. Hitchcock seems to have been entranced by it and soon took active steps to film it.

Yet now local events affected him more immediately. In August 1961, there was a sudden invasion of birds in the town of Santa Cruz, where he had once filmed *Shadow of a Doubt* and near his second home. Thousands of them seem to have been driven inland by fog, and the *Santa Cruz Sentinel* carried the main headline "Seabird Invasion Hits Coastal Homes" with a smaller headline "Thousands of Birds Floundering in Streets." It was reported that "sooty shearwaters, fresh from a feast of anchovies" had crashed into cars and houses, creating havoc among the local population.

He had found his story. After the intense and almost claustrophobic setting of *Psycho*, the new film would be on a broader and airier scale. He telephoned Joseph Stefano, who had written *Psycho* with such panache, but Stefano was not particularly interested in a story about birds.

Hitchcock turned instead to Evan Hunter, whom he had briefly met on the set of his television series. Hunter had an impressive list of previous works, among them *Blackboard Jungle*, and under the pseudonym Ed McBain he had also begun to write a significant series of crime fictions. Hitchcock told associates that he had hired him to earn some "artistic respectability." This may have been his response to the hysterical reception of *Psycho*. Hunter was a novelist, after all, and not a Hollywood scriptwriter.

In the autumn he happened to be watching the *Today* show on NBC television, when a commercial break arrested his attention. In an advertisement for a diet drink a pretty blonde turned her head to acknowledge a wolf-whistle. That was all. But Hitchcock was entranced. He believed that he had found a new female star. He arranged for her to be escorted to the studios at Universal where she showed the managers some examples of her work. On the following day she was told by her agent that "Alfred Hitchcock wants to sign you to a contract." It was for seven years at $500 a week. Hitchcock had neither interviewed her, nor seen her in anything other than the advertisement, but he was sure that she was the one.

When Tippi Hedren and Hitchcock eventually met for lunch, he never mentioned *The Birds*. He talked abut everything and nothing, but all the time he was watching her closely, observing her expressions and her gestures, her manners and her responses. He also decided that he liked the way she walked. Then he tested her in a number of set camera pieces, including scenes from *Rebecca* and *Notorious*. At one of the screen tests he whispered to her, "Remind me to tell you a story about doughnuts and their manufacture." The Hitchcocks then invited her to dinner at Chasen's, the restaurant in Hollywood where they dined every Thursday evening; as they sat at the table Hitchcock presented her with a decorative pin displaying three golden birds in flight. She knew then that she had been given the part.

She said later that "to put a totally unknown into a major motion picture was fairly crazy. That's taking a very, very big chance, and all the executives at Universal, people close to him, were saying 'Hitch, what are you thinking? Every actress in Hollywood would want to do this movie.'" She added that "I was never told exactly why. I think he becomes obsessed with certain people."

Hitchcock had told Evan Hunter, when they started to work

together, that he was about to begin a golden period in his career. The director may also have been revived by the prospect of a new start with another film studio, since his agent had arranged for his return to Universal after his brief but profitable dalliance with Paramount. He then proceeded to sell his own company and the rights for his television series to Universal, receiving in return enough Universal stock to make him its third largest shareholder. If he thought he could now control affairs in his own way, he was mistaken; but the contract, for five more films, gave him the safety and security he craved. His favoured unit of assistants, cameramen and technicians had in effect their own private space, a compound that included offices, an editing suite, conference rooms, a small cinema for screenings and a private dining room with kitchen. In February 1962 he was installed in his new kingdom.

He had already begun his script sessions with Evan Hunter. Hunter recalls that he would come to his office every morning and find Hitchcock sitting in a black leather wingback chair "clad in a dark blue suit with dark blue socks, and white shirt and black tie, his hands clasped over his wide middle, his feet scarcely touching the floor." His first request was always to "tell me the story so far." He would then follow it by questions about the next moves. "Why does she do that?" "Why does she go up the staircase?" "Why did she get out of the car?" So, as Hunter said, "he edited the script before any of it was actually written, commenting on character development and comic effect in these early scenes of the film."

These early, vaguely comic scenes, were important to set up the encounter between Tippi Hedren, as a rich Californian socialite, and the leading man, Rod Taylor, in the part of a conventional lawyer. Their relationship would establish the emotional rhythm of the film which is soon to be violently disturbed. As soon as the maleficent birds arrived, the plot would simply pile mayhem upon mayhem in a way that would thoroughly scare the audience. He had used the du Maurier story as an inspiration rather than as a source book. He told Hunter that he never wished to work in England again and that he did not want to shoot a film about a farmer and his family. He did, however, decide to keep its minatory ending.

Hitchcock and Hunter enjoyed a very friendly relationship that extended to their families. Hitchcock would call Hunter's wife to engage in amicable chit-chat, but never once asked to speak to Hunter. When they did meet, over a meal, he never asked the writer how he was proceeding with the script. Hunter also recalled that "he was a very possessive man. He virtually monopolised me and my family while we were in Los Angeles, even though the monopoly was one of kindness. He hosted us at dinners, took us to the races, made a Halloween visit to our children." He may not have been possessive, however; he may just have been lonely.

Evan Hunter recalled one moment of crisis, when a natural disaster threatened the Hitchcocks. In November 1961 a massive bush fire swept through the hills behind their house on Bellagio Road. Some 500 houses had already been gutted, and the Hitchcocks did not know what to do. "Anita," he told Hunter's wife on the telephone, "you don't understand. *Everything's* on fire." Should they take their possessions to the wine cellar or throw them in the pool? Then the wind changed direction and the Hitchcock house was spared. But it had been a close-run thing. According to his daughter he spent the day hosing down the roof and the adjacent land before retiring to bed. Other reports suggest that the Hitchcocks were evacuated to a local hotel. Whatever the circumstances, for a man of his fearful temperament, it would have been an ordeal of terror. But it was not unlike the disaster that he was imagining for the inhabitants of Bodega Bay in *The Birds*.

His cast was assembled without any difficulty; everyone wanted to work with Hitchcock. But there was to be no Cary Grant or Grace Kelly. "Evan," he told Hunter early in the proceedings, "there will be no stars in this picture. I'm the star—the birds are the stars—and you're the star." The last phrase was no doubt added to save the writer's feelings. The setting of the story was moved from the Cornish coast of du Maurier's narrative to the coast of northern California. The climate there was as close to that of England as Hitchcock cared to preserve. It was all low land and sky, the immense sky which would become the proscenium for the savage birds. "I chose Bodega Bay," Hitchcock said, "because I wanted an isolated group of people who lived near an articulate community." There was indeed a small community at Bodega Bay but it was transformed by an exercise in Hitchcock's imaginative geography. The look of the inhabitants was to be genuine, and they were all photographed for the benefit of the costume department, but the technicians and carpenters built a new estate complete with pier which looked better than any "real" setting. The downtown neighbourhood was also largely fictional.

The usual series of production meetings and script conferences ensued but, unusually, Tippi Hedren was invited to attend all of them. That was not necessarily a cause of complaint. She said later that "he gave me the best education an actor could have. With any other director it would have taken fifteen years, but he had me involved in every part of the film—script completion, wardrobe design, special-effects work, dubbing. It was his film from start to finish and he wanted me to learn how he put it together."

The director was clearly paying particular attention to his principal actress. He superintended every detail of her dress, hair and make-up. This was not in itself entirely unusual, since he had imposed this regimen on other actresses, but it was soon being whispered that he had asked members of the crew to follow her and report her movements. He took samples of her handwriting, and sent them to a graphologist for analysis. He presented her with flowers and wine. On one evening they were being driven to meet their colleagues; as soon as Hitchcock saw them, and knew that they could see him, he enveloped her in a passionate embrace. It was a piece of play-acting, but at some level he wished them to believe that they were having an affair. It was a childish form of wish-fulfilment.

Yet his obsession also affected his behaviour. Hedren recalled that "he started telling me what I should wear on my own time, what I should be eating, and what friends I should be seeing." She has also said that "he was developing this obsession for me, and I began to feel very uncomfortable because I had no control over him." Rod Taylor, her co-star, recalled that "he wouldn't let me or anyone else ride in the studio cars with her . . . He was putting a wall around her so that all her time would be spent only with him." Her own daughter, Melanie, stated that "Hitch was taking her away from me, and suddenly I wasn't even allowed to visit my mom at the studio." Alma had no doubt witnessed similar behaviour over the years. "Oh Tippi dear," Hedren recalled her as saying, "I am so sorry you have to go through all this—I am *so* sorry." It seems that there was nothing to be done.

Hitchcock himself once said that "romantic obsession has always interested me. Obsessions of all kinds are interesting but, for me, romantic obsession is the most interesting." Hedren was not the only object of his attentions; at the same time as he was supervising the world of Tippi Hedren, he found another young actress. Claire Griswold had played a small part in one of his television dramas, and he invited her to lunch where he announced that "Miss Griswold, you and I are going to do business." As soon as he had signed an exclusive seven-year contract with her, the same process of control began to emerge. He rehearsed her for a scene from *To Catch a Thief*, and it became clear to her that she was supposed to become a replica of Grace Kelly. He dressed and directed her as if she were a mannequin. She felt uncomfortable in this new role, naturally enough, and over the next few months she began to extricate herself from the situation. His interest waned, and she quietly returned to her old life. It is an indication, if nothing else, of his eagerness and readiness to adopt (or adapt) young women for his own directorial purposes.

The filming of *The Birds*, which began in the early spring of 1962 and continued into the summer, was wearying and difficult. There were, first of all, the birds themselves. They had to be trained, and protected. Some of them were coached to land on the necks of children, a macabre device but one rendered innocent by the fact that on screen the actual biting is done by glove puppets. A representative for the protection of birds was at hand and would say, according to Hitchcock,

"That's enough now, Mr. Hitchcock, I think the birds are getting tired." There were some prominent artistes. One trained gull was named Charlie, and a raven was known as Buddy.

Some of the birds were manufactured of papier mâché, and were tied to the characters with wires. Much of the real birds' behaviour, however, was entirely natural. A camera crew spent three days filming seagulls feeding in a rubbish dump. For another sequence a cameraman stood on a cliff off Santa Cruz Island as the birds dived to catch fish thrown towards them. Meat was sometimes strategically positioned on top of the camera. These shots were then edited and processed to take their part in the unfolding narrative. Other birds were painted on to the film, frame by frame. Hitchcock himself had a terror of birds and did not approach them during the filming. This may account for the atmosphere of panic that announces their arrival.

The human players were also something of a challenge. Hitchcock said of Tippi Hedren, in an interview for the London *Sunday Express*, that "you know she had never acted before . . . she had nothing to unlearn . . . I controlled every movement on her face." He watched her incessantly on the set. A journalist visiting the production noted that "he was directing Tippi like a robot." Or, as Hedren herself said, directing her "down to the movement of an eye and every turn of my head." The pressure on her was intense and unremitting. She said that "if he thought I wasn't doing exactly what he wanted, every day during preparation for *The Birds*, he would sulk or pout or seem hurt or disappointed."

He had planned every scene and every sequence of narrative in a series of graphics pinned to the walls of his office. He had to create a rhythm in his head. But then something happened. His mood was strangely altered and in the early stages of filming Robert Boyle, the production designer, remembered the cameraman, Robert Burks, saying, "Oh boy, I don't know what's happening this time, but this isn't Hitchcock." The director then confessed at the end of the day that "I got lost today—in my shooting." He admitted that he had a sudden desire to improvise. This was in part to give more depth to Tippi Hedren's performance.

Tippi Hedren under attack in *The Birds*, 1963.

Courtesy of Universal Studios/Getty Images

He explained in an interview with Truffaut that "I was quite tense and this is unusual for me because as a rule I have a lot of fun during the shooting. When I went home to my wife at night, I was still tense and upset." He added that "something happened that was altogether new in my experience. I began to study the scenario as we went along, and I saw that there were weaknesses in it. This emotional siege I went through served to bring out an additional creative sense in me." In particular he seems to have remembered the effect on him of the Blitz when he was staying at Claridge's in London. He was renewing his own anxieties to cope with a film that was all about anxiety. He invented new scenes concerning the attacks of the birds, elevating the panic of the participants, and added a different ending in which the imperilled family simply drives away as the birds look on.

The difficulties for Hedren were compounded by the filming of the most savage sequences of the film when, in an attic room, the throng of birds attacks her. She had been told that the birds were only mechanical. When she arrived on set, however, she realised that the bird handlers had arrived with protective gloves and boxes of furious birds. She was asked to stand in a corner of the set while the handlers threw pigeons, gulls and crows towards her, according to Rod Taylor, "one after another, again and again." It had, in appearance at least, all the marks of a ritual stoning. As the filming continued she became covered in bird excrement.

She said later that "the week was perfectly dreadful, really the worst week of my life." For one sequence on the fifth day of filming the birds were tied to her with elastic bands and so "they would bound and perch all over me." On that occasion one of the birds hopped on to her face and scratched her eyelid, at which point "I just sat and cried." The studio doctors ordained a few days' rest.

Hitchcock had remained out of sight for most of the proceedings, only appearing when the cameras were about to roll; as always, he preferred to avoid threatening or unsettling scenes. It is not at all clear, however, that he was engaged in an illicit act of hostility towards the actress. The attic scene would be the most powerful sequence in the film, and he wanted to ensure that it looked authentic. It also became clear to Hedren why he had wanted an unknown for the part; a more experienced performer would have balked at his demands. But she recovered and came back on set to film her awakening from the shock of the attack.

It had been decided from the beginning that no explanation would be offered or given for the attacks by the birds; it would be an entirely mysterious event without a cause. "You know," he told Albert Whitlock, the matte artist who created so many of the birds and so much of the landscape, "we're not making a science-fiction movie." Whitlock then asked him what it was they were making. The director was not sure. The new ending did not satisfy those members of the audience who wanted finality, or reassurance, or explanation. The film was as mysterious as the sudden appearance of the birds themselves.

He had decided to hold the European premiere at the Cannes Film Festival, a sure sign of the artistic ambitions he harboured for the film. He also arranged for a preview to be screened at the Museum of Modern Art, as a precursor to a season of Hitchcock films. *The Birds* was not precisely an art-house picture but it flaunted the conventions of the American cinema with its unsteady atmosphere and its refusal to close on a harmonious note. He deployed bird sounds, created both naturally and electronically, as the music; birds are always somewhere in the background, cawing and murmuring, yet with sudden silences to destabilise the audience.

In his publicity tour in America he struck a more jocular tone. He described *The Birds* to a reporter for the *San Francisco Chronicle* as "a fowl epic if ever I made one. Biggest cast of extras I ever had, too. Over 28,000 birds. Of course they all worked for chicken feed except for the buzzards which had agents."

"The ads quote you as calling it 'the most terrifying picture I have ever made.' Is that true?"

"Oh, indubitably. I financed it myself, and I'm terrified at the thought of losing all my money."

He did not lose all of his money, but he did not make a great deal.

The Birds did not come close to matching *Psycho* in terms of revenue. The audiences were not impressed by the apparently random nature of the bird attacks and therefore of the waywardness of the narrative itself. They were also surprised and annoyed by the inconclusive ending. Evan Hunter recalled that the audience at the special preview in the Museum of Modern Art "was, to say the very least, somewhat glacially polite in its reception. A stunned silence greeted the final complicated mosaic." When Hunter attended a public cinema he noted that "people actually turned to each other and mumbled, 'Is it over? Is that it? Huh?'" In trying to contrive an unusually mysterious ending Hitchcock had fatally misjudged the reactions of an ordinary audience.

The reviews were therefore mixed, with a tendency to criticise Tippi Hedren's performance as too controlled and unsympathetic. That is in fact a comment on Hitchcock's close direction rather than on any deficiencies in Hedren herself. He was particularly incensed by the attacks of what he called "the highbrows" who criticised the film as "corny." Once again he seems to have fallen into the gap between the artistic and the popular. Hitchcock said later that "Alma had never liked the original idea of doing *The Birds*. She didn't think there was enough story there. Well, she was right. Not enough story, too many birds."

The film has gained recognition in later years. It was not the first "disaster film" or "catastrophe film," as has sometimes been suggested, but it did set out the paradigm for every successful one that followed. All sorts of suppositions have been imposed upon it: the birds represent female aggression, the male will to power, or a universal attack upon the "meaning system." In one of his few remarks on *The Birds*, he said, non-committally, "if you like you can make it the theme of too much complacency in the world: that people are unaware that catastrophe surrounds us all." It is clear that he did not care very much what the film meant, as long as it had the required effect upon the audience.

Of Melanie, played by Tippi Hedren, he stated that "the girl is a nothing. She just represents complacency and smug satisfaction, in order to contrast that with the ultimate happening." That "ultimate happening" was the key. Every scene takes place in an atmosphere of mounting tension, so that any and every action becomes surrounded by a multitude of sinister possibilities. What was comfortingly solid at the beginning of the film is seen to conceal a world of threat. The tension is never reduced for a moment. This was his great gift. He maintained it on the set itself. He hired a timpanist to play an amplified drum close to the actors, so that they would instincively play to a relentless and menacing rhythm that might have been the beat of doom. He deployed red colours—of clothes, of hair, of umbrellas, of furniture, of balloons, and of interiors—to communicate danger and violence to the audience.

When the seagulls attack Melanie with diabolical cries, their savage shrieks might have been an echo of Hitchcock's earlier films where he equates the screaming of birds with violent death. The murderer in *Murder!* wore a bird costume in his circus performance; the stuffed birds in Norman Bates's office imply a sense of death and corruption in *Psycho*; a chirping bird in a cage greets Alice White after she has returned from a scene of murder in *Blackmail*; the caged canaries in *Sabotage* are the camouflage for a deadly bomb; screeching gulls fly over the corpse in *Young and Innocent*. Many other examples could be adduced for this primal image, not all of them susceptible to interpretation, but we may adduce William Blake's short poem from his "Auguries of Innocence":

> A *robin redbreast in a cage*
> *Puts all heaven in a rage.*

. . .

In a further bid to acquire artistic respectability he had agreed to a series of long interviews with François Truffaut, while the final editing of *The Birds* was taking place in the summer of 1962. He was not thinking of any English honours. In this year he turned down the award of CBE "because, in his view, it did not do justice to his contribution to British culture." Despite his statements to the contrary, he did have a full sense of his own worth.

When Truffaut wrote his letter of proposal, which entailed examining each of Hitchcock's films, concentrating upon "the birth of each film, the development and construction of the scenario, problems of direction in respect to each picture, the situation of a film within the body of your work," Hitchcock was sincerely touched. He replied that "your letter made me cry and how grateful I am to receive such a tribute from you." Truffaut was one of the leaders of what became known as the "nouvelle vague" and had already directed The 400 Blows and Jules and Jim. In private Hitchcock described the contemporary group as the "nouvelle vagrants," but he was not about to let his feelings show. Such homage from a younger director was richer than incense; it implied approval from those at the front edge of cinematic change. His tears were genuine; the sign of an emotional and fearful man, they represented the fulfilment of a long-awaited ambition.

At first he wanted to control the content of the interviews. In an unsent letter he insisted on seeing the transcript in advance and on having the power to alter any passage to which he took objection, with the terms of default set at half a million dollars. He did not send the letter, no doubt realising that it would be construed as a deep insult to a fellow professional.

The interviews were based on the relatively new concept of the director as "auteur," the sole begetter of the film just as an artist was the sole begetter of a painting. This was far from the case in Hitchcock's films where he required the active collaboration of many people, notably the screenwriter and the cameraman, but it suited his purpose to minimise their contributions. He described John Michael Hayes, who had crafted Rear Window, To Catch a Thief, The Trouble with Harry and The Man Who Knew Too Much, as "a radio writer" who simply "wrote the dialogue." It was a wilful twisting of the truth.

Through the middle of August Hitchcock would pick up Truffaut and his interpreter from the Beverly Hills Hotel at eight in the morning, take them by limousine to his offices in Universal Studios, and talk until six in the evening with an interval for lunch of steak and fried potatoes. Truffaut reports that at first Hitchcock adopted his familiar jovial and anecdotal persona and that "it was only on the third day he became more sober and thoughtful in spelling out the ups and downs of his career." This was not like any other interview Hitchcock had given. This was to be his testament.

Truffaut asked questions of a man whom he considered to be a "very fearful person" as well as a "deeply vulnerable, sensitive, and emotional man who feels with particular intensity the sensations he communicates to his audience." Small insights into his personality emerged in the interview but largely of a clipped nature. "Precisely." "Exactly." "That's right." "Right." Hitchcock preferred anecdotes and technical detail to any disquisitions on theme or meaning. He did not wish to enquire too deeply into his motives, or the reasons for any particular subject or film. He was only interested in content or plot in so far as they prompted his visual imagination. He had said, on more than one occasion, "I don't give a damn what the film is about." It had only to be seen, and not interpreted. No philosophical theory or analysis interested him in the least. Or, to put it another way, any film had different and multiple possibilities of meaning, which is perhaps the condition of life itself.

Yet he did plead guilty to certain aesthetic preferences. He explained to Truffaut that *Rear Window* was "the purest expression of a cinematic idea" that allowed him to create "a purely cinematic film." It was a film of gesture, of an image that only became significant when placed beside another image. He once said that an artist, painting a still life of a bowl of apples, would not care whether the apples were sweet or sour. That was a level of reality that did not interest him. He was preoccupied with order, and pattern, and symmetry. The spirals and staircases, the vertical bars and window blinds, all testify to that.

A film was more akin to a dream sequence, "daydreams probably," he told Truffaut, that were more powerful than reason or logic. He had previously said in an article for *The Stage* in 1936 that "I visualise my story in my mind as a series of smudges moving over a variety of backgrounds." He saw vague patterns, as if through a haze. Some poets have described the process of inspiration in a similar fashion. Music and colour affected him profoundly. Music was for him a medium "to express the unspoken," as he said on another occasion, and was often a simulacrum of the dream state he wished to invest in his work. Colour was also subtle and subliminal. He would orchestrate the colour of cars and advertisements in a street, of lampshades and flowers in a room. Cool colours such as pale blue and lime green were used to convey rationality and objectivity; hot colours such as yellow and red were designed to suggest emotional turbulence and danger. In *Dial M for Murder* Grace Kelly's outfits move from red to orange and then finally from grey to black; every passage of her emotional journey is dramatised by colour. For the heroine of *North by Northwest*, he imagined "a heavy black silk cocktail dress subtly imprinted with wine-red flowers in the scenes where she deceives Cary Grant."

He has often been described as an artist of the surface, and his films as the quintessential art of the surface, but in truth the surface covers the whole of life. He is close, perhaps, to the judgement of Lord Henry Wotton in Oscar Wilde's *The Picture of Dorian Gray* that "it is only shallow people who do not judge by appearances." Yet Hitchcock is aware all the time that "it's only a movie," that it is a game and an artifice. He delights in cinematic effects that are demonstrably artificial, or deliberately unreal.

But he is not an aesthete in the late nineteenth-century style. He had too strong a sense of his audience. "I don't make pictures to please me," he told an interviewer in 1972, "I make them to please audiences." "It all comes to this," he once said. "How do you apply glue to the seats of the audience?" The glue comes from fear, or anxiety, or terror, or suspense, or curiosity. Hitchcock knew how to elicit all of these. He was always asking his scriptwriters to keep the focus on the audience response. What do you want the audience to feel at this point? What do you want the audience to be thinking? How can you screw the audience to a pitch of unbearable tension? He also appreciated the fact that his audiences in Tokyo or in New York, in Paris or in London, were responding with the same emotions. His was a global medium quite unprecedented in scale and effect.

He was above all a pragmatist. If he had been asked to choose between art and commerce he might have hesitated, but only for a moment. "Do you think of yourself as an artist?" Peter Bogdanovich once asked; "No, not particularly." And to another interviewer he remarked, "I really hate the word artistic." He disliked all the associations of "the studio" in film-making and would have preferred it to have been known as "the factory." The studio system in which he laboured was imagined by him as a kind of prison. "We're inside on a stage," he once said, "the big doors are closed, and we're down in a coal mine." Truffaut recalled that in his interviews with Hitchcock the director more than once used the expression "when the heavy doors of the studio close behind me."

.   .   .

He kept on his treadmill. Characteristically he had been thinking of his next film long before he finished work on the last. He had remained interested in a novel, Winston Graham's *Marnie*, that had been sent to him before its publication in January 1961. It told the story of a female kleptomaniac, Margaret "Marnie" Edgar, who is forced into marriage with one of her rich victims, Mark Rutland, who has discovered her proclivities and blackmails her. It turns out that she has been traumatised by a childhood episode in which she had killed one of her prostitute mother's clients with a poker. From that time forward she had an aversion to men and to red, the colour of blood. It is psychological hokum, but it had possibilities for the screen.

The central idea, with all the opportunities it afforded for the portrait of an ambiguous lady, was strong enough for him to purchase the film rights immediately and even to take part in the advertising around the novel's publication in the United States. He is stated as saying that "the book is about one of the most unusual heroines I've ever encountered." He was still contemplating the return of Grace Kelly to the screen. He sent her a copy of the book, and awaited favourable news.

She had seemed at first excited and ready to recommence her career in film but suddenly, in the spring of 1962, she decided to turn down the role. It came as a severe blow to Hitchcock, who had put all his faith in her return to the screen under his auspices, and of course he also took it as a personal affront; his anger was compounded by disappointment. Kelly cited family reasons and the difficulty of travelling to Hollywood now that she lived in Monaco, but Hitchcock suspected that the cause was financial. She had hoped to make a great deal of money out of the film, which could then be used to assist Monaco, which was under financial pressure from France, but at a late stage another source of revenue was found. She was never going to do it for the sake of Hitchcock alone. Grace Kelly was not free to go, and certainly not to play the role of an obsessive thief. In a letter to her at the end of June 1962, he wrote that "after all, it was only a movie." But he was hurt.

Evan Hunter recalled that throughout 1962, while filming *The Birds*, "we discussed *Marnie* on the sixty-mile ride to and from location. We discussed *Marnie* during lulls in the shooting and during lunch and during dinner every night. We discussed *Marnie* interminably." At the beginning of 1963, just as *The Birds* was entering its final phase of post-production, Hitchcock began the preparations in earnest for a film about the beautiful but cold kleptomaniac. In the absence of Grace Kelly, he turned once more to Tippi Hedren. Although she had been shaken by her experience in *The Birds*, normal relations—or as close as Hitchcock ever got to normal relations—had been resumed, and in January he gave a dinner party for five people to celebrate her birthday. In February he began holding story conferences with Evan Hunter and Robert Boyle, the production designer. There was one planned sequence, which according to Hunter "disturbed me enormously." Hitchcock asked him, innocently enough, what scene that might be. Hitchcock knew exactly which scene it was. It was the scene in which Marnie's new husband, Mark Rutland, rapes her on the wedding night. "Oh don't worry about that," Hitchcock replied. "That'll be fine."

Hitchcock had paid much attention to the rape and, with the tape recorder switched off, had described all of its details to Hunter. The writer later told an interviewer that "he framed me up with his hands the way directors do, and said 'Evan, when he sticks it in her, I want that camera right on her *face!*'" But Hunter balked. He did not want to write the scene, simply because it was without motive. The new husband, played by Sean Connery, would be acting quite out of character. Hunter wrote an alternative scenario for the unfortunate honeymoon night, on yellow rather than white paper to differentiate it from the rest of the script, but it was rejected by Hitchcock, who wrote back quickly saying that he felt "there is still a lot of work to be done on it." He added ominously that it might need "a fresh mind altogether, and this probably will have to be the next procedure." He had effectively fired the scriptwriter.

He replaced Hunter with Jay Presson Allen, who began work at the end of May. She was not at all bothered by the director's insistence, and in fact believed that he had purchased the rights to the book for that scene alone. She told Hunter at a later date that, as soon as Hitchcock realised Hunter was not going to write the rape scene, he had purchased his ticket to New York. She herself managed to get past him a scene noticeable for its restraint.

Hitchcock and Allen were well suited. They shared a similar sense of humour and, from June to September, worked amicably. Allen said in an interview that "he gave me a feeling of total freedom. My feeling was that I could write anything in the world I wanted to write and that I could violate something that he had said he'd like with impunity." That was not of course the experience of Evan Hunter. It was perhaps a question of personalities.

Allen recalled also that "we became very, very good friends. I lived with Hitch and Alma for a good length of the time I was in California. They were unbelievably generous and fun." They all went out to dinner, visited the concert halls, and spent weekends at Santa Cruz. Allen recalled that they would "talk endlessly" in the first few weeks about plot and character. She said that "characterisation escaped him more than he would have wished it to." He was always more interested in images. She noticed, too, that Alma "had a marvellous sense of narrative." He also relied on his wife for stability and security. While they were discussing the psychological aspects of the film Hitchcock told

Allen of a recurrent dream he had in which his penis was made of crystal, a fact which he was obliged to conceal from Alma. Allen laughed and told him that the obvious interpretation was that "he was trying to keep his talent separate and safe from Alma." There may be other interpretations but, like most dreams, it may not require one at all.

Before filming began he made his usual meticulous preparations. He was always concerned about the costs involved, and was as thrifty in his art as he was in his life. James Hubert Brown, the assistant director, said that he "felt obligated to Universal and to himself to make pictures that were successful." "Back projection" was to be used for most of the external locations. This gave an oddly old-fashioned style to the film, but he did not mind that in the least. Costume designer Rita Riggs said that "even during the making of *Marnie* I felt a certain sadness. It was a very manicured form of film-making." There were occasions when she felt "frozen in time."

He was reassured by Sean Connery's professionalism as well as his ability, but he was more intent upon Tippi Hedren. Everything had to be perfect—the hair, the make-up, the costume. Hedren herself recalled that "many times before filming started, we had gone through the character, feeling by feeling, reaction by reaction . . . with me especially because Hitch was not only my director but also my drama coach, and I could have had no one better than Alfred Hitchcock."

The filming of *Marnie*, from October 1963 to February 1964, progressed well. Connery recalled that he gave "very little direction, didn't even look through the viewfinder." Once he trusted an actor, Hitchcock left him or her alone. Connery added that "I saw he didn't wish to over-discuss things, and *any* discussion was 'over-discussing.'" Hitchcock offered only what might be called technical advice: pause after each sentence; keep your mouth shut while other actors are talking; "Smile," he told one actress, "as if you have a mouth full of broken china." He started at eight, and finished at six. He had coffee for breakfast, read the newspapers and was then driven to the studio. One of his assistant directors, Hilton Green, said that "he was really demanding to work with because he expected everyone to be professional and know their job. But as long as you did it, you knew ahead of time what he expected on the schedule, there were never any surprises with him." Rita Riggs added that "things just ran smoothly, and there was 'please' and 'thank you.'"

This was not the case with Tippi Hedren. Once more she sensed that he was trying to get too close to her. A fellow actor, Diane Baker, recalled that "as the film progressed, I became more aware that Hitch's and Tippi's working relationship was coming to an end. Feelings were raw, tinged with innuendo." He purchased for her a luxurious trailer, complete with bathroom and bar, which was placed beside the bungalow from which he worked. He sent her champagne each day and according to one of his best biographers, Donald Spoto, he told her of a romantic dream or fantasy in which she played the central role. Diane Baker said that "I never saw Tippi enjoying herself with the rest of the cast and crew . . . She was never allowed to gather around with the rest of us. And he demanded that every conversation between her and Hitch be held in private . . . nothing could have been more horrible for me than to arrive on that movie set and to see her being treated the way she was. I had never seen that. I didn't expect it, and I didn't understand any of it." In an interview Hedren said that "he was almost obsessed with me, and it's very difficult to be the object of someone's obsession."

Hitchcock himself was not well. He was drinking more than ever, and often fell asleep after lunch. He had a general sense of ill health, and often seemed disturbed or anxious. He was tired all the time, and complained of various pains and ailments. He called in specialists, who could not find any specific cause for his problems, and he went for a medical examination twice a week. He told his associate Norman Lloyd that "you might have to finish this one for me." It seems that he started receiving injections of cortisone, which can induce insomnia, sweating and sudden changes of mood.

Towards the end of January 1964, Tippi Hedren had been invited to accept the Photoplay Award for the most promising actress of the year, to be televised on the *Tonight* show, but he refused her permission to fly to New York. He did not want her to be taken out of the character which he had so slowly and meticulously created for her. They were, after all, still filming. This led to a violent row on the set, in which she made a disparaging remark. Hitchcock said that "she did what no one is permitted to do. She referred to my *weight*." In some accounts she is supposed to have called him a "fat pig." They became more distant on the set, and communicated with each other through third parties.

It has been widely reported and believed that, shortly after this incident, he made some kind of sexual proposition to her which she rejected in disgust. Everything was said, nothing was done. He is supposed to have asked her to "touch me" in a certain place. She walked away. It was a bewildering minute. Diane Baker has also reported that he came unannounced into her own dressing room and "kissed her on the mouth." Eventually Baker became so sick with tension that she called a doctor.

Spoto reports that in March 1964, just as filming was coming to an end, Hitchcock called Tippi Hedren to his office and again asked her for sexual favours. Hedren told Spoto "that was the limit, that was the end." At the time she told Hitchcock that "I can't put up with another day—I want to get out of this contract." He is supposed to have replied, "I'll ruin your career. You'll never work again anywhere. I'll destroy you."

Others dispute this account. Jay Presson Allen has stated that "I was there throughout all that time and the problem that 'Tippi people' have talked about over the years was not that overt. Not at all. Hitch was only trying to make a star out of her. He may have had something like a crush on her, a *crise de coeur*, but there was nothing overt. Nothing. Nothing. He would never in one million years do anything to embarrass himself. He was a very Edwardian fellow." Joan Fontaine believed it to be likely that "knowing that pretty young actresses wanted to feel that he was a dirty old man, he would play it up." It may be recalled that on the set of *Rebecca* Hitchcock had also tried to isolate and manipulate Fontaine as a way of shaping her performance. It is at least possible that his threats and advances were designed to create the threatened and confused character of Marnie.

Yet it is also true that towards the end of his life, under the influence of drink or medication, he sometimes made improper suggestions to the female members of his staff. It may of course have been the habit of a lifetime, and was not to be taken very seriously. He was simply behaving like an old fool, and a drunken one at that.

He and Hedren met several times in 1964 to arrange public appearances for the promotion of *Marnie*, and he stated to one of the distributors that "I feel that her performance in the picture is so impressive that I'm going to have her interviewed only by journalists who have seen her performance in the film." This may of course have been a subtle way of limiting her media coverage. Hedren never worked for Hitchcock again, although she remained on the payroll for a few months. When she refused to appear in one of the episodes of *The Alfred Hitchcock Hour* on television, the contract was finally dissolved.

Marnie was released on 8 July 1964 in London and a fortnight later in New York. He had wanted the film to impress the more serious critics as an exercise in psychology and sexual drama, but he failed in his purpose. The reviewer of the *New York Times* noted that "a strong suspicion arises that Mr. Hitchcock is taking himself too seriously—perhaps the result of listening to too many esoteric admirers." It failed at the box office too, where the absence of suspense and the unruliness of the plot made the film unpopular even among Hitchcock enthusiasts. It was his first outright failure in ten years.

Contradicting his own statement before the film's release, Hitchcock seems to have blamed Hedren. She had not been "the volcano" he had wished for. "It had wonderful possibilities, or so I thought," he told one interviewer. "I thought I could mould Miss Hedren into the heroine of my imagination. I was wrong. She couldn't live up to her character."

This was wholly unfair. *Marnie* lacks clarity of purpose of which the inconclusive ending is proof. Hitchcock's own feelings are perhaps too overt, to no good purpose. At one point Mark says to Marnie, "I've tracked you and caught you and by God I'm going to keep you." The director could have whispered the words as they were spoken. The fact that Tippi Hedren invests her role with an almost continuous note of barely controlled hysteria may be a tribute to her skills as an actress but it may also be the consequence of bullying or tension on the set. It was sometimes said that she was too "stiff," but that was precisely what she was supposed to be; her rage beneath her apparent composure is beautifully conveyed. Yet although the film brings many troubled feelings to the surface, it fails to make them cohere.

Marnie also has an air of vivid unreality in its use of matte painting and backdrops as an aid to setting and to scene. It is not clear whether Hitchcock used them as a deliberate device to emphasise the artificiality of the film, or as a measure of economy. In one scene a ship is seen at the bottom of the street in the port of Baltimore; this was from a recollection of Hitchcock. "I was fascinated as a kid in London to go down to the docks—there was an ordinary street and right across the end was a huge liner with a smokestack." Yet the effect did not quite work on the screen; it looked like what it was, a badly painted backdrop. In an interview at the National Film Theatre one of the audience suggested to him that the distorted image of a ship was "presumably symptomatic of her [Marnie's] tortured childhood." "No," he replied, "we had a lousy scene painter." The fact is that he let it pass. By the end of the film, he did not seem to care.

Truffaut has suggested that, after the critical and commercial failure of *Marnie*, Hitchcock "was never the same . . . its failure cost him a considerable amount of self-confidence." But the fact that he never ventured again into the sphere of psychological cinema, if it may so be called, was the result of official as much as private pressure. Universal Studios wanted him to revert to the formula of thrill and suspense that he had used so successfully in the past. He was required to employ stars to bring in the audience. He was expected to devise much tighter narratives. He pondered. He was at a loss what to do. He was unsure of himself. He may not have wanted to go back to the old formulae, but he had no choice in the matter. It was expected of him.

·   ·   ·

At the end of 1964 he took a holiday with Alma to St. Moritz and Italy, where he could contemplate the future. First thoughts of a comedy thriller began to emerge. He met two Italian scriptwriters with whom he discussed the idea of a New York hotel entirely staffed by the Mafia, but it came to nothing after rattling around in a few conferences and meetings.

Hitchcock already had another idea. The global success of the James Bond franchise set him thinking about the possibilities of spies and espionage as the basis for a successful film. In November 1964 he had written to Vladimir Nabokov outlining the plot of a scientist defecting with his secrets to Eastern Europe; his wife supports his defection but soon realises that he is in fact a double agent working for the Americans to elicit East German secrets. It is a convincing story that Nabokov might have rendered even more intriguing. Hitchcock told the novelist that his previous writers "usually adapt other people's work. That is why I am bypassing them and coming direct to you—a storyteller." Nabokov did not bite.

Hitchcock's damaged self-confidence, if such it was, was partly healed by the recognition he received in the early months of 1965. On 18 January he was asked to host the inaugural gala for President Lyndon Johnson. His sense of humour did not desert him. Of one performer he said, "I always thought that Woody Allen was a national park." Two months later the Screenwriters' Guild presented him with their Milestone Award for his "historic contribution to the American motion picture." He adopted his television demeanour and delivered a number of sly and acidulous remarks. "The invention of television," he told the audience, "can be compared to the introduction of indoor plumbing. Fundamentally it brought no change in the public's habits. It simply eliminated the necessity of leaving the house." The American Society of Newspaper Editors then invited him to address their annual dinner in Washington. He had by degrees become a cultural icon, an intrinsic part of the American imaginative landscape.

He was still considering a film of espionage, despite the disinclination of Nabokov, and brought to the project an Irish novelist, Brian

Moore, who had a reputation as a writer of thrillers. Hitchcock wrote to Truffaut in October 1965 that "in realising that James Bond and the imitators of James Bond were more or less making my wild adventure films, such as *North by Northwest,* wilder than ever I felt that I should not try and go one better. I thought I would return to the adventure film which would give us the opportunity for some human emotions."

Brian Moore quickly realised that, despite their amicable relationship, "we were in for trouble. I found that he had absolutely no concept of character—even of two-dimensional figures in a story. He kept switching from the woman's to the man's point of view, and the original story idea began to shift and fade uncontrollably." Moore also realised that in the absence of an inspired or creative imagination the film—to be called *Torn Curtain*—was becoming a ragbag of old effects and old devices. Moore added that "the film is little else than a Hitchcock compendium." He even went so far as to tell the director that, if it had been a novel, it would have to be dumped or completely rewritten.

Hitchcock did not take kindly to this advice, and Moore found himself relieved from duties. In his place Hitchcock invited Keith Waterhouse and Willis Hall—English screenwriters who had gained deserved popularity for their stage adaptation of Waterhouse's novel *Billy Liar*—to rewrite Moore's script, but in the event they seem to have made only minor adjustments and alterations. The script would remain the major problem of the entire production.

Universal Studios had insisted upon employing star names for the project. So the binary galaxy of Julie Andrews and Paul Newman was introduced into the equation. Hitchcock invited Newman to dinner at Bellagio Road. It is said that the actor offended the director by taking off his jacket and by drinking beer rather than wine; Newman himself recalled that "when Hitchcock first invited me to his house and described the story in detail, it sounded like an exciting story, so I agreed to do it." Andrews has said that "I accepted for the chance to work with Hitchcock, and he taught me more about film and lenses than anyone." Yet there was no true response on either side, and Hitchcock still entertained the illusion that she was a singing star who had inadvertently found herself in film. John Russell Taylor wrote that "Hitch speaks politely of her. She speaks politely of him. But obviously there was no spark of communication between them."

It is perhaps not surprising that the high hopes originally harboured for *Torn Curtain* soon began to falter. The script seems to have been a dead weight. Hitchcock went into production even before it was finalised, and Newman stated that "I think I could have hit it off with Hitchcock if the script had been better." The actor sent the director a long letter outlining all of the faults he perceived in the writing, a gesture that Hitchcock regarded as an affront to his competence. Newman has also stated that "all during the shooting we all wished we didn't have to make it." Andrews herself believed that the atmosphere on the set deteriorated. Neither she nor Newman were accustomed to a director who rarely, if ever, commented upon their performances or gave them any indication how they were to proceed.

Samuel Taylor, the scriptwriter who had remained in touch with him ever since their days on *Vertigo*, recalled that "he just lost heart during the shooting. He had been told by the studio that he was getting the two biggest stars of the day, and he discovered that they didn't fit the Hitchcock mould or the Hitchcock method. He just couldn't get a chemistry going with them, and he got very depressed, and just went through the motions." It has been claimed that he spent most of the time complaining about them, out of earshot, and berating their joint cost of $1.8 million. He also did not appreciate Newman's style of "method" acting. When the actor questioned whether he should be wearing a particular pair of shoes, Hitchcock told him that "we are cutting at the second button of your coat, so don't worry about your shoes." When he queried Hitchcock about his motivation, the director gave his usual reply: "Your motivation is your salary."

According to Keith Waterhouse, Newman once asked Hitchcock how he should be relating to Andrews in one scene where he receives a suspect parcel from her. "Well, Mr. Newman, I'll tell you exactly what I have in mind here. Miss Andrews will come down the staircase with the package, do you see, when you, if you will be so good, will glance just a little to the right of camera to take in her arrival; whereupon my audience will say, 'Hello, what's this fellow looking at?' And then I'll cut away, do you see, and show them what you are looking at." Waterhouse added that "I have heard no better or more concise an analysis of what film-making is all about either before or since."

Hitchcock had wanted something different in the way of music for *Torn Curtain*. He cabled Bernard Herrmann with the message that "this audience is very different to the one to which we used to cater. It is young, vigorous and demanding. It is this fact that has been recognised by almost all the European film-makers where they have sought to introduce a beat and rhythm that is more in tune with the requirements of the aforesaid audience." Instead Herrmann produced a score that was noticeable for its violins, flutes and strings. One of the horn players remembered Hitchcock saying, "What is this? It is not what I want." There seems to have been a confrontation between the two men in the recording studio, where Herrmann asked him, "What do you want with me? I don't write pop music." Herrmann left in the early months of 1966, and never worked with Hitchcock again.

Torn Curtain is in fact a highly entertaining thriller with no pretensions to being anything else, a well-made narrative with constant attention to the suspense of time and circumstance. The most notorious scene is one in which the American professor and his accomplice are obliged to murder their East German minder, named, perhaps coincidentally, Hermann Gromek. It is a long and painful process, involving a knife and a shovel and a gas oven, and was designed by Hitchcock to prove how difficult it can be to kill a man. "In my films," he said, "killing does not happen casually." But the most effective scenes are those in which the raw dramatic powers of anticipation and anxiety are excited, leaving the audience in a state of perpetual tension. This was the one area of cinema in which Hitchcock was still the absolute master.

Yet the public, and the critics, already accustomed to the sensationalism and special effects exploited by "James Bond" films, did not see it that way. It was considered to be old-fashioned and simplistic;

compared with such films as *From Russia with Love* and *Thunderball*, it seemed to the critic of the *New York Times* that it "looks no more novel or sensational than grandma's old knitted shawl." Its reception was for Hitchcock a severe disappointment; it seemed that he had lost his spark, that he was becoming increasingly out of touch with contemporary cinema.

. . .

Through the later months of 1966, after the manifest failure of *Torn Curtain*, he seemed to withdraw into the seclusion of Bellagio Road with Alma at his side. "I dread being alone," he said. "Alma knows that, too." They spent Christmas at the Palace Hotel in St. Moritz. A friend, Whitfield Cook, remarked that "I'll never forget Alma saying that 'Hitch insists on getting into ski pants, which takes him about an hour, and then he sits on the porch smoking the whole time!'" That was what he liked to do on holiday—sit and watch.

He was preparing the ground. He had for a long time been interested in the careers of British killers, with John Christie, John George Haigh and Hawley Harvey Crippen near the top of his list (Crippen had actually been born in Michigan, but his reign of terror in London may grant him honorary British citizenship). Hitchcock had also become interested in Neville Heath who had brutally killed two women in 1946. This was the man for Hitchcock, and by the end of the year he was planning a film based upon a serial killer who had necrophiliac leanings. After the expensive disaster of *Torn Curtain* he decided that the film would be stripped down to its essentials, in the style of *The Wrong Man*. He asked Benn Levy to become the scriptwriter; significantly Levy had written some of the script for *Blackmail*, the first British talkie made by Hitchcock in 1929. The director was returning to his London roots.

Levy flew to Hollywood in February 1967, and worked for the next two months on the film Hitchcock was inclined to call *Kaleidoscope Frenzy*. It concerned a psychotic killer, homosexual and deformed, who tried to lure into his net a female police officer. When the treatment had reached a conclusive phase Hitchcock handed the material to Howard Fast, the American novelist perhaps best known for *Spartacus*. "My God, Howard!" he said, "I've just seen Antonioni's *Blow-Up*. These Italian directors are a century ahead of me in terms of technique! What have I been doing all this time!" It was a rare admission that he had indeed allowed the modern cinema to pass him by. Hitchcock decided to borrow some of the techniques of the Italian directors for his new film, including a hand-held camera and natural light. He was also ready for scenes of male and female nudity, with which he had only flirted in *Psycho*. After the debacle with Newman and Andrews, he was happy to use unknown actors. He wrote to Truffaut in April 1967 that "I am, at present, preparing a new picture. It has no title but deals with a psychopathic murderer of young women. It is roughly based on an English crime case. It is a purely realistic story, and the central figure is a young man who has some kind of relationship with his mother."

Fast recalled that "Hitchcock gave me a very free hand. He seemed mostly interested in working out elaborate camera movements." But it was all for nothing. The executives at Universal were horrified by the theme and by the central character; they rejected the script. Fast recalled that "they had belittled Hitchcock's attempt to do precisely what they had been urging him to do—to attempt something different, to catch up with the swiftly moving times." It has been said that he broke down in tears at the studio's response. It is possible. There was always a small sphere of hysteria in the director's psyche.

· · ·

So what on earth was he supposed to do? He was too valuable a property to waste. His international fame, and his television popularity, would always entice an audience. In the summer of 1968 Universal came up with a film for which they had purchased the rights, an international thriller entitled *Topaz*; his doubts were compounded by his uneasy relationship with its author, Leon Uris, who seemed quite impervious to all of Hitchcock's blandishments, bad jokes and brandy. They were both possessed of too large an ego to acquiesce to each other's personality. Uris had been hired to write the screenplay but he recalled that Hitchcock was trying to dominate him, consigning him to the status of an employee. It was not going to work.

The director turned instead to Samuel Taylor with whom he had worked on *Vertigo*, and also brought in old colleagues such as Henry Bumstead, the production designer, and Edith Head, costume designer. He would need all the help he could get. He had wasted too much time on the Uris script, and the film was scheduled to commence. "I'm in bad trouble, Sam," he told Taylor. "I've got a script I just can't shoot." So why not delay it? "I have to go with it now. It's in production." Taylor, therefore, was obliged to write fast.

The story was not uninteresting. It concerned an agent for the French secret services who, through certain contacts in Cuba, learns that the Soviet Union is sending missiles to Cuba. In deference to the international scope of the film, Hitchcock decided to hire relatively unknown foreign actors to play the principal parts. This was a mistake. Significant episodes of *Topaz* were to be filmed in Paris and Copenhagen. This was expensive and unnecessary.

The filming did not go well. Henry Bumstead said in 2004 that "*Topaz* was a nightmare. I got high blood pressure on that picture. I'm still taking pills for it . . . There was just no time for prep [preparation], and I'll tell you, prep is the most important time on a picture."

Hitchcock did not have any natural rapport with his cast. The French, Danish and German actors involved were not prepared for his dark humour and sexual innuendo, and his cockney badinage eluded them. Samuel Taylor recalled that "one of the tragedies of *Topaz* was that Hitchcock was trying to make something as if he had Ingrid Bergman and Cary Grant in it." Another actor on the set, John Forsythe, said that "He was no longer the great brain that sat in the chair watching . . . He would go away for fifteen or twenty minutes, and lie down if he could, and it was sad to see." There was at least one occasion when he fell asleep during a long take, and no one was brave enough to wake him. Eventually he opened his eyes and said, "Well, how was it?" And then he laughed. He had, perhaps, finally lost interest in the proceedings. There were times when in the middle of filming in the studio he would decide to take his composer, Maurice Jarre, out to lunch at Chasen's. When asked if he wanted to stay for the rest of the scene he replied, "No, the actors are ready; the cameramen are ready. If not, I'll cut it."

His detachment or lack of interest manifested itself in the three different endings he filmed, on the understanding that Universal would pick the one they most liked. The most anodyne was chosen. "I could have fought the decision," he said later, "but it didn't seem worthwhile." When not downright bored, he seems to have been anxious and dispirited throughout the proceedings. He agreed with critics and audiences alike that it had been a disaster. "*Topaz*," he said, "was a most unhappy picture to make." Pauline Kael in *The New Yorker* concluded that "the embarrassment of *Topaz* is that Hitchcock is lazy and out of touch."

. . .

His daughter, in her memoir of Alma, stated "those were trying times for Daddy and the only thing that kept him balanced were Mama and his family." He was, as he might have put it in the English phrase, "ticking over." He read endlessly—"reading properties," as he put it—in case inspiration struck; he watched every new film he could locate and had to endure the visits of studio executives who reminded him that his next project, if it should come, would have to be on a much smaller scale than the doomed *Topaz*. He also visited the local theatres and made trips to the racetrack. He vacated his second home in Santa Cruz, and it was eventually sold. The journeys to the estate had become too tiring.

Yet there was no sense of an ending. "I am looking for a new film project," he wrote to Truffaut, "but it is very difficult. In the film industry here, there are so many taboos. We have to avoid elderly persons and limit ourselves to youthful characters; a film must contain some anti-establishment elements; no picture can cost more than two or three million dollars. On top of this, the story department sends me all kinds of properties which they claim are likely to make a good Hitchcock picture. Naturally, when I read them, they don't measure up to the Hitchcock standards." Yet one project, suggested to him towards the end of the year, seemed to fulfil all of his requirements.

11

BACK TO BASICS

He was sent or given a novel, Arthur La Bern's *Goodbye Piccadilly, Farewell Leicester Square*, that might have been written for him. It concerns a psychotic killer, sexually impotent, who preys upon women in central London; the wrong man is arrested, and he flees from prison to take revenge upon the real killer. Three years after *Kaleidoscope Frenzy* had been rejected by the studio, a similar story of serial killing and sexual innuendo was now accepted. On this occasion the studio acceded to his wishes in the knowledge that it could be made cheaply and quickly while trading on Hitchcock's name. It would be filmed in London, thus distancing the murderous plot for American audiences, and Hitchcock would be given a budget of less than $3 million. He seemed to have jettisoned his original plans for an "experimental" film, complete with hand-held cameras and natural lighting, in favour of what might be called conventional Technicolor.

Hitchcock moved quickly. He asked Anthony Shaffer, who was then enjoying great success with *Sleuth* on the English and American stages, to be his scriptwriter. He had telephoned the writer on New Year's Eve 1970, and Shaffer believed at first that it was a practical joke perpetrated by one of his friends. But by the middle of January he was having lunch in New York with the director; the subject was a film called *Frenzy*.

Hitchcock was about to travel to Paris to be made a Chevalier of the Légion d'honneur, but he took the opportunity of returning to London in order to visit possible locations with Shaffer. Hitchcock wanted what were essentially the settings of the city with which he had been familiar as a boy, most notably Covent Garden which his father had known well. The dark Thames would flow through the film, and there was a role for Wormwood Scrubs prison in East Acton. The public houses would be of the old school. He objected to more modern pubs on the grounds that "they look wrong. There's nothing like dark wood in a good pub."

The original novel had been located in London during the Second World War but Hitchcock wanted a contemporary setting. Yet in the end there was hardly any difference. Hitchcock's version of the new city was thoroughly old-fashioned, as if it had stopped growing after he had left it, so that the scenes and dialogue have a somewhat dated flavour. But that did not affect his vision, which was as powerful as ever.

Shaffer arrived in California on 21 January 1971, and by late February he and Hitchcock had fashioned a treatment of fifty-five pages. They worked well together, fortified by steak and salad at lunchtime as well as a recourse to cocktails at four. Shaffer once gently objected to the monotonous diet, and on the next day a fifteen-course meal arrived for him. Shaffer described his director as "lugubrious," but that never impaired their professional relationship. On 27 February Shaffer returned to New York where he worked on the first draft of the completed script.

It was not a pretty story. The hero or anti-hero, Richard Blaney, falsely accused of being a serial killer, is querulous and unsympathetic. The real psychopath, Bob Rusk, is a genial fruiterer at Covent Garden who lives with his mother in a flat off the market. The naked body of a woman is seen floating down the Thames; another murder scene is preceded by a long and vicious rape that Hitchcock insisted on filming in detail. When Rusk loses his tie pin, and realises that it had been clutched *in extremis* by another victim, he is forced to rummage through a consignment of potatoes in which he has dumped her body.

Food, sex and violence—the holy trinity of Hitchcock's imagination—culminate in a scene where Rusk, covered in potato dust, is eventually forced to break the fingers of his victim in order to recover the pin.

By the beginning of April Shaffer had completed the first draft of the screenplay, which was scrutinised by both Hitchcocks. It was now 160 pages long, and met with their broad approval. It was time to move the office to London, where Hitchcock's staff booked a suite at Claridge's from the middle of May to the end of September. He was received at Pinewood Studios, where some of the film was to be shot, as a king from over the water. Even though he was now nominally an American, he had in truth become one of the most famous Englishmen of the age.

He began the rigorous business of casting. He had already offered the part of the serial killer to Michael Caine, who turned it down on the grounds that the part was "really loathsome, and I did not want to be associated with it." Hitchcock never spoke to him again, even when by coincidence they dined in the same Hollywood restaurant. His other choices were less recalcitrant. Alec McCowen, who was cast as the principal police officer, and Vivien Merchant, who played his wife, were better known as stage actors; but they seemed to relish the opportunity of working with Hitchcock.

Only one member of the cast, Jon Finch, playing the innocent accused, proved troubling. He gave an interview before filming in which he suggested that Shaffer's script was a little out of date. But that is how Hitchcock had wanted it. Finch also proffered suggestions of his own about the dialogue. This was not what Hitchcock wanted. His cameraman, Gilbert Taylor, recalled that the director "was very angry, and he was thinking about recasting." It is fortunate that he kept the actor, who gave a thoroughly convincing portrait of an unsettled and unhappy man. It may have been Hitchcock himself who managed to unsettle him, of course, once more eliciting a convincing portrait from one of his cast through provocation and bullying.

At the beginning of June Alma suffered a stroke; it was fortunate that Hitchcock's personal physician was travelling with them, and was able to begin treating her immediately. She did not want to be taken to an English hospital, and so was given continual care at the hotel. One of her arms was paralysed, and she had difficulty in walking. The effect on Hitchcock was acute. He was as disturbed and as anxious as he had been thirteen years before when Alma had been diagnosed with cancer, and the film was effectively suspended until she began to recover; any necessary meetings were held at the hotel, so that he could remain with her. Eventually she was well enough to fly back to California for further treatment. It may have been fortunate that she was staying at Claridge's at the time and she told the associate producer, Bill Hill, "Well if I'm going to have a stroke, I can't imagine a better place to have it."

Relieved of his immediate alarm Hitchcock began filming at the end of July. Although he was still staying at Claridge's he set up his office in the Strand Palace Hotel, a hundred yards from Covent Garden market. He knew the setting well enough from his childhood, and someone remarked that Hitchcock's father had once been a fruiterer. "No," he replied, "my father was not a costermonger here. He was a wholesale cabbage buyer. He would buy acres of cabbages. *Acres.*" In the eventual trailer for the film Hitchcock said, "This is the famous London wholesale fruit and vegetable market, Covent Garden. Here you may buy the fruits of evils and the horrors of vegetables."

The filming proceeded well, despite the fact that there had been early problems. On the Friday before filming started Hitchcock fell badly in his hotel suite and was confined to bed for the weekend, but he was ready by early Monday morning. On this first day of filming Bill Hill recalled that "I was driving into London very early and on the radio I heard someone saying 'If you are in London today or going to London today, will you please avoid Covent Garden because Alfred Hitchcock is starting his new movie there today.' So naturally, when we got there, we couldn't move." Hill found Hitchcock sitting in his limousine, a Rolls-Royce Silver Shadow, apparently unperturbed by the crowds around him. Hill persuaded him to get out of the car and walk towards the camera already set up for him; the people took their photographs, and then left the area. "There you are," Hill told them, "that's it." Filming in the market then commenced. Later in the day a union official approached Hitchcock's staff and told them that the last take could not be completed because it was approaching six in the evening. Hitchcock protested, saying that he had understood he had been given permission to finish any take he had begun, and that in any case the interruption was bad for the actors. He threatened to take the entire film to Hollywood, thus creating a very bad advertisement for the British film industry. The union official relented, and he was not troubled again.

Bill Hill recalled that after these early stumbles, "everything went very, very smoothly. Everybody had a great respect for him and he was very pleasant with a *great* sense of humour . . . We all learned very early that you don't change anything he says. If that's what he wants, that's what he is going to get." Such was the regard for him that he was given permission to film inside Criminal Court Number One at the Old Bailey, where Blaney is wrongly convicted. There are photographs of him sitting, plump and imperturbable, in his chair labelled "Mr. Hitchcock." There was one ominous notation on the call sheet for 24 September, with a reference to "Mr. Finch late and shooting held up from 9:45 to 10:50." It has been said that Hitchcock made Finch apologise to each member of the cast, but it is more likely that Finch did so voluntarily.

The filming on the set was as tight and as disciplined as the work on location. He wrote to one relative, eager to see him, that "life is just a matter of going from the hotel to the studio and back to the hotel during the week, and weekends are spent resting as much as possible to be ready for the week ahead." He had now reached his seventy-second year. He had spent thirteen weeks in London, including sixty-three shooting days that began at six in the morning and finished in the early evening. There were also six nights of filming which must have taxed his strength. According to some members of the cast and crew he still had a tendency to doze after a large lunch, waking up suddenly to ask his assistant director, Colin Brewer, "How was it for you, old bean?" When Brewer replied that it was fine, he would say, "OK, print it." On one occasion Hitchcock was asked on waking whether he would like to repeat the scene. "Yes—and tell them to do it louder." His favourite tipple was vodka and orange, which he sipped from a flask.

Finch recalled that "I don't think he was that interested in what the actors were doing, but he was always aware of the camera, and he knew when someone was being shot too short or too long. When passers-by at Covent Garden asked me who the star of the film was, I told them 'Alfred Hitchcock.'" Anna Massey, playing Blaney's girlfriend, remembered that at the beginning of production "he had immense creative energy and a real mental zest . . . but then he got slow physically."

The rape scene, in which the killer strangles and violates his victim at the same time, was the most gruelling for the actors. It took three days to film, and Hitchcock demanded the utmost fidelity to the horror of the matter. Barry Foster, who played the part of the psychopathic killer, recalled that "it was a very unsavoury business, and in the rape-strangling scene we were all trying to keep a firm grip on our stomachs." In that scene Foster whispers "Lovely! Lovely!" as the victim begins to pray. The audience finally see her face in death, her eyes protruding, her tongue sticking out of her mouth, and her neck red. It was the sequence Hitchcock had been waiting to film for some years, and had been rehearsing for it ever since *The Lodger*. His personal assistant, Peggy Robertson, wrote to a colleague in Hollywood that "we've finished the rape and murder of Brenda sequence, and it is absolutely terrifying! I've seen the rushes three times now and am still absolutely petrified." This was Grand Guignol in the Hitchcock style. He described it as the one "meaty" episode in the film. In a scene in a public house two businessmen have a conversation about the serial killer. "He rapes them first, you know." "Nice to know every cloud has a silver lining."

At the end of October 1971, Hitchcock returned to America after completing all of the principal photography. He could now also confer with an almost completely recovered Alma on the shaping of the film, and the post-production process went smoothly enough. There was, however, a problem with the music. He had publicly disagreed with Bernard Herrmann on *Topaz*, and now was disappointed with Henry Mancini's work on *Frenzy*. It did not reflect the pop music that Hitchcock had in mind—this was, after all, still the era known as "swinging London"—and so the director hired the British composer Ron Goodwin instead. At their first meeting Hitchcock opened a box and brought out an exact model of his head. It was to be used for promotional purposes. "What do you think of that?" he asked the baffled composer. "Very nice," Goodwin replied. It was the right answer. But what else could he have said?

In the middle of December the Hitchcocks flew to Marrakech for a vacation in the sun, but they returned at the beginning of the new year for more work on post-production. He then prepared himself for the rigours of promotion. *Frenzy* was given its premiere at the Cannes Film Festival in May where, as François Truffaut recalled, Hitchcock looked "aged, tired, and tense" and seemed to be "very much like a young man about to take a school examination." But Hitchcock need not have worried. He was given a standing ovation at the end of the screening and, as Truffaut recalled, a week later he looked "fifteen years younger." When he returned to the United States he was engaged in a relentless sequence of interviews, lunches and ceremonies through the month of June. He had never been so much in demand.

The reaction to the finished film was overwhelmingly favourable, and gave Hitchcock his greatest success since *Psycho*. It seems that the director had recovered his touch for suspense and for the macabre after the failures of *Torn Curtain* and *Topaz*. The headline above the review in the *New York Times* announced "Hitchcock in dazzling form," an appreciation which became in *Time* magazine "Hitchcock is still the master." The author of the original novel, Arthur La Bern, was not so impressed. He sent a letter to *The Times* of London in which he concluded that "the result on the screen is appalling. The dialogue is a curious amalgam of an old Aldwych farce, *Dixon of Dock Green* and that almost forgotten *No Hiding Place*. I would like to ask Mr. Hitchcock and Mr. Shaffer what happened between book and script to the authentic London characters I created." They had simply passed through the medium of Hitchcock's imagination.

The film itself has not dated. It is too intensely realised to age. An innocent man is on the run, and a killer is on the loose in a seedy and dilapidated London. This is the world of Hitchcock, with all the patterns and parallels it produces. He has gone further in realisation than he had ever done before, but his instincts and preoccupations are the same as those with which he started in the silent cinema. He himself said of the film in an interview that "it's true all the way through—true in its setting, true in its characters, and true in its humour."

.   .   .

He may have come full circle with his return to London but he had no thought of retirement. "If I can still put as much vitality into a movie as I've put into *Frenzy*," he said, "what's the point of retiring? I used to be called the 'boy director' and I still am." Now seventy-three, though, he was necessarily slower than before; he was eating and drinking more than the doctors would recommend, and his weight was becoming an increasing burden.

By the autumn of 1973 he had grown tired of inactivity. "I'm going to look around," he told another interviewer. "See about some new forms of murder." In a similar vein he said that "I have no hobbies, so I will just have to see where the next body will turn up." That body turned up in his next film, *Family Plot*. He had come upon a novel, Victor Canning's *The Rainbird Pattern*, that held distinct possibilities. It concerned a medium, Madame Blanche, and her boyfriend who have agreed to find the nephew of a wealthy spinster; inadvertently they disturb the plans of a kidnapper and his partner. When Hitchcock outlined the story to colleagues they were bewildered; it seemed to be going in several directions at once. But Hitchcock found in it the elements of a game, or a black comedy, in which the threads would finally

Hitchcock with Alma, celebrating his seventy-fifth birthday, 1974.
Courtesy of NBCU Photo Bank

be tied in a satisfying knot. The book was set in rural England, but he moved the story to California.

He brought in his experienced scriptwriter, Ernest Lehman, who at once noted that "he had slowed down considerably. He had none of his former stamina, and I found that I had far less inclination, in the beginning of our story conferences, to do creative battle with this legendary and physically weakened man."

By spring 1974 Lehman had prepared a script, and within a week the director had sent it back with multiple queries and emendations. Hitchcock also outlined the visual details of the opening scene and questioned matters of motivation and construction. He seemed to have recovered his energy. But then difficulties arose between them. "I found myself refusing Hitch's ideas," Lehman said, even though "those ideas were coming from a legendary figure." He meant that he refused to be overawed.

They had one fundamental difference which, in other circumstances, would have been fruitful. Hitchcock worried about plot, while Lehman worried about character. The writer stated later that "Hitchcock sort of dropped things in to pay lip service, but he didn't really want them in the picture. I pleaded with him, so he put them back in the script and shot them, then edited them out of the picture." Hitchcock wrote to his former colleague from London days, Michael Balcon, that Lehman was "a very nervous and edgy sort of man" who was giving him "a rather difficult time." Lehman professed to believe that *Family Plot* would never actually be made.

In the autumn Hitchcock began to suffer spells of dizziness which were diagnosed as a weakness of the heart. He was taken by ambulance to UCLA hospital where, after treatment, he was prescribed a pacemaker under the skin below his collarbone. The procedure was followed by pronounced fever and a bout of colitis, inflammation of the colon; the ordeal was completed with the removal of kidney stones. Lehman was now not the only one who believed that the projected film would come to nothing. But the director, for the moment incapacitated, continued to correspond by letter with Lehman.

By the early months of 1975 Hitchcock was back at work, preparing the sequence of a car chase that occurs at a crucial moment in the film. He had been tardy in choosing actors. In this film, more than any other, characters were simply parts of the design. The studio had suggested Liza Minnelli and Jack Nicholson for the parts of the medium and her boyfriend, but Hitchcock demurred. He did not want to spend more money on salaries than absolutely necessary. So he hired instead Barbara Harris and Bruce Dern who, as it turned out, were entirely suited to their parts. Karen Black and William Devane completed the quartet of pursued and pursuers who remain at cross purposes throughout the film. Hitchcock seems to have struck up a particular friendship with Dern, who acted as his cheerleader when fatigue set in. "I got to jack him up a little," Dern said. "Get him ready for the day. He's bored with the whole fucking thing." But Dern also noticed that, when he was fully engaged, there was no one more attentive on the set than the director. "He noticed everything—a shadow on a performer's face, a bad angle for a prop, a few seconds too long on a take." There were times, however, when the director annoyed him. Dern once said to him, "Let me do another take on that, I didn't go deep enough." Hitchcock replied, "Bruuuuuce, they'll never know in Peoria." He was alluding to the old theatrical phrase, "Will it play in Peoria?," as the standard of a typical American town. But Hitchcock knew that Dern, and Harris, were quirky and engaging performers. He told Dern that "I never know what you're gonna do next. I know that the frame is perfect. I know the shot works perfectly. All I want is to be entertained." He actually encouraged the actors to improvise which was, for him, a very unusual intervention. In this, his last film, he just liked seeing the actors perform.

Filming began in the middle of May 1975. Just before the cameras turned Hitchcock decided that he wanted the narrative to be set in the middle of nowhere rather than in San Francisco. He told his first assistant director, Howard Kazanjian, that he wanted all signs and references to northern California removed. "I don't want any names on police cars. I don't want names on any badges . . . I want it no city." This was to be an abstract space. He had retained his aversion to filming on location, and much of the action took place on specially designed sets. Bumstead, still with him after all this time, recalled that "Hitch always drove right on the stage with his car, took six or seven steps to his chair, and now he says 'This is more like it. This is nice.'" He sat in his chair, speaking only to the director of photography and his first assistants. But he rarely said anything at all. On the first day of filming he shook hands with all the performers. He kissed Barbara Harris on the cheek and whispered to her, "Barbara, *I'm* scared. Now go and act."

But he was growing tired; he had some trouble in standing on his legs weakened by arthritis. By July he seemed to be exhausted, and hurried up the work so that he might finish early, and by the autumn he assigned the post-production work to his assistants. He did, however, supervise the score by John Williams who had just earned much praise for the music of *Jaws*. "He talked a lot about English music," Williams recalled, "which he was very interested in: Britten, Walton, Elgar, Arthur Bliss and Vaughan Williams." From John Williams Hitchcock wanted something light and exuberant since, as he told the composer, "murder can be fun."

Family Plot is indeed filled with "fun," albeit of a macabre kind. It is an absurdist thriller which does not take itself seriously at all. It harbours a stylised, and sometimes almost diagrammatic, pattern built on the illusions of balance, contrast and symmetry. There is no room for the exploration of character except in the most rudimentary way. William Devane said that "I played the clothes"; when he put on his costume, he had his part.

Hitchcock did not know what to call it. "It will be called Alfred Hitchcock's 'Something,'" he said, "perhaps Hitchcock's 'Wet Drawers.'" For his obligatory cameo he had himself filmed in silhouette behind frosted glass in the door of a "Registrar of Births and Deaths." It may be an allusion to his omnipotence as a film director, but it was also a way of disguising his face, which was becoming increasingly livid and puffy from injections of cortisone. Yet he appeared in the advertising posters, his rotund face suspended in a crystal ball, winking at his public. He seems to be intimating that, after all, it's only a movie. It is a

Hitchcock on the set of *Family Plot*, his final film, 1975.

Courtesy of Hulton Archive/Getty Images

game, with all its rules on show. It suggests also that although he is the director, he is somehow detached from the whole process.

Family Plot was released in March 1976 to generally favourable reviews, reflecting both the obvious stature of the film-maker and the genuine public warmth that his longevity had aroused. Frank Rich in the *New York Post* observed that "like many modern painters (such as Klee and Kandinsky) great movie directors often become more intrigued by the abstract possibilities of style as they get older." This is a very astute comment, underlined by Hitchcock's allusion to Mondrian in one "overhead" sequence of a chase in a cemetery with a careful blocking out of routes and outlines.

.   .   .

His domestic routine, cherished for many years, was now shattered when Alma Hitchcock suffered a second and debilitating stroke. She was confined to the house in Bellagio Road and needed constant nursing; Hitchcock cooked for her two or three times a week while otherwise relying upon deliveries from Chasen's restaurant. "Little did I believe," he wrote to Michael Balcon, "that after all these years and the accumulation of a little wealth that I should approach my seventy-eighth year being a cook in the kitchen!" However much he may have tried to conceal it, he was much agitated. His granddaughter recalls, "I remember my grandfather being so upset about Alma—with tears in his eyes he kept asking 'What am I going to do?'"

He himself was afflicted by arthritis that made it difficult for him to rise each morning; he wore reading glasses and was growing slightly deaf. He still went to his office each day at ten in the morning. It was a capacious room in a bungalow built for him, with a very large desk and comfortable leather sofas; the desk was of course a picture of neatness, and no librarian could have arranged the open bookshelves more precisely. Lunch was brought to him punctually at 12:30 in a dining room next door to the office. The meal invariably consisted of steak and salad. He had a flask or bottle of vodka in the top drawer of his desk and at four o'clock, just before returning home to Bellagio Road, he took a drink. Whether he took two or three is an open question, subject only to rumour, but he had good reason to fortify himself.

An old colleague, Hume Cronyn, recalled that in these latter years Hitchcock had become "a sad and rather isolated figure. I visited him often and found him weeping. He said not only that the work was not proceeding well, but that he never went out, never saw anyone, was never invited anywhere." But he had in truth wished this fate for himself; he had never been gregarious and had never cultivated any lasting friendship except that with his wife. With Alma now only a sad presence in his life, he was fundamentally alone. It was, at his age, hard to bear.

·   ·   ·

In the autumn of 1976 he wrote to Truffaut that "at the moment I am completely desperate for a subject." He had no intention of retiring. A new pacemaker had been fitted, and for a while it seemed to have rejuvenated him. In an interview with *Sight and Sound* he remarked that "my health is pretty good, despite a few arthritic aches and pains. I have a heart-pacer but that works more reliably than nature. And my films are sufficiently successful for other people to want me to go on working."

Then he found one more project. He had been reading Ronald Kirkbride's novel, *The Short Night,* a romantic espionage thriller about a double agent who is spirited out of Wormwood Scrubs prison. Hitchcock also took the precaution of buying the rights to Sean Bourke's *The Springing of George Blake,* concerning the escape from the Scrubs of a real double agent, George Blake, who then fled to the Soviet Union. The narrative of Blake on the run interested him, but he was also intrigued by the story of Blake's wife and three children. This was to be the core of the film which was to be only loosely based on the facts of the matter. He enlisted an American writer, James Costigan, and through the spring and summer of 1977 they worked together; but nothing came of it. Hitchcock then turned once more to Ernest Lehman, but they parted company when the director began to insist upon introducing a brutal rape scene that Lehman resisted. It had been the same situation with Evan Hunter and *Marnie*. Lehman recalled that "sometimes I think we both knew, on this one, that we were going through the motions. Were we, or weren't we? I'll never know. He *wanted* to make it, didn't he? I *wanted* him to make it—isn't that why I wrote it? But did either of us believe that he could?"

In the summer of 1978, after Lehman's departure, Hitchcock called on another old friend, Norman Lloyd, to help with the script. "He couldn't lick the story," Lloyd said later. "Nobody could lick the story. Nobody knew better than Hitch that it was old hat. He'd had it on his shelf for eleven years and, interestingly enough, while we're talking about it we kept looking for something else." The doubts multiplied as Hitchcock's health continued to deteriorate. One day he turned to Lloyd. "You know, Norm, we're not ever going to make this picture." When asked the reason he replied, "Because it's not *necessary*."

His moods of enthusiasm and dismay now fluctuated with his health. Hitchcock suddenly informed Lloyd that they should break off the treatment and start work at once on the actual script. "Not me," Lloyd replied. "I don't think we're ready." The writer saw the pained look of betrayal on Hitchcock's face. "He just cut me off," Lloyd said, "like I'd never known him. He had a right to."

On the following day Lloyd returned to Hitchcock's bungalow, where Hitchcock was sitting with the treatment in his hands. "I really would like to work on it with you," Lloyd said.

"Never mind, I can do it myself."

This may have been at the time Hitchcock telephoned Anthony Shaffer, the writer of *Frenzy*, in London. He first apologised for not employing him in *Family Plot*. Then according to Shaffer his voice changed. "Tony! They're all betraying me! Everyone's leaving me! You've got to come and rescue me! I'm all alone!"

In the autumn of 1978 he suffered a bad fall. He slipped on a carpet laid upon the marble floor of his bathroom, crashed against the shower door and fell against the wall. He was taken to hospital and no permanent damage was found. But rails were put up within the house, and he began to use a cane.

In December, another scriptwriter was brought in to work on *The Short Night*. David Freeman, in *The Last Days of Alfred Hitchcock*, noted when they met that "he's short, five feet five inches or less, with almost unwrinkled skin. He's very fat." Their first interview did not seem to go well, and "the truth is that I'm starting to get uncomfortable. I begin to think he doesn't know why I am here." But this was Hitchcock's old technique, of talking about anything other than the film in hand. Freeman believed that the director had so donned the mantle of his public self that he was ultimately "unknowable." He was as fixed as the faces of Mount Rushmore.

When the two men did eventually turn to the film, Hitchcock was full of technical questions. He needed to know the precise topography of the area around Wormwood Scrubs prison, from which George Blake escaped. What time did the street lights go on? Was there a roundabout near the main road? When he disliked one of Freeman's ideas he gave his standard reply. "No, that's the way they do it in the movies." He seemed to be most interested in the possible sex scenes. "Yes, yes. That will work. Very exciting." There are unconfirmed reports that it was at this stage in his life that he made sexual propositions to female members of his staff, and that one or two secretaries were paid for their silence. It is all too probable that he lost his inhibitions as he fell slowly into senility.

He was often in pain from arthritis and still relied upon injections of cortisone to relieve it, but Freeman noticed on one of his visits to Bellagio Road that "on the bureau opposite his bed there are about fifty bottles of pills." Freeman also observed that Hitchcock began to drink brandy which he kept "in a brown paper bag stashed in the bathroom of his office"; Hitchcock "wrapped his lips around his glass with urgent bite, bent his head back until his throat and several chins seemed flat, and poured the brandy down into his throat in one continuous gulp."

Pain was not the only stimulus for drink. There was also fear. His personal assistant, Peggy Robertson, told Freeman that before one story meeting he had told her "that he couldn't continue." He asked her repeatedly, "When do you think I'll go? When?" The occasional visits of old friends seemed to increase his distress, and Ingrid Bergman recalled that "he took both my hands and tears streamed down his face, and he said 'Ingrid, I'm going to die.'" The news of the death of contemporaries also reduced him to tears, but perhaps from hysteria as much as grief. When Hume Cronyn came, they just held hands and cried.

A version of Freeman's script was completed by the spring of 1979, but it was stillborn. Some tentative preparations had been made for production of *The Short Night*. A location scout had been sent to Helsinki, where much of the action was to be filmed, and the narrative was turned into a sequence of storyboards. The game of casting was played. Clint Eastwood? Sean Connery? He tinkered with the script.

But the play-acting could not go on indefinitely. He called his old associate Hilton Green into the office and asked him "to go to Lew Wasserman and tell Lew that I'm all through."

"What do you mean you're all through?"

"I'll never direct again."

In another version he is supposed to have said, "I can't make this picture. I'm never going to make a movie again." Whatever the exact words, he knew that he was pronouncing his own death sentence. No one could argue him out of it.

. . .

In March 1979 he was celebrated as the recipient of a Lifetime Achievement Award by the American Film Institute. He did not relish the occasion that had all the hallmarks of an expensive funeral; he refused to cooperate with the staff of the institute until the last minute, and sat through the proceedings with a blank stare. His face was puffy, he was obese, and he walked to his table with great difficulty. He hardly seemed aware of what was going on around him. Yet he had strength enough for a short and elegant speech. "I beg permission to mention by

name only four people who have given me the most affection, appreciation and encouragement, and constant collaboration. The first of the
four is a film editor, the second is a scriptwriter, the third is the mother
of my daughter Pat, and the fourth is as fine a cook as ever performed
miracles in a domestic kitchen, and their names are Alma Reville." At
the last moment, Alma had been able to attend. For the final time he
was surrounded by old friends, Ingrid Bergman and Cary Grant among
them. They had all come essentially to deliver their farewells.

Two months later Hitchcock cancelled *The Short Night* and
announced to his staff that he was closing down the office and the
company. He had given them no advance warning, although most of
them must have anticipated his decision, and he had made no provi-
sion for their futures. Some were slow to forgive him for this final act of
thoughtlessness or selfishness. He came back for a while as if nothing
had happened.

Freeman recalled that "he'd found a new secretary and resumed
his rituals, unencumbered by the fiction of being a film-maker, or the
trappings of power and authority." But the pantomime did not last for
long. He did return at the beginning of 1980 when, in a private ceremony on a sound stage, he received the knighthood bestowed on him
by the Queen in the New Year's Honours List. When asked about the
long wait for the honour, he replied that "I guess she forgot." There was
very little else to say.

He slowly faded away. He lost interest in the world. He refused food
and drink. He was cold, and even hostile, to visitors. He screamed at his
doctor. He had turned his face to the wall. He seemed to have forgotten
that Alma was still in the same house. Once more he was lying alone
in the darkness, with the scythe of death descending ever closer to him.
He died of renal failure on the morning of 29 April, 1980. His body
was cremated and his ashes scattered over the Pacific Ocean. Alma was
bewildered for a while but then retreated into a world where he still
lived. She died in 1982.

BIBLIOGRAPHY

Allen, Richard: *Hitchcock's Romantic Irony* (New York, 2007)

Allen, Richard and Ishii-Gonzales, Sam (eds): *Alfred Hitchcock* (London, 1999)

——: *Hitchcock* (London, 2004)

Auiler, Dan: *Vertigo* (New York, 1998)

——: *Hitchcock's Secret Notebooks* (London, 1999)

Badmington, Neil: *Hitchcock's Magic* (Cardiff, 2011)

Barr, Charles: *English Hitchcock* (Dumfriesshire, 1999)

——: *Vertigo* (London, 2002)

Bellour, Raymond: *The Analysis of Film* (Bloomington, 2000)

Belton, John (ed): *Alfred Hitchcock's* Rear Window (Cambridge, 2000)

Bennett, John Charles (ed): *Hitchcock's Partner in Suspense* (Lexington, 2014)

Bogdanovich, Peter: *The Cinema of Alfred Hitchcock* (New York, 1963)

Bouzereau, Laurent: *Hitchcock* (New York, 2010)

Boyd, David (ed): *Perspectives on Alfred Hitchcock* (New York, 1995)

Boyd, David and Palmer, R. Barton (eds): *After Hitchcock* (Austin, 2006)

Brill, Lesley: *The Hitchcock Romance* (Princeton, 1988)

Brougher, Kerry and Tarantino, Michael: *Notorious* (Oxford, 1999)

Chandler, Charlotte: *It's Only a Movie* (New York, 2005)

Cohen, Paula Marantz: *Alfred Hitchcock* (Lexington, 1995)

Cohen, Tom: *Hitchcock's Cryptonomies* (two volumes, London, 2005)

Condon, Paul and Sangster, Jim: *The Complete Hitchcock* (London, 1999)

Conrad, Peter: *The Hitchcock Murders* (London, 2000)

Corber, Robert J.: *In the Name of National Security* (London, 1993)

DeRosa, Steven: *Writing with Hitchcock* (London, 2001)

Deutelbaum, Marshall and Poague, Leland (eds): *A Hitchcock Reader* (Chichester, 2009)

Dufreigne, Jean-Pierre: *Hitchcock Style* (New York, 2004)

Duncan, Paul: *Alfred Hitchcock* (Cologne, 2011)

Durgnat, Raymond: *The Strange Case of Alfred Hitchcock* (London, 1974)

——: *A Long Hard Look at* Psycho (London, 2010)

Falk, Quentin: *Mr. Hitchcock* (London, 2007)

Fawell, John: *Hitchcock's* Rear Window (Carbondale, 2001)

Finler, Joel W.: *Hitchcock in Hollywood* (New York, 1992)

Foery, Raymond: *Alfred Hitchcock's* Frenzy (Plymouth, 2012)

Freedman, Jonathan and Millington, Richard (eds): *Hitchcock's America* (Oxford, 1999)

Freeman, David: *The Last Days of Alfred Hitchcock* (London, 1985)

Giblin, Gary: *Alfred Hitchcock's London* (Baltimore, 2006)

Gottlieb, Sidney (ed): *Hitchcock on Hitchcock* (London, 1995)

——: *Alfred Hitchcock Interviews* (Mississippi, 2003)

Gottlieb, Sidney and Brookhouse, Christopher (eds): *Framing Hitchcock* (Detroit, 2002)

Gottlieb, Sidney and Allen, Richard (eds): *The Hitchcock Annual Anthology* (London, 2009)

Grams, Martin jnr and Wikstrom, Patrik: *The* Alfred Hitchcock Presents *Companion* (Hollywood, 2001)

Haeffner, Nicholas: *Alfred Hitchcock* (Harlow, 2005)

Hamilton, John: *Hitchcock's Blonde* (Bristol, 2009)

Hunter, Evan: *Me and Hitch* (London, 1997)

Hurley, Neil P.: *Soul in Suspense* (London, 1993)

Jacobs, Steven: *The Wrong House—The Architecture of Alfred Hitchcock* (Rotterdam, 2007)

Jensen, Paul M.: *Hitchcock Becomes Hitchcock* (Baltimore, 2000)

Kapsis, Robert E.: *Hitchcock* (Chicago, 1992)

Kolker, Robert (ed): *Alfred Hitchcock's* Psycho (Oxford, 2004)

Kraft, Jeff and Leventhal, Aaron: *Footsteps in the Fog* (Santa Monica, 2002)

Krohn, Bill: *Hitchcock at Work* (London, 2000)

———: *Alfred Hitchcock* (Paris, 2010)

LaValley, Albert J. (ed): *Focus on Hitchcock* (New Jersey, 1972)

Leff, Leonard J.: *Hitchcock and Selznick* (London, 1987)

Leigh, Janet: *Psycho* (London, 1995)

Leitch, Thomas: *Find the Director* (London, 1991)

———: *The Encyclopaedia of Alfred Hitchcock* (New York, 2002)

Leitch, Thomas and Poague, Leland (eds): *A Companion to Alfred Hitchcock* (Chichester, 2011)

McDevitt, Jim and San Juan, Eric: *A Year of Hitchcock* (Plymouth, 2009)

McGilligan, Patrick: *Alfred Hitchcock* (Chichester, 2003)

Modleski, Tania: *The Women Who Knew Too Much* (London, 1988)

Mogg, Ken: *The Alfred Hitchcock Story* (London, 1999)

Moral, Tony Lee: *Hitchcock and the Making of* Marnie (Maryland, 2005)

Morris, Christopher D.: *The Hanging Figure* (Westport, 2002)

Naremore, James (ed): *North by Northwest* (New Jersey, 1993)

O'Connell, Patricia Hitchcock and Bouzereau, Laurent: *Alma Hitchcock* (New York, 2003)

Orr, John: *Hitchcock and 20th Century Cinema* (London, 2005)

Paglia, Camille: *The Birds* (London, 1998)

Païni, Dominique and Cogeval, Guy: *Hitchcock and Art* (Montreal, 2001)

Perry, Dennis R.: *Hitchcock and Poe* (Maryland, 2003)

Perry, George: *The Films of Alfred Hitchcock* (London, 1965)

Phillips, Gene D.: *Alfred Hitchcock* (Boston, 1984)

Pomerance, Murray: *An Eye for Hitchcock* (London, 2004)

Raubicheck, Walter and Srebnick, Walter: *Hitchcock's Rereleased Films* (Detroit, 1991)

Rebello, Stephen: *Hitchcock and the Making of* Psycho (New York, 1991)

Rohmer, Eric and Chabrol, Claude: *Hitchcock* (New York, 1979)

Rothman, William: *Hitchcock—The Murderous Gaze* (London, 1982)

Ryall, Tom: *Alfred Hitchcock and the British Cinema* (Beckenham, 1986)

Samuels, Robert: *Hitchcock's Bi-Textuality* (New York, 1998)

Sharff, Stefan: *Alfred Hitchcock's High Vernacular* (New York, 1991)

———: *The Art of Looking* (New York, 1997)

Skerry, Philip J.: Psycho *in the Shower* (New York, 2009)

Sloan, Jane E.: *Alfred Hitchcock* (New York, 1993)

Smith, Susan: *Hitchcock: Suspense, Humour and Tone* (London, 2000)

Spoto, Donald: *The Art of Alfred Hitchcock* (New York, 1979)

——: *The Dark Side of Genius* (London, 1994)

——: *Spellbound by Beauty* (London, 2008)

Sterritt, David: *The Films of Alfred Hitchcock* (Cambridge, 1993)

Strauss, Marc Raymond: *Alfred Hitchcock's Silent Films* (Jefferson, 2004)

Sullivan, Jack: *Hitchcock's Music* (New Haven, 2006)

Taylor, Alan: *Jacobean Visions* (Frankfurt, 2007)

Taylor, John Russell: *Hitch* (London, 1978)

Thomson, David: *The Moment of* Psycho (New York, 2009)

Truffaut, François: *Hitchcock* (New York, 1983)

Walker, Michael: *Hitchcock's Motifs* (Amsterdam, 2005)

Weis, Elizabeth: *The Silent Scream* (London, 1982)

Wood, Robin: *Hitchcock's Films Revisited* (New York, 1989)

Yacowar, Maurice: *Hitchcock's British Films* (Detroit, 1977)

Youngkin, Stephen D.: *The Lost One* (Lexington, 2005)

Zizek, Slavoj: *Everything You Always Wanted to Know About Lacan (But Were Afraid to Ask Hitchcock)* (London, 1992)

INDEX

All films are directed by Hitchcock (AH) unless otherwise stated.

A Note About the Author

Peter Ackroyd is the author of *London: The Biography*, *Albion: The Origins of the English Imagination*, *Shakespeare: The Biography*, and *Thames: The Biography*. He has written acclaimed biographies of T. S. Eliot, Dickens, Blake, and Sir Thomas More, as well as several successful novels. He has won the Whitbread Book Award for Biography, the Royal Society of Literature's William Heinemann Award, and the South Bank Award for Literature. His last book was a biography of Wilkie Collins.

A Note About the Type

The text of this book was set in Electra, a typeface designed by W. A. Dwiggins (1880–1956). This face cannot be classified as either modern or old style. It is not based on any historical model, nor does it echo any particular period or style. It avoids the extreme contrasts between thick and thin elements that mark most modern faces, and it attempts to give a feeling of fluidity, power, and speed.